Living with Animals

Explorations in Contemporary Social-Political Philosophy (ECSPP)

Series Editors: Naomi Zack (University of Oregon) and Laurie Shrage (Florida International University)

As our world continues to be buffeted by extreme changes in society and politics, philosophers can help navigate these disruptions. Rowman & Littlefield's ECSPP series books are intended for supplementary classroom use in intermediate to advanced college-level courses to introduce philosophy students and scholars in related fields to the latest research in social-political philosophy. This philosophical series has multidisciplinary applications and the potential to reach a broad audience of students, scholars, and general readers.

Titles in the Series

Living with Animals

Rights, Responsibilities, and Respect

Erin McKenna

ROWMAN & LITTLEFIELD
Lanham • Boulder • New York • London

Published by Rowman & Littlefield
An imprint of The Rowman & Littlefield Publishing Group, Inc.
4501 Forbes Boulevard, Suite 200, Lanham, Maryland 20706
www.rowman.com

6 Tinworth Street, London SE11 5AL, United Kingdom

British Library Cataloguing in Publication Information Available

Library of Congress Cataloging-in-Publication Data

Names: McKenna, Erin, 1965– author.
Title: Living with animals : rights, responsibilities, and respect / Erin McKenna.
Description: Lanham : Rowman & Littlefield Publishing Group, 2020. | Series: Explorations in contemporary social-political philosophy | Includes bibliographical references and index. | Summary: "This accessible work of scholarship brings a pragmatist ecofeminst perspective to discussions around animal rights, animal welfare, and animal ethics, urging readers to make existing relations better"— Provided by publisher.
Identifiers: LCCN 2020037391 (print) | LCCN 2020037392 (ebook) | ISBN 9781538128206 (cloth) | ISBN 9781538128213 (paperback) | ISBN 9781538128220 (epub)
Subjects: LCSH: Ecofeminism. | Animal welfare. | Human-animal relationships. | Animals and civilization.
Classification: LCC HQ1194 .M35 2020 (print) | LCC HQ1194 (ebook) | DDC 304.2082—dc23
LC record available at https://lccn.loc.gov/2020037391
LC ebook record available at https://lccn.loc.gov/2020037392

Contents

Editors' Foreword

In *Living with Animals: Rights, Responsibilities, and Respect*, Erin McKenna investigates the requirements for ethical coexistence between human and nonhuman animals from the perspectives of philosophical pragmatism, ecofeminism and ecowomanism, and Native American thought. Throughout this very readable and engaging book, McKenna shares a wealth of knowledge about many different "beasts," from chimps and cattle to wolves and whales. She also offers close readings of many popular novels and films with nonhuman animal protagonists in order to explore the ambivalence that many of us experience when we use animals for food, sport, live entertainment, medical research, domestic companions and protection, and clothing and other commodities. In addition, she reflects on her own encounters with nonhuman animals in various research, home, and farm settings.

McKenna finished this book just as the magnitude of the COVID-19 pandemic became apparent and our lives were reshaped in dramatic ways. Her book raises questions that have become significantly more urgent, such as this one: How do we enter into dialogue with people who treat nonhuman others in troubling ways so that we can find solutions to many problems? These problems include the spread of zoonotic viruses, the contribution of meat consumption to climate change, the loss of habitat for nonhuman others on the planet and its consequences, and the mass suffering of sentient and conscious nonhuman creatures. For a book that confronts deep moral issues, it is surprisingly nonmoralistic, nonpreachy, nondogmatic, nonrigid, and respectful toward opposing perspectives.

Living with Animals makes an original contribution to social-political philosophy by demonstrating how pragmatist ideas and methods can enrich other theoretical approaches, such as ecofeminism. Moreover, this book shows how the pragmatist strands of ecofeminism/womanism can address contemporary social and political problems. With each chapter, McKenna deepens and elaborates this pragmatist and ecofeminist approach, while offering concrete proposals about how we can coexist with nonhuman others in a morally defensible way.

Laurie Shrage and Naomi Zack
Series Editors

Acknowledgments

First, I would like to thank Rowman & Littlefield for hosting this series, titled Explorations in Contemporary Social-Political Philosophy. The books in this series will be valuable resources for teaching and learning about important issues within philosophy. I would also like to thank Laurie Shrage and Naomi Zack for editing this series, with special thanks to Laurie Shrage for her suggestions and edits along the way.

In addition, I would like to thank the University of Oregon's philosophy department for their support of this project. The work of two research assistants—Kit Connor and Ansel Harris Smith III—was valuable in finding sources and assembling the bibliography. The University of Oregon library staff also deserve my thanks for their help as I checked out stacks of books from our own (and partner) libraries. The students who have taken my classes on Val Plumwood and on ecofeminism and ecowomanism are all a part of this project as well.

As usual, I would like to thank the community of scholars who gather at the Society for the Advancement of American Philosophy and the Summer Institute in American Philosophy for their support of my work. In this case, special thanks go to Tess Varner, Zach Piso, Lee McBride, Lisa Heldke, and Scott L. Pratt.

I would also like to thank the following people for their many suggestions for animal stories I could use. I could not include them all, but the suggestions did help me shape the project: Mary Trachsel, Alison Schmitke, Grace Groom, and Erin Bucklew. My colleague Bonnie Mann also deserves thanks for home delivery of some much-needed library books.

As always, I want to thank the myriad of animal beings with whom humans share this planet. Special thanks go to those dog beings who share in my daily life and put up with many hours watching me sit at a computer or read a book: Kira and Scully.

Preface and Introduction

I have been living with, and thinking about, other animal beings my whole life. Questions about my own responsibilities to animals arose early. My family raised and slaughtered sheep, steers, chickens, and rabbits on a small scale. I objected early on and tried to refuse to eat the animals we'd raised. It took many more years for me to decide to follow a vegetarian diet. A horse I cared for colicked when I was very young. I felt responsible. Being too small to throw her hay into her feeder, I had not always gone to the trouble of climbing the fence with the hay so I could put it in her feeder. Instead, for a few days, I had fed her on the ground, where she likely ingested whatever caused the blockage in her intestines. She recovered, but I had gained a new sense of the responsibility that comes with living with, and caring for, another living being. Similarly, when I adopted a kitten from a feral litter, I learned a lot about interspecies communication and community. More sadly, when a neighbor's dog came to our home to escape his abusive owner, my parents made me return the dog when the owner came looking for him. I never forgave myself for that and have never forgotten how that dog looked as he was taken away. These are just a few examples of strong memories I have from my childhood—all by the time I was eight. Later, when I had to write an eighth-grade career report, I researched the job of a zookeeper since that is what many ethologists seemed to do to make a living. I wanted to be like Jane Goodall, but I couldn't see myself working at a zoo after interviewing a zookeeper and seeing captive elephants in their very small indoor enclosure.

I wrestled with such problems personally. When I found philosophy at college, I found something that could help me wrestle with these problems more deeply and that could help me move from thinking about such issues to acting on them. While my early focus was on social and political philosophy, concerns about the environment and other animal beings have always been a part of my written work and my teaching. Working to rethink human relationships with other animal beings has also meant working to rethink much of Western philosophy. It has been important to me to write and teach about these issues in order to encourage more people to see philosophy as practically important and to encourage more people to see other animal beings (and the rest of the environment) as both interdependent with human beings and worthy of respect in their own right. While philosophy has often been an obstacle to acknowledging other beings (and the rest of the environment) in these ways, it can be an important tool for helping to change many of the dominant ways of thinking about, and acting toward, the rest of nature.

The recent pandemic provides a good example for why such a change is important. COVID-19 is a zoonotic disease. Most of the diseases that catch the public's attention are zoonotic: Ebola, SARS, MERS, HIV, West Nile, rabies, malaria, E. Coli, toxoplasmosis, Lyme disease, and several strains of influenza.[1] Human mobility is clearly a factor in spreading these diseases, but the initial jump into the human population is fueled by human destruction of environments, trade in wildlife (for food and pets), and industrialized agriculture. In a recent *Washington Post* article, Karin Brulliard writes that "a global wildlife trade worth billions of dollars, agricultural intensification, deforestation and urbanization are bringing people closer to animals, giving their viruses more of what they need to infect us: opportunity." She goes on to note that "70 percent of emerging infectious diseases in humans are of zoonotic origin, scientists say, and nearly 1.7 million undiscovered viruses may exist in wildlife."[2]

Spillover occurs through hunting and eating wild animals, gathering animals together in markets, human encroachment into wildlife habitat, and displacing wildlife through environmental disturbance and destruction. In one example, the "clearing of rainforests for palm oil and lumber and livestock displaced fruit bats, some of which ended up on new pig farms where mango and other fruit trees also grew. . . . Bats 'drop more than they eat,' Gillespie said, 'and their saliva and feces infected pigs below.'"[3] While this particular example resulted in the spread of the Nipah virus, the swine flu (H1N1) of 2009 spread more widely. As noted in *Zoobiquity*, "During its infectious journey around the world, the 'human' flu virus had acquired genetic material from pig and bird flu viruses."[4] This is possible because of how much human beings share in common with other animal beings.

> Biologists are rapidly uncovering ancient genetic similarities that link diverse species—mammals, reptiles, birds, and even insects. The discovery is astonishing: nearly identical clusters of genes have been passed down for billions of years, from cell to cell and organism to organism. . . . *Deep homology* is the term coined . . . to describe these genetic kernels we share with nearly all creatures. . . . Deep homology traces our molecular lineage to our most ancient common ancestors. It proves that all living organisms, including plants, are long-lost relatives.[5]

Learning to respect these relatives is imperative for the health of humans and the rest of nature. "There needs to be a cultural shift from a community level up about how we treat animals, our understanding of the dangers and biosecurity risks that we're exposing ourselves to," said Kate Jones, chair of ecology and biodiversity at University College London. "That means leaving ecosystems intact, not destroying them. It means thinking in a more long-term way."[6]

It also means rethinking a number of the common ways human beings relate to other animal beings. Hunting chimpanzees resulted in HIV emerging in the human population; industrialized agriculture gave us mad cow disease and more common outbreaks of E. Coli and influenza; trapping and hunting wolves and coyotes eliminated important predators and allowed for the faster spread of Lyme disease. While the issue of such disease transfer is not the focus of this book, the kind of respect that is argued for here would be an important step in helping to mitigate or prevent more virulent outbreaks. Arguing for restrictions on meat markets and the trade in wild animals, Jane Goodall notes, "We have moved into this destructive and greedy period of human history where we are destroying the environment and putting economic growth ahead of the environmental protections, even though we are thus destroying the future for our own children. Now we see this resulting in this current pandemic, which is having a horrific effect on the planet." She goes on to point out that the risk of zoonotic diseases does not just come from human interactions with wildlife: "[W]e also have to remember that some of these epidemics have started with viruses jumping from domestic animals in awful intensive farms, where the conditions are horrendous, with crowding and poor hygiene." She argues that our lack of respect for the personalities and intelligence of other animal beings, and our lack of respect for the natural world, is coming back to bite us. Goodall's hope for change does focus on changing laws to promote conservation, but it doesn't rest there. Her hope rests with young people. Importantly, her Roots & Shoots program for young people insists on working with the connections among projects focused on helping humans, projects focused on helping other animal beings, and projects focused on helping the environment.[7] Humans need to remember that their lives and deaths are intertwined with the rest of nature; they need to remember that to be human is to be related to the rest of life—not separate from or superior to it.

OVERVIEW

In what follows, I present examples of what it might mean to take a pragmatist ecofeminist approach to thinking about how humans currently do (and could potentially) live with other animals (I explain these terms and theoretical approaches in chapter 1). Any such undertaking cannot hope to be exhaustive. I have chosen to focus on a set of specific animals, and I have connected the ethical and political discussion of their lives and deaths with examples of children's and young adult literature and films. I primarily discuss *Charlotte's Web*, *Chicken Run*, *Babe*, *Curious George*, *Black Beauty*, *The Jungle Book*, *The Call of the Wild*, *White Fang*, *Julie of the Wolves*, and *Moby-Dick*. In all of these books, the animals themselves are central, communicate about their needs and desires (obviously as understood by the author), and challenge the idea of seeing other animal beings as simply existing to use as humans see fit. All these books not only have promising possibilities for helping us rethink our relationships with other animals in Western industrialized countries but also highlight (often without comment) many of the troubling legacies of Western industrialization and colonization. While I cannot explore any of these works in their full and rich complexity, I do try to highlight important examples of both the potential and the limitations of each story. Further, where appropriate, I have integrated Native American stories about the animals being discussed in order to present some challenges to the dominant discourse and policies. In keeping with the idea of drawing on children's and young adult literature, these are largely drawn from *Keepers of the Animals: Native American Stories and Wildlife Activities for Children*. The authors of this book write that "Native North Americans emphasize a close relationship with nature versus control over the natural world," and they emphasize that it is important "to take a journey into the realm of our animal relations in order to better understand them."[8] Stories provide a way to enter this realm of knowledge and propose ethics for sustaining those relationships.

Chapter 1 provides some context for the array of animal issues raised throughout the book and introduces the philosophical perspectives of pragmatism, ecofeminism, and ecowomanism. After sketching the history of human relationships with other animal beings, the long-standing human desire to fully connect and communicate with other animal beings is discussed, using the story of Dr. Dolittle as an example. The importance of rethinking relationships between humans and other animal beings is then motivated by an analysis of the environmental impacts of eating meat. Brief accounts of some of the common approaches to animal ethics are presented and then general accounts of pragmatism, ecofeminism, and ecowomanism are introduced. The pragmatist philosophies of Charles S. Peirce, William James, John Dewey, and Jane Addams are discussed, along with the ecofeminist view of Val Plumwood and the ecowomanist view of Alice Walker.

Chapter 2 focuses on the plight of the great apes, with special focus on chimpanzees as a particular example. Ethical questions about the capture, killing, and use of these apes are raised, and the question of extending moral standing to apes is examined. The proposal to extend rights to apes is also discussed. I argue that there are limitations to the rights approach and, relying on the work of Val Plumwood, I argue that the rights approach reinforces human exceptionalism. Human exceptionalism continues to limit who among the other-than-human realm will ever count morally or politically. We need to develop an approach based on respect and solidarity instead of following an extensionist model. The stories of *Curious George* are examined in conjunction with the real-life example of Washoe—a chimpanzee involved in language studies.

Chapter 3 is grounded in a discussion of *Black Beauty* in order to examine the lives of contemporary horses in cities, in competition, and at work on cattle ranches. While fewer horses in the United States are engaged in work in city streets than when *Black Beauty* was written, there are still contentious debates about using horses for carriage rides in cities. While the well-being of the horses is commonly the reason given for ending such activities, the result is a removal of horses from most people's lives. Those humans who do have sustained relationships with horses often compete with them, and in those activities, there are not infrequent occasions of abuse and harm. There are also frequent occasions for real bonding between horse and human, though. In contrast to the money- and prize-driven worlds of showing and the rodeo, horses are still frequently used on working ranches. In fact, those who resist the industrial model of concentrated animal feeding operations (CAFOs) for raising cattle are quite likely to use horses as a working partner as they move cattle from pasture to pasture. Ranch horses' lives connect to the lives of cattle, and grazing cattle are often in competition with "wild" horses in the United States. These overlapping lives result in complex situations where someone eating grass-fed beef (perhaps in an effort to not participate in the animal suffering and environmental degradation caused by industrial farming) may unwittingly contribute to the death of wild horses. Instead of putting horses and cattle in competition with each other, though, contemporary cattle ranches might be a place to enhance the long-standing partnership between humans and horses and horses and cattle. This chapter explores that possibility through an ecofeminist lens based in the work of Charlotte Perkins Gilman, Karen Warren, Carol Adams, A. Breeze Harper, and Val Plumwood.

Chapter 4 examines the conditions of pigs and poultry in contemporary industrial farming, as well as the emerging alternatives of pasture-based agriculture, through a discussion of *Babe* and *Chicken Run*. The work of ecofeminists Carol Adams and Val Plumwood is again integrated in this discussion, and the work of Alice Walker is developed. The work of John Dewey is then combined with these ecofeminist perspectives in order to develop a pragmatist ecofeminist ethic of respectful use. Together, these theorists point to the importance of using a pragmatist approach to discuss and evaluate what these different systems mean for the animals themselves, for the environment, for farmers, and for consumers.

Chapter 5 focuses on whales and fishes and moves from a discussion of *Moby-Dick* to examine the increased critical attention focused on keeping dolphins and whales in captivity and using them in entertainment. The rise of industrial fishing practices and industrial fish farming, though, has changed these relationships. Fishes[9] have increasingly come to be seen simply as a resource. Overfishing has caused fisheries to collapse, and the wasted bycatch means less food in the oceans for other sea creatures. The human relationships with the mammals of the ocean have also changed. Not so long ago whales and dolphins were seen as resources for food and oil, but now many see them as intelligent sentient creatures and object to hunting them or keeping them in captivity. Films such as *The Cove* and *Blackfish* highlight growing concerns over the use of whales and dolphins in entertainment and as food. Both films received a great deal of public attention, and *Blackfish* resulted in many boycotting Sea World and Marineland. The public response to the films demonstrates a growing concern for sea mammals and a growing respect for their intelligence and their cultures. The critical pragmatism of Alain L. Locke is used to argue for the possibility of understanding an exchange among human and other animal cultures. The native philosophies of Vine Deloria Jr. and Robin Wall Kimmerer are introduced to begin an examination of more inclusive ways of understanding human relationships with other animal (and plant) beings.

Chapter 6 examines human relationships with animals commonly considered pests. While these relationships are often antagonistic and lethal for the other-than-human animals, such an approach fails to appreciate human interdependence with those animal beings seen as pests and often results in creating further problems and perceived divides. The philosophy of Rachel Carson is discussed to critique the model of trying to dominate and control nature (especially in the form of insects), and Lori Gruen's view of entangled empathy is used and critiqued in an attempt to develop a more inclusive ethics. Using the story of *Charlotte's Web*, special attention is focused on spiders in order to ask whether an ethic of empathy can be used to gain a greater understanding of "pests" such as insects, spiders, prairie dogs, and coyotes. Once an animal is labeled as a pest, humans generally feel justified in killing individuals of that species rather than looking for ways to coexist (throughout human history the same can generally be said about groups of humans who get labeled as a nuisance as well). Under this guise, the United States called for the extermination of wolves and continues a war with coyotes. While there is increasing research showing that such predators should be seen as integral to an ecosystem rather than as pests, there are fewer champions of the "pests" most of us encounter on a more regular basis: flies, mosquitoes, ants, mice, rats, spiders, and snakes.

Chapter 7 focuses on big cats and wild canines and includes discussion of *Born Free*, *The Lion King*, *The Jungle Book*, *The Call of the Wild*, *White Fang*, and *Julie of the Wolves* in order to examine how humans often respond to those animals who can kill and eat them. Not only are these predators seen as dangerous, but they also often fall in the pest or nuisance category when they are perceived to threaten the livestock animals that humans raise for food. In addition, they are seen by many as a threat to their domesticated cousins—the dogs and cats with whom we share our homes. The ecowomanist philosophy of Alice Walker (discussed in chapters 1 and 4) will be used to rethink relationships based on fear and domination and to argue for respectful coexistence and honoring the sacred. The pragmatist philosophy of Jane Addams is also used as an example of how to address complex and controversial issues, such as wolf predation, in a productive manner.

Chapter 8 concludes by briefly returning to the complicated interactions among many of the ways humans live with other animal beings. This chapter challenges the reader to think carefully in the midst of this complexity rather than seeking a single position on issues such as diet or scientific research. The work of Plumwood, Walker, and Kimmerer is once again offered as a pragmatist ecofeminist way forward.

Chapter One

Living with Animals

Humans are animals, and we have lived with, thought about, used, and killed other animal beings throughout our history. While it seems that early hominid species were both predator and prey, many human beings today see humans as the top predator in control of the rest of nature. Any other animal beings who treat a human, or those animals with whom humans live in close contact (pets and livestock), as prey are declared to be dangerous and are killed or relocated to a place farther away from humans. As humans continue to expand their presence in the world, though, there is less and less space left for other animal beings to inhabit without risking violating some felt human right to be unaffected by the lives of other creatures.

This has not always been how humans lived with other animals, though, and it is not even how all humans live with other animals today. In the past, and in many indigenous cultures today, human beings see other animal beings as kin of one kind or another. Early humans probably scavenged from the kills of other animals such as wolves, large cats, and bears. To do this, they had to have intimate knowledge of these animals' lives, as well as those of other scavengers such as vultures, ravens, and crows. To remain safe, they had to be aware of the large predators who might see them as a meal. While wolves, large cats, and bears rarely attack humans, crocodiles, alligators, hippos, and many parasites seem less discriminating. Humans also had to learn about snakes and spiders who might present the threat of a venomous bite, and had to negotiate living with rodents who had an interest in our garbage and food supplies. These examples just begin to tell the story.

The importance of other animals for the human animal can be seen in the fact that much of the earliest art by humans is about other animal beings. The depiction of animals in this early art often focuses on Lascaux, France, but such depictions occur around the globe, with prominent examples in Africa, Australia, and the Americas. Animals are also featured prominently in myths, religious stories, and fables. Animals were often used in religious sacrifice, and religious texts wrestle with the issue of whether humans should eat other animals and, if so, which ones. Along with particular taboos, one can find directions for the proper slaughter and consumption of specific animals. Fables abound with stories about animals, though in these there is often a shift from an attempt to understand and portray the animals themselves to using the animals as a stand-in for humans and human behavior.

As humans began to live in close proximity to tamed and then domesticated animals, important changes in the ways humans lived with other animal beings occurred. While some hunter-gatherer societies see some other animals as competition for the foods they themselves want and need, they also seem to understand that other animals have a role to play in maintaining the health of the plants and prey on which the humans depend. It is also possible that they simply lacked the means by which to try to eliminate a perceived competitor. Either way, they tended to live in balance with the sources of their food and with other animals who shared this dependence. Many animals limit their reproduction when faced with conditions of drought or famine. This limit was lifted for many humans with technologies that allow humans to farm and so provide food more reliably year round and through many environmental shifts.[1]

This settling down to farm and raise livestock altered not only human relationships with each other and their own bodies but also their relationship with the rest of nature. Here my focus is on how it altered how humans lived with other animals. The dog is believed to be the first domesticated animal, becoming domesticated about fifteen thousand years ago. Domesticated dogs are related to wolves, and their existence provides indirect evidence of the close relationship humans had with wolves in the past. Taking in and taming wolf pups is not an easy task, even today. Many scientists now agree that there must have been some willingness on the part of some wolves to make domestication possible. This means humans were living among wolves in ways that were not completely adversarial in order for this process to begin. This occurred before humans had domesticated livestock animals such as goats, sheep, cattle, and pigs. Humans were still scavenging and hunting, and probably working in cooperative relationships with wolves to do so.

Livestock animals became domesticated around eleven thousand to thirteen thousand years ago, though it is likely that humans managed and partially contained herds and flocks before then. Dogs were (and are) potential predators of livestock animals, though some dogs specialize in guarding and herding livestock animals. Wolves, bears, and big cats, though, increasingly came to be seen as threats to livestock animals, dogs, and humans. What had been some kind of cooperative coexistence became an antagonistic relationship as humans sought to protect animal beings they viewed as property. Just as uncultivated fields came to be seen as wasted resources awaiting human improvement, undomesticated animals came to be seen as having no value of their own and as presenting a threat to those animals who did have value.

In addition to predators being seen as a threat, rodents were seen as a threat to the increasing amounts of stored grains; snakes and burrowing animals were seen as creating a problem by filling fields with holes that presented hazards; other grazing animals came to be seen as competition for the grazing land humans wanted for livestock. In short, the rest of nature was seen as needing to be support for human farming and livestock production. Any parts of nature that did not support these endeavors were basically worthless, and any parts of nature that threatened these endeavors needed to be eliminated.

And yet something still remains that lures at least some humans back to a more cooperative relationship with the rest of nature, at least in their imaginations (if not always in real life). Literature and movies abound with examples of humans living in close relationship with other animal beings, communicating with other animal beings, and helping and being helped by other animal beings. One telling example is the story of Dr. Dolittle. Another version of the film was released in February 2020, demonstrating the continuing allure of humans communicating with other animals. The story of Dr. Dolittle began in the 1920s as a series of children's books written by Hugh Lofting. Dr. Dolittle is an observer of nature and learns to speak to animals in their own languages with help from Polynesia the parrot. The books have been adapted for stage, radio, television, and film. The 1967 film with Rex Harrison largely followed the stories as written (with added romance), while the 1988 film with Eddie Murphy updated the story to contemporary times.[2] The 2020 film starring Robert Downey Jr. returns once again to the time and place more akin to the books. In this version, Dr. Dolittle and an array of animals live in a sanctuary on land given by the queen for the duration of her life. When the queen is poisoned by one of her ministers, Dolittle and the animals embark on a voyage to find a special tree whose fruit will save the queen and so save their sanctuary. Along the way, Dolittle remarks on the cruelty of hunters, the greed of humans, and the kindness and intelligence of various other animal beings.

The stories are set in the early 1800s in England. It was not uncommon at that time for people of means to house collections of animals captured and brought to England from various colonies in Asia, Africa, and the Americas. The Dr. Dolittle stories are intertwined with the history of the rise of Enlightenment science, increasing industrialization, European colonization of the globe, and the emergence of capitalism. Dr. Dolittle both participates in the logic of domination found in these frameworks and challenges it. For example, in *Dr. Dolittle's Circus* he exhibits the pushmi-pullu (a two-headed creature) in order to make money, but he goes to great lengths to free Sophie the seal, whose husband (back in Alaska) has not eaten since she was captured. When Dr. Dolittle makes the case that Sophie should be returned home, her owner says he needs her to make money and points out that Dolittle does the same. "'Well, that isn't the same as me at all,' says the Doctor. 'The big difference is that the pushmi-pullu is here of his own accord and Sophie is kept against her will. It is a perfect scandal that hunters can go up to the Artic and capture any animals they like, breaking up families and upsetting herd government and community life in this way—a crying shame!'" When Dolittle realizes he doesn't have enough money to buy her, he argues that Sophie "doesn't belong to those men, anyhow. She's a free citizen of the Arctic Circle. And if she wants to go back there, back she shall go."[3] He ends up helping her escape and eventually returns all the animals to the jungle. In other stories, Dolittle calls fox hunting a childish sport and notes that foxes are vilified for eating in order to live, a dog is a witness to a murder and testifies in court, and polar bears ask him not to reveal the North Pole to the rest of the world because they worry humans would do anything to get to the coal buried there.[4] The stories can be used to demonstrate the intertwined logics of domination that we continue to live with today.

Some aspects of the stories can also be used to dismantle those logics as many humans seek real communication with, and understanding of, other animal beings in order to make more respectful relationships possible in the future. The Enlightenment logic of domination in the original stories is reinforced by the hierarchy of power represented in the class relations, the racist identification of black people with monkeys, and the colonial relations with the "Indians" on the island where Dolittle becomes king and brings fire, clean water, and democracy to the indigenous societies. At the same time, Dolittle's respect for Long Arrow (son of Golden Arrow), a "Red Indian" from South America, as the greatest naturalist who ever lived challenges the presumed superiority of the "civilized" British. There are also numerous asides indicating that the "less civilized" humans and the other animals have insight and knowledge that the "enlightened" British lack. Nonetheless, the logic of colonization remains clear, even as aspects of the story challenge the logic of domination with regard to the human treatment of other animal beings. In the latest film these same tensions remain, as the queen is dismissive of Dolittle and the animals even after they save her life.

Dr. Dolittle is just one example from children's and young adult literature that explores closer relationships between human and other animal beings. In this book, I explore the ethics and politics of human relationships with a subset of animal beings by exploring both the evolutionary history of these animal beings and some of their representation in children's and young adult literature. The focus here is primarily on literature commonly read in the United States, though stories from other cultures are also included. I think this focus is necessary because it is primarily the Western industrialized countries, and the United States in particular, that have created and promoted the idea of human exceptionalism in ways that reduce other animals to objects to be used and consumed by humans. The heavy focus on meat production and consumption in the United States (and now being spread around the globe) both follows from this view and is now a primary motivator for maintaining the primacy of this view of other animals. I will argue that this itself is a story, and one that is inaccurate, unethical, and unsustainable. Children's stories often offer an alternative.

Alice Walker writes about humans as closely connected with the rest of nature. When she moved to the country, she regained that sense of connection herself: "I became aware of that very thin membrane, human-adult-made, that separates us from this seemingly vanished world, where plants and animals still speak a language we humans understand, and I began to write about the exhilarating experience of regaining my childhood empathy."[5] Children are often quite open to the idea that human and other beings have a great deal in common, that they can communicate with other animals, and that we owe other animals care and respect. Most children are captured by stories with animal characters and seek the company of both toy stuffed animals and real live animals. This closeness and respect for other animals does not always last into adulthood, as society sends messages about animals as less capable and less valuable than humans and promotes the idea of other animal beings existing primarily for use by human beings. Many children face a decision about their relationships with other animal beings when they realize that the meat on their plate is the dead remains of an animal. Ironically, that meat is sometimes presented in the form of another animal, such as dinosaur-shaped chicken nuggets, in order to get them to eat it. Some children object to eating animals, though family and societal habits often make acting on this view difficult for children to achieve. Alice Walker's story "Am I Blue" was censored for being anti-meat, demonstrating that many worry young people might choose not to eat meat if given the choice. There is some evidence that this is happening, despite the overwhelming promotion of meat consumption. The Humane Society of the United States reports that "[v]egans and vegetarians remain a small portion of the U.S. population. But a third of people responding to a recent U.S. poll said they ate at least one meatless meal a week, and one-quarter of Americans between the ages of 25 and 34 are vegan or vegetarian."[6]

While some of this change is primarily focused on human health and the realization that too much meat in one's diet causes a variety of health concerns, much of it is also concerned about the health of the planet. Climate change is a pressing concern, and livestock production is a contributing factor. Livestock production contributes methane and carbon dioxide emissions in addition to the pollution caused by fecal waste. In their article "Reducing Food's Environmental Impacts through Producers and Consumers," Poore and Nemecke write, "With current diets and production practices, feeding 7.6 billion people is degrading terrestrial and aquatic ecosystems, depleting water resources, and driving climate change." They also report that "[p]ork, poultry, meat and milk show higher correlations between acidification and eutrophication." Eutrophication is the increased nutrient load in water that results in dead zones and algae blooms. Food production is a major contributor of greenhouse gasses (GHG). Not all of this is from animal or animal-related farming, but much of it is. "Methane from flooded rice, enteric methane from ruminants, and concentrate feed for pigs and poultry are sizeable globally, representing 30% of food's GHG emissions."[7] Poore and Nemecek are particularly concerned about animal products because "the impacts of animal products can markedly exceed those of vegetable substitutes" since "meat, aquaculture, eggs, and dairy use ~83% of the world's farmland

and contribute 56 to 58% of food's different emissions, despite providing only 37% of our protein and 18% of our calories." They conclude that a shift to diets that exclude animal products stands to beneficially transform environmental conditions: "For the United States, where per capita meat consumption is three times the global average, dietary change has the potential for a far greater effect on food's different emissions, reducing them by 61 to 73%." They note that even cutting one's animal consumption in half can have a substantial impact, though they realize that "widespread behavioral change will be hard to achieve in the narrow timeframe remaining to limit global warming and prevent further, irreversible biodiversity loss."[8]

By contributing to climate change, livestock production also contributes to the decline in a variety of nondomesticated animals around the globe. Many of these animals cannot adapt to the shifts in climate due to the speed at which these shifts are occurring. Changes in ocean temperatures and currents impact whales, dolphins, and fishes. Extremes in temperature and precipitation impact many land animals, as do more intense and more widespread fires. Livestock production also more directly impacts the health and well-being of these nondomesticated animals. Chemical and manure runoff from crop production that is targeted for animal consumption pollutes ground water, rivers, and oceans. Manure lagoons leak and fail. Diseases found in farmed animals can spread to their nondomesticated cousins. Forests are cleared to make room to graze animals, destroying habitat for many other animal beings and introducing competitors for their food sources. Monkeys, apes, and birds are often harmed when land is cleared for either crop production or grazing. Many "wild" animals are killed to protect livestock animals. Wolves, coyotes, and cougars are primary examples in the United States.

The complex systems of environmental, wildlife, and livestock protection and use in the United States mean that we are all implicated in the suffering and death of billions of animals each year. Even for people who do not directly consume animals themselves, the protection of cropland results in the death of millions of animals. Some of those same people may call for a cougar to be shot from fear of the cat preying on pets. It is important to begin to try to understand the complex intertwining of our human lives and deaths with the lives and deaths of other animal beings. Political fights over land and water are connected to which animals humans think matter the most. Political fights over farm subsidies are connected to who and how humans think we should eat. Disagreements about climate change are connected to who and how humans currently do eat.

It's not just about food, though. Political fights over biomedical research are also connected to how humans view other animal beings. Many of the same animals that humans seek to eradicate from their farms and houses (mice, rats, and rabbits) are intentionally bred to be used in biomedical and other scientific research (often to research diseases caused by humans eating too many other animals). Monkeys and apes have been captured and bred for use in research and teaching as well. Whales and dolphins are studied in captivity and often are used in the entertainment industry. Marine parks, zoos, circuses, and the use of animals in film and television present yet another host of ethical and political questions regarding humans' relationships with other animal beings.

PHILOSOPHICAL PERSPECTIVES

Philosophers have been on the front lines in thinking about these issues. Until recently, the response to many of these practices was to frame them as ethical problems and examine them through the dominant lenses of either a utilitarian ethic (most famously presented by Peter Singer) or a deontological ethic (most famously presented by Tom Regan).[9] The utilitarian approach brought greater consideration for the lives and deaths of animals by examining their pain and suffering. Generally those taking this position argue that the pain and suffering of other-than-human animals is an ethical wrong that should be avoided unless it is outweighed by a greater benefit to a large number of beings. This line of reasoning helped give rise to the animal welfare movement, which seeks to improve conditions for animals in farming, research, and captivity. Except in some instances where there is a judgment that no welfare changes can make certain conditions humane, or where there is a judgment that no real and necessary benefit is achieved by the use of animals, those advocating this approach do not call for the end of all use of other-than-human animals in these kinds of practices.

By contrast, those taking a deontological approach generally argue for the abolition of all use of other-than-human animals by humans. On this account, since animals are "subjects of a life" they are due rights such as the right not to be killed or tortured. This argument usually entails the end of all farming and use of all other-than-human animals for food or fiber, the end of all research involving other-than-human animals, and the end of all entertainment and competition involving other animal beings. Some use this approach to argue that all domestication of animals is wrong and we should end the practice of living with any other-than-human animals no matter the conditions of those lives. This approach moved from seeing the questions about how human beings relate to other animal beings as solely ethical questions and introduced the questions to the political realm, and the rise of animal rights (not welfare) was born.

While there are clear tensions between these two approaches, in public discourse the two are generally collapsed under the heading of animal rights. Though many animal welfare advocates do support granting limited legal rights and/or personhood to some other animals as a means of protecting them from abuse, and so materially improving their welfare, they stop short of saying that other-than-human animals have inviolable rights that prohibit any use of them by humans. On both accounts, it should be noted, there remains a certain amount of anthropocentrism and human exceptionalism. The animals to be granted personhood and rights, and whose suffering counts the most, are usually those whom humans deem to share the most in common with us: apes, dolphins, whales, elephants. These are all big-brained social mammals with long lives and long childhoods. It is thought that this results in social complexity, communication, and intelligence enough like our own to deserve greater ethical and political consideration.

These approaches, while having achieved concrete changes for the lives of other-than-human animals, still tend to work with the idea of the human as the model ethical and political subject. This book will explore some alternatives to these approaches based in a pragmatist ecofeminist perspective. I have presented elements of such an approach in my books on pets and livestock.[10] Here I give a general account of pragmatism and ecofeminism, which will be filled out more fully in the chapters that follow by examining the current situations particular animals face through the frameworks provided by theorists such as John Dewey, Charlotte Perkins Gilman, Alain L. Locke, Val Plumwood, Karen Warren, Carol Adams, Lori Gruen, A. Breeze Harper, Vine Deloria Jr., Robin Wall Kimmerer, and Alice Walker.

Pragmatism is a school of philosophical thought primarily developed in the United States in the late 1880s and early 1900s. Writing in the wake of the American Civil War, and in the middle of a paradigm shift ushered in by competing theories of evolution, pragmatism was concerned with understanding the changing nature of the world. Theories of evolution altered our understanding of the formation and place of the earth in the universe, as well as of all the life on earth. While there were marked differences among the competing theories of evolution, they all served to place human beings in direct relationship with all the other living beings. This meant it didn't make sense to understand humans as completely distinct from other animals. We came to understand that we shared an evolutionary past, shared genetic material, and shared traits of consciousness and communication. Rather than being outside of nature, humans were in the middle of networks of relations with the rest of nature. While some continued to understand humans' place as at the top of some kind of hierarchy—the Great Chain of Being reimagined in evolutionary terms—most thought that evolution suggested that humans were not a final perfected product of evolution. Instead, humans represented one among many possible ways of being in the universe. Dolphins represented another, with abilities and intelligences that humans did not have. Wolves represented still another, with abilities and intelligences that humans did not have. Chimpanzees represented still another, and so on.

This ontological realization of relatedness has yet to fully integrate itself into human ethics and politics. The pragmatists were largely focused on working this out, though. They saw that the changing nature of reality meant the possibility of the changing nature of ideas, ethics, and politics. The Civil War demonstrated the possibility of change in these areas. It also provided a cautionary example of the potential power of ideas when lived out in action—both constructive and destructive power. In the Civil War, there were competing ideas about what it is to be human and who is human. There were competing ideas about political power and order. There were competing ideas about what was ethically required of individuals in the face of situations they believed to be unjust. All beliefs have power to change things. The manner in which one holds those beliefs also matters. If one holds to an idea with unquestionable certainty, one is likely to view any means as justified in the pursuit of the end posited by the idea. This way of holding an idea did not make sense to the pragmatists given their understanding of the changing nature of things. It made more sense to hold ideas tentatively, acting on them as long as experience supported them, but being willing to revise them as new experience or information emerged. Holding on to an idea or belief tenaciously does not allow for intelligent modification of beliefs and action.

The pragmatists thought ideas were not to simply be debated in the realm of other ideas and concepts but, instead, put to work in the world. Someone owning slaves was putting an idea to work in the world. So was someone hiding people on the underground railroad, as were the fugitives themselves. Someone using a chimpanzee in biomedical research is putting an idea to work in the world. So is someone destroying the research lab and taking the chimpanzees. How to judge between competing ideas can be complicated in the present moment. The hindsight of history often makes it clearer which ideas served to improve lives for more people and which only benefited a select few, but in the middle of such a dispute, things are less certain. While few now debate the human status of those humans who were enslaved and are now granted at least all the formal rights of personhood, there is strong debate about the status of chimpanzees as persons with rights not to be tortured and killed in biomedical experiments. Working ideas out in practice is what constitutes human histories. Power and privilege can cover over problems with ideas, though, so there needs to be a pluralistic, inclusive, and democratic process of inquiry that helps make it possible (though it never guarantees) for all voices to be present and heard.

Various thinkers in the pragmatist tradition focused on different aspects of understanding and living through this ontology, epistemology, ethics, and politics of change. Here I will discuss some aspects of the work of Charles S. Peirce, William James, John Dewey, and Jane Addams. The work of Charlotte Perkins Gilman and Alain Locke is also connected with the pragmatist tradition, but I save the discussion of their work for future chapters. For convenience I will use Peirce to present a pragmatist epistemology, James to present a pragmatist ontology, Dewey to present a pragmatist ethic, and Addams to present a pragmatist politics. These are highly artificial separations since ontological views inform ethical views, and views of epistemology inform views of politics, and so on. This is just a convenient device for getting some of the main ideas of a pragmatist approach on the table.

Peirce understood that for limited and fallible creatures such as human beings, understanding a changing world required a diverse community of inquirers engaged in ongoing experimentation and refinement of knowledge claims. Such knowledge claims, or truths, are always provisional, though we treat them as settled as long as they are working. Peirce thought that nature was only knowable by beings who shared aspects of its ordering and functioning. Knowledge about the rest of nature, including other animals, is only possible because humans are continuous with the rest of nature and share features such as consciousness and communication, even if these take very different forms in different organisms. He writes, "[W]e are all of us natural products, naturally partaking of the characteristics that are found everywhere throughout nature."[11] We look for regularities in nature, even as we also take note of the differences.

Those regularities, or habits of nature, can be seen in evolution when different species in different eras evolve similar ways of interacting with their environment, be that how they breathe or how they see. Such habits can be seen within a species and in individuals as well. Those regularities allow humans to know patterns and better take note of the exceptions to those patterns. While the universe is not set and determined in Peirce's account, there is still predictability even in the face of ongoing change. Such predictability means that we cannot believe just anything we want about the rest of nature. Instead, our knowledge is formed and constrained by our experiences with the rest of nature. This speaks against taking an anthropocentric approach to knowing the rest of nature. Focusing only on human experiences and interests would mean missing much that is revealed in the experiences of other organisms' interactions with their environments. Current interest in biomimicry is an example of how and what humans can learn in this way.

The shared capacity for communication is another example of a shared capacity taking many different forms. Peirce concluded that there is "some kind of language . . . among nearly all animals. Not only do animals of the same species convey their assertions, but different classes of animals do so, as when a snake hypnotizes a bird."[12] Various vocalizations, facial expressions, and other body language found among many animals help make his point, as do forms of chemical and olfactory communication. Difference in communication and consciousness are real but do not mark a sharp ontological break. If they did, knowledge of "others" and relationships with them would not be possible. The experience of human history tells us that such relationships are not only possible but also important to living well.

Similar to Peirce, James found the universe to be full of sameness, full of difference, and full of relationships. On his view, the relations that connect experiences must themselves be experienced relations, and *"any kind of relation experienced must be accounted as 'real' as anything else in the system."*[13] Things are related but not fixed. The same is true of experiences. This means that at any given time and place some things and experiences are connected and others are not. Change and novelty are real possibilities and so, too, are the possibilities of tragedy and amelioration. On this view, there is no guarantee that things will improve. Indeed, they can go very wrong as the world contains real risk and at times requires decisions that remove certain possibilities from any future state of the world (the extinction of a species, for example). James's pluralistic ontology also entails a pluralistic epistemology and a value pluralism. Given the uncertainty of the world and our choices in it, some fall back on dogmatic belief to give them comfort. James believes that this is when most injustices and cruelties emerge, for "[o]bjective evidence and certitude are doubtless very fine ideals to play with . . . [b]ut where on this moonlit and dream-visited planet are they found?" What we have instead is "the practical faith that we must go on experiencing and thinking over our experience, for only thus can our opinions grow more true."[14] Knowledge claims that are provisional and held tentatively allow for greater tolerance for the views, experiences, and values of others, including those of other-than-human beings.

Dewey argues that "[t]he intelligent acknowledgement of the continuity of nature, man, and society will alone secure a growth of morals which will be serious without being fanatical, aspiring without sentimentality, adapted to reality without conventionality, sensible without taking the form of calculation of profits, idealistic without being romantic."[15] Given the continuity of humans with the rest of nature, and the realization that past and present relationships with the rest of nature condition the possibilities for the future, it is important to critically examine those relationships. For Dewey, organisms are always in transactional relationships with the rest of their environment (physical, social, and cultural). That is to say, they are shaped and modified by their environment, as they also shape and modify that environment. This means there can be no sharp divide between an organism and its environment, and there are no sharp divides between culture and nature. It also means that for organisms to be in sustaining and sustainable relationships with their environments, organisms must consider others when acting in the world.

Human history shows that humans have paid attention to animals and modified their behavior in anticipation of responses from other animal beings. This was necessary for early humans in order for them to eat and not be eaten. With domestication, it was necessary for humans to understand the needs and desires of other animal beings and consider these as they worked to find ways to live together with more intimacy and dependence. The more recent move to industrialized animal agriculture, though, fails to maintain sustaining and sustainable relationships among humans and the majority of the animals raised for food. Instead, these relationships now present a problematic situation connected to pollution, climate change, the overuse of antibiotics, unsafe meat, zoonotic diseases, and poor working conditions for farmers and workers in the slaughter industry. The treatment of workers in a contemporary, centralized, and fast-paced slaughterhouse actually mirrors the lack of respect for the animals being slaughtered.

In Dewey's view, when a situation is problematic (it is not sustaining and sustainable) humans should engage in critical inquiry and then work to revise habits based on what they come to understand about the desired ends-in-view and the possible means to achieving those ends. Humans are often resistant to changing habits, individually and socially, and so are quite good at ignoring problems or trying to find small fixes that leave the general habit in place. The earlier discussion of the impact of meat eating on climate change is a good example. This connection has been known for quite a while, and there have been calls to reduce the human consumption of meat from a variety of groups, and yet meat consumption continues to increase. Similarly, concerns about feeding meat animals antibiotics to promote growth were raised almost as soon as the practice began, but the practice continued. As more evidence mounted that this was contributing to antibiotic resistance, some specific antibiotics were pulled from use in livestock production, but the general practice continued. This kind of response is what Peirce called the method of tenacity. One refuses to see the problems that are arising and continues with a set of beliefs and their related actions despite the problems. For an intelligent moral response, Dewey's method of inquiry requires individuals to think carefully about the situation, including how it arose in the first place and the purposes it was trying to achieve. Individuals then need to develop a variety of possible responses with which to experiment and then use what they learn in making these adjustments to continually refine their responses. A pragmatist ethics requires an open and critical approach to ongoing and changing situations, not fixed and dogmatic beliefs. This is also the case for a pragmatist approach to political organization and action.

Addams is probably best known for her peace activism and work at Hull House, a settlement house in Chicago. In both of these endeavors, she was guided by a deep commitment to an inclusive democracy. She also thought that it is better and more effective to work with people in a problematic situation to change that situation than it is for someone from outside or above to try to impose a solution. Working with others, one is more likely to have a fuller understanding of the problems at hand and to propose solutions that will have the support of those involved. Working in this way, she found that "progress has been slower perpendicularly, but incomparably greater because lateral."[16] She embodied this approach as she and other residents at Hull House worked to improve or ameliorate conditions of poverty, sanitation, sweat shop labor, child labor, and political corruption in Chicago. To ameliorate a problematic situation means to make it better, not to fix it completely or once and for all. This approach requires humility with regard to one's own positions, recognizing that we are all fallible and only have a partial perspective on any given issue. It also requires respecting those involved in both the problem and the proposed responses. This means respecting, listening to, and working and compromising with those with whom one disagrees. This takes courage as well. It is easier for people to act on their convictions when they are sure they are correct and they are in a position to impose their will on a situation. It is harder and scarier to be open to having one's ideas changed and to be willing to compromise in order to achieve concrete improvements for those in need. A good example of this concept is Washington State's Wolf Advisory Group (WAG), which is made up of livestock producers, hunters, and wolf advocates. They work together to agree on policies that make it possible for wolves to continue living in Washington State. This endeavor requires listening to other perspectives and being willing to accept less-than-ideal policies in order to make policy and habit change possible (this will be discussed more fully in chapter 7). Addams's commitment to this kind of approach rested on her understanding of individuals and communities as always in complex relationships and situations that require collective inquiry and sympathetic understanding. For her, ethics and politics both needed to move beyond a focus on individual rights and responsibilities to embrace a social perspective.

Generally pragmatists are committed to the idea of an open, pluralistic, and changing universe in which humans try to navigate their continuously developing embodied and conscious existence amid the lives of other continuously developing embodied and conscious existences. Doing this constructively and respectfully requires acknowledging one's own limited perceptions, knowledge, and understanding and living consciously as a fallible being. It requires that one seek out the perspectives, knowledges, and understandings of others who are differently situated in order to live intelligently and experimentally. Rather than fixing knowledge in place once and for all, espousing beliefs that are warranted by one's experience and putting them to work in the world to improve or ameliorate conditions becomes the task at hand.

It is important to notice that on this pragmatist perspective the role of the philosopher working on social, political, and ethical questions is not the role of an expert bestowing a theoretical position onto practitioners who will then put the theory into action. Instead, the philosopher needs to be engaged with the issues so that theory and practice inform each other. This idea has strong similarities to most feminist philosophy. Further, the philosopher is often in the position of trying to understand, clarify, and adjudicate among competing claims. When this happens in real life, rather than on the written page, it means working to find common ground among differently situated beings while trying to make room for respect for genuine differences. This, too, is the kind of on-the-ground advocacy work in which many feminist theorists also engage. Feminist theory, despite its own deep diversity, shares much in common with pragmatism and can be a useful ally in formulating respectful ways of negotiating a complex, situated real life.

Ecofeminism and ecowomanism are two historically rich and contemporarily complex areas of philosophy that are important for thinking through ways humans can improve how they live with other animal beings. I think it is necessary to augment the pragmatist insights with some of the key insights of ecofeminism and ecowomanism in order to fully embrace and improve humans' ongoing relationships with the rest of nature.[17] Ecofeminist philosophy is both old and new. Assumptions about how women and nature are related have long been part of religion and philosophy. In much of Western philosophy, the presumed dualistic relationship of reason and emotion was mapped onto the dualism of male and female. This concept was also connected with a dualism of culture and nature (which the pragmatist tradition rejects, as seen in the earlier discussion). While feminist philosophy generally challenges the reason/emotion dualism, the culture/nature dualism is often left intact, and women are to move to the side of culture to become fully human. This idea also implies that women need to become more rational to become fully human. Ecofeminists critique not only the emphasis on reason (and its separation from emotions) in Western philosophy but also the idea that being fully rational entails being separated from, and dominating, the rest of nature. Ecofeminism embraces an intersectional understanding of the complex relationships among gender, race, class, and species. Emerging out of the work of Alice Walker, ecowomanism pays particular attention to how race and class further complicate the possibilities for rethinking human relationships with the rest of nature.

Alice Walker coined the term *womanist* in 1983 in *In Search of Our Mothers' Gardens: Womanist Prose*. Her full definition is long and complex but includes this famous statement: "Womanist is to feminist as purple is to lavender." This idea is further explained: "From womanish. (Opp. of 'girlish,' i.e. frivolous, irresponsible, not serious.) A black feminist or feminist of color." "Not a separatist, except periodically, for health. Traditionally a universalist, as in: 'Mama, why are we brown, pink, and yellow, and our cousins are white, beige and black?' Ans. 'Well, you know the colored race is just like a flower garden, with every color flower represented.'"[18] Womanism deepens and enriches feminist analysis through particular attention to the thought and experience of women of color. Walker's writings often include environmental themes (discussed more in chapter 7), and soon some womanists, working to emphasize the inclusion of concerns about the environment, coined the term *ecowomanism* and focused on the parallel oppressions of the land, animals, and people of color (especially African American women). They also argued that concern for the well-being of the environment and other animals is connected to the possibility of the health and well-being of humans—especially the health and well-being of those suffering environmental injustice. Ecowomanism broadened the concerns addressed by many ecofeminists and made more room for spiritual connections among humans, the land, and other animals. While some ecofeminists also made room for spiritual connections, there has generally been tension between spiritual ecofeminism and philosophical ecofeminism. This situation has sometimes resulted in a limited understanding of the connections humans have with the rest of nature and limited the attention paid to various indigenous philosophies and spiritualties.

Val Plumwood's work, which does take up indigenous philosophies and spiritual connections, is an important example of what can come from combining ecofeminist analysis with a pragmatist approach to inquiry. While both ecofeminism and pragmatism generally share an openness to the continuity of humans with the rest of nature, the ecofeminist views understand this in a deeper way than most of the classical pragmatists, and ecofeminism deepens such an understanding with particular attention to the positionality of gender, race, class, and species. While ecofeminists challenge traditional rational approaches to moral theory, and so often turn to the ethics of care, pragmatists can offer a more pluralistic ethic and mode of inquiry. The pragmatist approach to knowledge results in multiple ways of knowing and experiencing the world that inform a generally pluralistic and process-oriented ethics and politics that honors relationships as real and shaping factors of one's life and environment (material, social, and political).

The approach offered in this book is focused on providing an introduction to a variety of animal issues through a pragmatist ecofeminist lens. The hope is to provide a better understanding of the complexity of human relationships with other animal beings and to introduce an approach to these issues that builds off of more standard approaches to animal ethics but also problematizes some of the philosophical discourse on these issues. No set of pragmatists or ecofeminists are in complete agreement about anything, so an array of figures are discussed in an effort to show the pluralism of the fields and the need for multiple voices.

Chapter Two

Chimpanzees and Other Primates

This chapter focuses on the plight of the great apes, with special focus on chimpanzees as a particular example. Ethical questions about the capture, killing, and use of these apes are raised, and the question of extending moral standing to apes is examined. The proposal to extend rights to apes is also discussed. I argue that there are limitations to the rights approach and, relying on the work of Val Plumwood, I argue that the rights approach reinforces human exceptionalism. Human exceptionalism continues to limit who among the other-than-human realm will ever count morally or politically. We need to develop an approach based on respect and solidarity instead of following an extensionist model. The stories of *Curious George* are examined in conjunction with the real-life example of Washoe—a chimpanzee involved in language studies.

CAPTURING AND KILLING APES

Most people in the United States support the conservation of the great apes (also referred to as large-bodied apes): chimpanzees, bonobos, gorillas, and orangutans. People find them cute and are regularly exposed to images of juvenile chimpanzees as playmates and pets in advertising. Many are also aware that apes are quite smart, live in complex social groups, make and use tools, solve problems, and have documented systems of communication (verbal and nonverbal). Individuals of all the large-bodied ape species have learned to use a human-created language as well. For some, this situation raises questions about whether it is ethical to use apes in research or keep them in zoos, but most people living in the United States don't think that their daily actions have anything to do with the lives and deaths of chimpanzees, bonobos, gorillas, or orangutans. They are wrong.

People living in the United States (and around the world) consume products that endanger these apes. Logging and mining impacts chimpanzees, bonobos, and gorillas. Logging, rubber plantations, and palm oil plantations impact orangutans. Everyone using electronics is implicated in the killing of apes, as is everyone consuming processed foods. While many are aware that ivory products endanger elephants, many fewer realize that things they use and consume every day endanger apes. There is no easy way to extricate ourselves from these global systems, but it seems imperative that people be aware of the consequences of their choices and more informed about the beings who are maimed, killed, and abused within these systems (human and other animal beings alike). Further, it is important for humans to consider the consistency of some of their own positions. While many in the United States call for conservation efforts on behalf of apes, they are quite happy to have wolves, big cats, and alligators shot to keep them away from human homes. And while many in the United States call for people to stop eating apes (and whales), they rarely examine the ethics of their own diets.

Why this abhorrence of eating apes? For many, it's because they are so much like humans. But then why is it seen as acceptable to keep them in zoos, use them in research, or have them as pets? These issues are all interconnected, as hunting apes for food creates orphaned infants who are sold as pets and used in entertainment. In the past, this was also how individuals were captured for zoos and research. Ironically, this process is chronicled in the *Curious George* books written for children from the 1940s to the 1960s. While George is identified as a monkey in the books, he is a juvenile chimpanzee. In the first book (1941), George is captured by a man wearing a yellow hat to bring back to the United States and put in a zoo. Of course, it is George's curiosity about the yellow hat that allows the man to capture him and put him in a sack.[1] Capturing a young chimpanzee to put in a zoo was realistic at that time, as is the fact that he would be put in a sack. But the rest of the reality is much darker.

Humans who live among chimpanzees have historically had taboos against hunting and eating them (seeing them as kin), or they have highly managed sustainable hunting practices that take into account the fact that chimpanzees give birth only about every five years and usually to only one infant. With European colonization of Africa, however, hunters from the

United States and Europe decimated chimpanzee populations. The first impact came with trophy hunting and hunting them to bring back bodies to stuff and put in natural history museums. This practice often entailed taking large males, which destabilized family groups. Then people wanted live chimpanzees to put in zoos, use in entertainment, keep as pets, study in laboratories, or use in space programs. Given the size and strength of an adult chimpanzee, it was not possible to bring back adults. To capture babies, though, hunters had to shoot the mothers and any other chimpanzees with the mother and baby. Since chimpanzees forage in social groups, and since young chimpanzees stay close to their mothers for protection, the idea that the man who captured George found George all by himself is far from the reality of chimpanzee experience.

Mothers often carried their young up trees to get away from hunters. When they were shot and killed, the fall from the tree frequently killed the baby. If the baby was successfully captured alive, s/he was actually stuffed in a sack like George was. But while George is depicted as being sad, his curiosity brings him around and he has fun on the boat crossing. He's told how much he will like the zoo. Some of what's missing from the story is that these youngsters often wouldn't eat or drink due to shock and grief. Young chimpanzees are not weaned until they are about five years old, and they then stay with their mothers for several more years (and sometimes for life). According to Dale Peterson in *Eating Apes*, this "makes them among the species most easily and readily decimated by an ordinary platoon of determined hunters."[2] As large-brained social mammals, they sustain a complex array of social relationships. Being ripped away from their mothers and their communities was devastating for both the infants and the chimpanzees left behind. It is estimated that for every chimpanzee brought into captivity, ten chimpanzees died.[3] For a species who reproduces only once every five years or so, it is hard to bounce back from such devastation (current estimates are that there are fewer than 130,000 living "freely" in Africa). Beyond the numbers, such death and kidnapping disrupts complex social organizations and often results in fighting and death within and between groups of chimpanzees left behind in the wake of this violence.

Further, human encroachment and habitat destruction have made apes more vulnerable. With colonization, African countries suffered great resource extraction. In addition to taking chimpanzees and gorillas directly (as in the story about George), logging and mining operations degraded the apes' habitat and increased the human hunting of apes for food. Rather than spend money to bring in food to feed loggers and miners, many of these corporations armed their workers so they could hunt to eat. While it is now (since the Commission on International Trade in Endangered Species [CITES] in 1975 came into force) illegal to hunt chimpanzees and gorillas due to their protected status, this law is hard to enforce. Further, there is a growing market for exotic meats, so it is quite profitable for hunters to sell chimpanzee and gorilla meat to tourists. The bushmeat trade is a lucrative one, and "if the present trend in forest exploitation continues without a radical shift in our approach to conservation, most edible wildlife in the equatorial forest of Africa will be butchered before the viable habitat is torn down."[4] It seems chimpanzees and gorillas have good reason to be wary of human beings. No other predator so systematically and unsustainably destroys entire populations of other species and their habitats.

THE ETHICS OF CROSS-FOSTERING AND LANGUAGE STUDY

So the reality is that George's mother and others in her social group would have been killed and sold for meat while he made his way to the zoo. In the story, George first goes to the man's house. There he eats at the table with a bowl and spoon, is dressed in pajamas, sits in a cushy chair to smoke a pipe, and then sleeps in a bed. When the man leaves, though, George's curiosity about the phone lands him in trouble when he calls the fire department. Interestingly, he is put in prison, where he is clearly not happy, and he escapes. He is eventually found by the man who captured him and taken to the zoo. The book ends by declaring that the zoo is a good place for George to be.[5] Several aspects of this story stand out. The human is not given a name, but George is. This is an aspect of the book that resists the more normal human/animal divide that sees humans as named individuals but lumps all other animal beings together and denies them individual personalities and uniqueness. The book also subtly shows the similarities between the prison and the zoo, though in the end the message is that the zoo is a good place for George (however, he later escapes the zoo in *Curious George Takes a Job*).[6] This is a tension throughout the series. George doesn't really end up living in the zoo, though he encounters other animal beings in zoos and circuses regularly. There is no direct critique of zoos or circuses, but the fact that George doesn't stay in such places is meaningful.

George spends most of his time living with the man who captured him. The way he is raised shares some similarities with another famous chimpanzee—Washoe. Washoe, cross-fostered by Drs. Alan and Beatrix Gardner, was the first chimpanzee to learn to communicate with American Sign Language (ASL). Being cross-fostered meant she was raised in a human home, dressed in human clothes, ate with a spoon and bowl, and slept in a bed—just like George. She was raised as if she were a deaf human child and taught ASL. She was originally captured in Africa for the National Aeronautics and Space Administration (NASA) to use in the space program, though. This means Washoe was taken from her mother at a very young age amid the violence of killing necessary to remove an infant chimpanzee from her family. She was captured in 1965, when NASA was focused on a moon landing.[7] Back in 1957, though, Curious George was given a medal as the first space monkey in *Curious George Gets a Medal*. This story is interesting for several reasons. First, George lets a number of farm animals (goats, pigs, chickens, and cows) out and gets the farmers mad at him. Then he ends up in the natural history museum, where he finds wild animals who have been stuffed and put on display so people can look at them. While he does not find any stuffed apes, he does end up posing with a dinosaur and then breaking things in the museum. Professor Wiseman, who runs the museum, is very angry and wants George to be put in jail. Then he realizes this is the same George to whom he has just written a letter. The letter asks George to participate in the space program where he will be trained to go up in a rocket, push some levers, and then land safely back on earth. While no ape was ever *asked* to participate in the space program, many were captured for this purpose and subjected to harsh training tactics and life-endangering activities. While Wiseman had started out by asking George to participate, Wiseman now blackmails George by promising to forgive the damage done to the museum if George goes into space. When the time comes for George to press the levers, the author writes that he seems to be in a daze (an accurate description of many chimpanzees used in this way). George eventually comes around, pushes the lever, and successfully parachutes down. He is celebrated as the first living being in space, and it is declared the happiest day of his life.[8]

Unlike George, Washoe never went into space. At around ten months old, she was judged to be too big for the space program and found herself living with humans, being dressed in human clothes, being fed in a high chair, and sleeping in a bed with stuffed animals. Since she was under a year old, and would have still been dependent on her mother for twenty-four-hour care, socialization, and learning, a host of graduate students helped care for Washoe. They used sign language around her and actively taught her by molding her hands into signs. She was not drilled in language as other experiments tried to do (Project Nim). The idea was that since chimpanzees use gestures to communicate in their own communities, she would be able to pick up a gestural language in the course of everyday activities. There had been attempts to get chimpanzees to speak, but since their vocal box is constructed differently, it is hard for them to make consonant sounds.[9]

Chimpanzees do vocalize to communicate, but usually in moments of high excitement, and they seem to have less conscious control over vocalizations than they do over gestures. The work with Washoe was deemed a success, as she acquired more than three hundred observed signs and more than two hundred reliable signs and created novel signs such as "water bird" for a swan. It is important to note that in this work there was a strict protocol for counting a sign as reliable. There was a list of observed signs, which required that three different observers observe the sign on separate occasions. To be reliable, a sign had to be observed fifteen days in a row without solicitation. So if on day thirteen Washoe didn't want to talk about dogs, the sign for dog wouldn't make the reliable list. This strictness was put in place so the Gardners could answer the inevitable doubt and criticism that accompanies such research with various animal beings. In the 1970s, the Gardners sent Washoe to Oklahoma along with Roger Fouts, who was one of the graduate students who'd been working with Washoe. The Gardners then adopted four infant chimpanzees who'd been born in U.S. labs and removed from their mothers at just a few days old. Moja, Tatu, Pili, and Dar were also cross-fostered but had each other to sign with as well as humans who were native signers themselves (though Pili died at a young age). While this research was going on, Washoe (having lost an infant of her own) adopted a son—Loulis. Loulis's mother was being used in research and was unable to care for him. He was brought into the sign language research to see whether Washoe would teach her offspring what she had learned. So humans stopped signing around Washoe and only spoke English. Washoe did teach Loulis to use signs, and he acquired a list of about 120 observed signs and about 60 reliable signs.[10] Eventually these five chimpanzees were united into one family at Central Washington University at the Chimpanzee-Human Communication Institute (CHCI).[11]

I was a summer apprentice at CHCI and then continued to volunteer there for more than a decade. I was constantly amazed at the communication I saw among the chimpanzees and between the chimpanzees and their caretakers. Dar, though he was the largest of the five chimpanzees, was rather shy. On several occasions, when treats were being given out, I saw him hang back and then catch the caretaker's eye and point to another room. He would slowly move to the other room while the others were busy with their treats. The caretaker would then move to the other room and give Dar his treats in peace and quiet. I witnessed Tatu do the same. Washoe was a master mediator if a fight broke out. She would hug each of the chimpanzees involved in the fight and then bring them together to hug or groom each other. She did this by using signs, showing that the chimpanzees could use and respond to signs in moments of high excitement. Tatu talked to me about hurting bees, Moja asked to see my sunglasses and to smell my hair, Washoe asked to see my shoes, Dar asked me to play chase, and Loulis laughed while he tickled my feet through the glass window in the observation room (signing "more" any time I tried to stop).

It is important to note that, as amazing as being around these chimpanzees was, Roger and Debbie Fouts (and the students at CHCI) argued that it was not ethical to have chimpanzees in captivity, that it was not ethical to remove infants from their mothers (as cross-fostering requires), and that it was not ethical to use chimpanzees in research. They believe that chimpanzees should be respected and treated ethically just on the basis of their chimpanzeeness, not on how much like humans they can be. However, once some individual chimpanzees had been cross-fostered, these individual chimpanzees had to be cared for in a way that respected their unique upbringing and abilities. The Foutses made choices about where to be and what to do based on what they thought would be best for the chimpanzees and dedicated their lives to this extended family. They were there with Washoe in 2007 when she died at the age of forty-two.

In the book *Next of Kin: My Conversations with Chimpanzees*, Roger Fouts provides an interesting account of how working with Washoe changed his life and the life of his family. While many researchers worked with apes between the 1960s and 1980s, most did not come to see that they had an ethical obligation to the well-being of these individuals or to the species as a whole. The Foutses did see this obligation and have done much to point out the ethical problems with the very language studies in which they participated. One problem with cross-fostering, and other ape language studies, is that the chimpanzees get older and bigger. Adult chimpanzees are much stronger than humans and can bite through bone. They eventually end up losing their freedom to chains and cages. Many chimpanzees used in language and psychology experiments ended up in biomedical research labs (as did many used in the space program when they got too big for the capsules). [12]

APES AND HUMAN EXCEPTIONALISM

Conditions in these biomedical facilities were (are) not good on many counts. First, chimpanzees are social creatures who spend a great deal of time in physical contact with each other and form complex social hierarchies. In research facilities, chimpanzees were typically housed alone in a cage that was five feet by five feet by seven feet. This is not enough room for most adult chimpanzees to stretch out and is a far cry from the three miles of territory a free-living chimpanzee might roam in a day while foraging for food in a much larger territory. The size and strength of chimpanzees means that for most of this research they need to be unconscious. Trying to dart and take a chimpanzee living in a group is quite difficult since they will protect each other (as they do when hunters shoot them), so they are kept alone in these small cages. These cages also have a back wall that can be moved toward the front of the cage to squeeze the chimpanzee between the two and immobilize them for blood draws and injections. I got into such a cage when I visited the former Colston lab and breeding facility in Alamogordo, New Mexico. It was quite unnerving.

The chimpanzees at this facility were being transitioned to a sanctuary in Florida. At that time (2007), half the chimpanzees had already left for Florida, and yet I was still overwhelmed by the number of chimpanzees. Given that they now had more space, the cages had been enlarged, and the work of creating social groups had begun. I spent the day helping to put food into puzzle boxes and making other enrichment items. I then accompanied one of the staff as he delivered dinner. They had me dress in a lab coat (which couldn't have put the chimpanzees at ease) and wear a hat with a face shield. They said this was because the chimpanzees inevitably throw feces at humans. This is not an unusual behavior for captive chimpanzees who are hurt and dominated by humans. While the staff member walked into the housing facility standing upright and talking loudly, I used the chimpanzee etiquette I had learned at CHCI. I walked in a bent posture, kept my teeth from showing, nodded my head in greeting, and offered a bent wrist. Not only did no one throw feces at me, but several chimpanzees also returned my greeting and quieted down. This response had nothing to do with me personally, just the power of good manners and some acknowledgment of the other. Etiquette and ethics are often closely related.

Knowing that what I saw that day wasn't nearly as bad as the conditions had been while the facility was active, I still left that day feeling horrified, sad, and ashamed. While today the U.S. government has phased out its own colonies of chimpanzees used in biomedical research (Chimpanzee Health Improvement, Maintenance, and Protection Act [Chimp Act] of 2011) and set standards for their care that "require" social housing and enrichment, there are still many concerns. For those chimpanzees who are born and die in captivity, these regulations are far from respectful of their complex needs and abilities. Now consider ripping an infant chimpanzee from her mother, raising her in a human social setting, teaching her sign language, and then dumping her in a five-foot-by-five-foot-by-seven-foot cage amid the noise and confusion of hundreds of chimpanzees imprisoned in similar cages, with no enrichment and no one who can "talk" to her or "listen" to what she is saying. This was the fate of many chimpanzees used in language research, and the Foutses worked hard and made sacrifices to make sure it was not Washoe's fate, nor the fate of those who became her adoptive family.

How is it that some human beings can treat those other animal beings most closely related to them (according to the Smithsonian, humans and chimpanzees share 98.8 percent of their DNA; humans and bonobos, 98.8 percent; humans and gorillas, 98.4 percent; and humans and orangutans, 96.9 percent) in ways that dismiss their needs, diminish their uniqueness, and deny our relatedness while depending on it? After all, the results of biomedical and psychological research on apes would be worthless for humans unless there was great similarity in the biological, cognitive, emotional, social, and behavioral realms. Even those who refuse to believe that many animals other than humans have language, reasoning, and problem-solving skills or agency usually grant some special status to these apes. Among the other-than-human animals (all lumped together), apes usually stand out based on their similarity to humans. They are often the focus of attempts to grant personhood to beings other than human beings, and they are the focus of many animal rights protests regarding scientific research and captivity. Other large-brained social mammals come to be included in this sphere of moral consideration: whales, dolphins, and elephants. The basis given for this increased consideration usually is that these animals have more aspects of what makes human beings so special when contrasted with mere "animal" beings. They have large brains that allow for complex reasoning, social recognition, memory, problem solving, deceit, and language (or some form of communication discernible to humans). This is a form of moral extensionism that rests on a version of human exceptionalism.

Human exceptionalism can take a number of forms, but basically it's the idea that human beings have an exclusive claim to traits deemed of a higher order. The list usually includes reason, language, culture, tool use, tool making, and higher-order emotions such as shame and guilt. Pretty consistently various other animals have been shown to have one or more of these supposedly exclusive traits, so the game has to shift. When tool use was observed in apes, birds, and octopuses, the line of human exceptionalism was redrawn at tool making. When tool making was observed in apes and birds, the focus returned to language. The language debates continue to rage. But why should the ability to learn and use a human language be the marker of moral worthiness? It seems that language is the last best hope for many who fear the blurring of what they see as a distinct separation between human and other animal beings. The long history of Western philosophy (and many religions) has been focused on maintaining humans above, or outside of, the rest of nature. But this is not reality. Humans are related to, in relationship with, and interdependent on the rest of nature. This entails certain responsibilities.

The work of the ecofeminist philosopher Val Plumwood is helpful for understanding some of what is problematic about human exceptionalism. In her book *Environmental Culture: The Ecological Crisis of Reason*, she points out that human exceptionalism is at the root of what ecofeminists call the logic of domination or the colonial mind-set. This way of thinking tends to homogenize, stereotype, and background the rest of nature, and so operates under the delusion that humans are not dependent on (much less interdependent with) the rest of nature. This allows the resource model of limitless extraction to continue without accountability or guilt. According to Plumwood, excluding humans from the realm of nature enables humans to deny their own continuity with the rest of nature and then to dominate or conquer all that is other than human. Humans operating with this dominating mind-set tend to homogenize and stereotype the rest of nature. That is, they disregard differences among all those other-than-human animals. Different beings are seen not only as alike but also as interchangeable and replaceable (e.g., farmed salmon are the same as wild salmon). Denying their dependence on the rest of nature (for food, fiber, water, air), humans push the rest of nature into the background so that this dependence and continuity does not have to be acknowledged. Doing so allows humans to instrumentalize nature, seeing other beings as only having value in terms of how humans use them and having no agency or value of their own. This is done to land, water, other animals, and other humans who are seen as "primitive" or closer to nature. Therefore, the rest of nature, other animal beings, and some human beings are seen as not ethically considerable, and so the privileged humans are invited to invade and use as they will.[13]

This denial of dependency promotes a hyperbolized version of autonomy that Plumwood finds in most versions of liberalism (i.e., classical liberalism or social contract theory). While there are many variations, basically the idea of social contract theory is that rational, autonomous, atomistic individuals, operating out of self-interest, will arrive at a social and legal structure that promotes the optimal balance of positive and negative liberties for each rights-bearing individual who is a party to the contract. For example, in John Rawls's version, humans are asked to engage in a thought experiment: Pretend you don't know who you are—that is, you don't know your age, race, ethnicity, sex, gender, class, religion, occupation, and so on. From behind this "veil of ignorance," what laws and social arrangements would you rationally agree to? Would you agree that salaries for the same job should differ based on sex? Would you agree that it should be legal to deny education to someone based on their religion?[14]

This kind of thought experiment can be useful for helping us see what might be considered fair, just, and ethical. Feminists have critiqued social contract theory for many reasons, though. One critique is that humans are social, not atomistic, and so relationships matter politically and morally. One can't completely disembed oneself in order to do this thought experiment. Further, humans are not purely rational, and reason and emotion cannot be separated from each other. For Plumwood, reason without emotion often is a liability for survival, as it is likely to allow some humans to dominate and commodify other humans and the rest of nature. More problematic, though, is the idea that not everyone is included in the contract. In fact, historically, women and people of color have been commodified objects of the contract (property) and not the rational subjects being consulted in forming the contract.[15] For my purposes here, all other-than-human animal beings (and the rest of nature) are still commodified objects of the contract—property. However, many who object to the ongoing objectification of the latter are calling for ending the property status of other animals and granting them rights. This kind of extension has (at least on paper) happened for women and people of color, and today many theorists and activists want to follow the extensionist model for other animals. In this way, other animal beings would have rights that could be defended in a court of law, and they would be seen as morally considerable beings. This approach should help place some limits on humans instrumentalizing them, commodifying them, and using them at will. Several suits have been brought to courts around the world on behalf of great apes. For example, Sandra, an orangutan who was granted personhood in Argentina in 2015, is now living at the Center for Great Apes sanctuary in Florida.

APE RIGHTS?

The specter of equal rights for animals strikes fear in the hearts of many. If animals have rights, how can they be used for food? Could they be used in research? Could humans keep them in captivity in zoos or homes? There are advocates for the rights-based approach who think all these things would be a violation of other animals' rights and should be illegal. For others, though, rights need to be contextualized to the needs and desires of specific species. The right to liberty, for example, may well differ for a human, a chimpanzee, a pig, and a dog. Even just considering chimpanzees, the right to liberty may not be the same for all. For example, Washoe's right to liberty was violated by her capture and subsequent captivity. As the Foutses came to see that her situation was unjust and unethical, they looked for ways to make her situation better. One thought was to return her to Africa. However, turning a human-raised chimpanzee out to forage for herself, even with a great deal of transitional training, may not be just or ethical. This was attempted with a chimpanzee named Lucy. The whole process caused her a great deal of stress, as she was again separated from the social setting with which she was familiar. In the end, Lucy's relations with humans made her an easy target for poachers, and she was killed.

The Foutses came to the conclusion that while cross-fostering was wrong in the first place, once it had occurred they had to work within that context to provide Washoe (and the rest of her family) with as much liberty as possible. So, rather than remove human clothing, dishes, utensils, and such from her environment, these things were made available each day, and she could use them or not. Sometimes she ate with a spoon, sometimes she drank from the bowl, and sometimes she ate with her fingers. Sometimes she put on clothes—shoes being her favorite item. Moja, however, put on clothes pretty much every day, and Loulis often dumped his food on the floor and ate it from there. A larger enclosure was built that included multiple rooms and spaces where no one could see them, so the chimpanzees could be alone if they wanted. Access to the outdoors was provided every day, and there were many different climbing structures and swings. Humans who were around the chimpanzees used ASL, but they also used chimpanzee postures and gestures. Anyone the chimpanzees did not like was not allowed to be in close proximity to them. Participation in research at CHCI was purely observational or voluntary on the part of the chimpanzees. If a chimpanzee did not want to participate in a study, they didn't have to. For example, in a study to see how the chimpanzees would distinguish a cracker from a cookie by varying the levels of sweetness and saltiness, several of the chimpanzees lost interest when the cookies lost their sweetness. Similarly, when there was a study to see about preferences for nest-building material, different materials were put out each day. When Dar repeatedly asked to have his blankets and said he'd be good, the study was ended and the blankets were again put out every night.

It is important to note that, as this family of chimpanzees got older (and stronger), they were weaned off most direct human physical contact. The main reason for this was the safety of the chimpanzees. If a chimpanzee hurt a human by accident (by playing too rough), or out of excitement or fear, the chimpanzee would be blamed and probably killed (given current laws and human exceptionalism). So, in a complicated twist, these chimpanzees were more free to behave and play as they wished if humans remained outside the enclosure. There was still lots of social interaction and limited contact through the caging. However, Roger Fouts is quite clear that this situation was far from ideal, as they were still in prison.

> I have to accept the Darwinian fact that Washoe is a person by any reasonable definition and the community of chimpanzees from which she was stolen are a people. I have to accept the responsibility for unjustly imprisoning a relative of mine who has done nothing wrong. I have to accept the fact that I cannot undo the damage that has been done to her. I have to accept the fact that I cannot return her to her family, nor bring her mother back to life. Because of these things, I act. Because the five chimpanzees for whom I am responsible are marooned in this prison for life, I insist that their interests and well-being are our first priority. In their home, human arrogance of any sort is forbidden. They only take part in research if they wish; they are not bribed with food or forced with threats or socially harangued into submission.[16]

But given their early lives, he felt the environment at CHCI was a more just and ethical option than abandoning them to other research or to life "in the wild" (if that were even possible). On a strict animal rights view, though, what the Foutses did would still be wrong.

This shows one concern with the rights approach. Rights are to be universal, but this means sometimes important particularities of context are lost. Species are not all the same, and individuals within any given species are not all the same. Further, while Washoe and her family are well positioned to be considered as rights-bearing beings, what about other animal beings and the rest of nature? As I've mentioned, the big-brained social mammals are those to whom most people are willing to consider extending rights and ethical consideration. Washoe and her family, having learned to communicate using a human language, might warrant even more inclusion on this model. However, this approach of extending rights and moral consideration to those animal beings most like human beings simply perpetuates human exceptionalism and further marginalizes other animal beings (not to mention plants).

To avoid these problems, Plumwood does not take up the rights or extensionist approach. Instead, she suggests humans need to see their continuity with, and dependence on, the rest of nature in a way that helps them embody a form of solidarity with the lives, deaths, and strivings of all creatures. While this doesn't rule out enacting certain legal protections for other animal beings, that alone does not solve the deeper problem of a worldview (a metaphysics or ontology) that understands humans as outside of nature. Since the rights approach rests on just such a worldview, a rights approach is not enough to make the needed change and may even get in the way at times. For Plumwood, developing the needed solidarity entails recognizing the agency of all living beings and working to understand the world from other points of view. She draws on indigenous sources to arrive at her version of animism, which understands the world as full of minds and of persons of various kinds. In describing some of the commitments found in the indigenous philosophies on which Plumwood draws, Deborah Rose writes, "There is a multiplicity of perspectives and knowledges, and there is no privileged perspective. Where one person's or species' knowledge stops, someone else's knowledge picks up the story."[17] Plumwood argues that communication is already always happening, but humans (especially in industrialized countries) rarely listen. Humans need to be attentive and open to other living beings and work to decenter themselves. This is what would make just and ethical relationships even a possibility.

But we currently lack this solidarity with most other animal beings. This lack of solidarity can be seen with regard to chimpanzees, bonobos, and gorillas, as the mining, logging, and bushmeat trades continue to threaten their existence. Orangutans face a different, but related, threat from this way of thinking. Orangutans live in the Southeast Asia islands of Borneo and Sumatra, with only an estimated 7,500 left. They live a more solitary life than the other large-bodied apes but do come together to mate. Females give birth about every eight to ten years, keeping their offspring with them until they are eight years old. There is much for a young orangutan to learn: how to judge the strength of branches as they walk through the canopy and when and where various trees fruit.[18] The Malay consider orangutans "people of the forest," and orangutans have enjoyed the protection of taboos against hunting and eating them since they were considered kin, similar to many traditional views about chimpanzees, bonobos, and gorillas. This view was disrupted by colonization, and the habitat of orangutans was disrupted by rubber extraction. There was also pressure from hunting them to bring babies into captivity as pets, for zoos, and for use in labs. Today, the main threat comes from palm oil production (ironically used in most commercially prepared vegetarian and vegan foods). The palm oil plantations remove habitat, cut up traditional territories, and put roads in the orangutans' way. Injury and death by car is common, and the illegal pet and bushmeat trades continue to cause many deaths. Even famous individuals, such as Chantek, have not been treated well. Chantek was a cross-fostered orangutan who learned ASL.[19] When he got older and bigger, fears of lawsuits resulted in the University of Tennessee at Chattanooga returning him to the Yerkes research facility, where he was locked in one of the biomedical cages I described earlier—without room to move, without much enrichment, and no one with whom to sign. When his former caretakers did visit, Chantek asked them to take him home. While he was eventually moved to the Atlanta zoo with a large enclosure, the keepers there did not want him to have the human objects with which he was raised and didn't want him signing, as that was not "natural" behavior. He died in 2017 at the age of thirty-nine.[20]

PROTECTIONS FOR PRIMATES

The various apes used in language research have died or will soon reach the end of their lives. We have learned a great deal from them, even as we have treated them badly. One way to honor their lives is to make sure the lives of other great apes are better than theirs were. And yet we still see movies and commercials featuring the great apes (and monkeys). While more computerized images are being used, it is important to remember that when you see one of these apes in a film, on a TV show, pictured on a greeting card, or performing in a circus, you are most likely seeing juveniles who should still be with their mothers. You should remember that that individual has probably been trained with food deprivation and physical punishment and that, when they eventually become too big to control, they are likely to end up in an unaccredited zoo (now that research labs are cutting down on the use of apes and accredited zoos are at capacity). The same is true for those great apes kept as pets. They, too, will outgrow their human homes and face a similar fate. It is easy to see why people are attracted to the idea of having one of these amazing beings as a pet. They are cute and smart. But as with Curious George, they often make a mess of human homes and lives, and they end up being killed for being aggressive (as was Travis, a chimpanzee used in entertainment and kept as a pet, who severely mauled a woman in Connecticut in 2009) or sent to a zoo, lab, or sanctuary. To be fair, the Curious George books pointed out the destruction George did just by following his own nature, and he continually ended up back at the zoo or in a lab. But in reality, these are not such happy places for physically active, socially complex, and intelligent animal beings.

There is a growing sanctuary movement. While still places of captivity, most sanctuaries are designed around the needs and desires of the various apes being housed rather than around the desires of human caretakers or visitors. For example, Chimpanzee Sanctuary Northwest tries to provide the best home they can for chimpanzees who spent most of their lives being used in biomedical research.[21] Their mission is simple: "Chimpanzee Sanctuary Northwest provides lifetime quality care for formerly abused and exploited chimpanzees while advocating for great apes." If they are successful, there will be no need for sanctuaries because there will no longer be apes kept as pets, used in entertainment, or experimented on in biomedical facilities. "We envision a world where our closest genetic relatives are respected and honored and allowed to thrive and behave as they were born to. We envision a world where chimpanzees are allowed to be, simply, chimpanzees."[22] Each of the chimpanzees living at this sanctuary has a name, a history, and a distinct personality and set of preferences. For example, Foxie loves troll dolls, Jamie likes patrolling the large outdoor enclosure, and Jody enjoys making large nests with lots of blankets. Run by Diana Goodrich and J. B.

Mulcahy, who were graduate students at CHCI the summer I was an apprentice, this sanctuary embodies the "chimpanzees first" philosophy that helps humans decenter themselves and come to be in solidarity with individuals of another species. This idea is emphasized with donors and visitors. This respect and solidarity is extended to other animal beings as well, and Diana and John practice a vegan diet.

While it is important to note and respect the amazing abilities of the various great apes, and while we owe them a particular debt given their use in research, entertainment, and zoos, they are not the only animals who matter morally. The Cambridge scientists' 2012 Declaration on Consciousness states:

> [N]on-human animals have the neuroanatomical, neurochemical, and neurophysiological substrates of conscious states along with the capacity to exhibit intentional behaviors. Consequently, the weight of evidence indicates that humans are not unique in possessing the neurological substrates that generate consciousness. Non-human animals, including all mammals and birds, and many other creatures, including octopuses, also possess these neurological substrates.[23]

While some scholars (particularly philosophers) may still resist, most people are starting to change how they think. It seems there is no kind of evidence, or any amount of evidence, that will convince someone who is wedded to human exceptionalism. But money and support for sanctuaries and for conservation are one indication of a shifting mind-set. At the same time, however, money continues to go toward keeping a wide range of animal beings in captivity in zoos, circuses, research facilities, and human homes. For instance, more than a billion dollars was granted by the U.S. government to the National Primate Research Centers in 2007.

Unlike the great apes, who receive special protections due to their endangered status, monkeys are widely used in research, in entertainment, as assistance animals, and as pets. Monkeys are still captured in the wild and then bred in labs to produce research animals. Rhesus macaques are the monkeys most commonly used in research, but marmosets, squirrel monkeys, and tamarins are also used. According to the United States Department of Agriculture (USDA), more than one hundred thousand monkeys are currently kept in U.S. labs. They are used in research on diseases, nutrition, dentistry, toxicology, vaccines, drug testing, transplantation, cloning, and more. The research often requires long periods of restraint, multiple surgeries, deprivation of food and water, and lethal dose testing.[24] Social housing is often overridden by the specifics of the experiments, and little enrichment is provided despite the requirements in the Animal Welfare Act that says, "Dealers, exhibitors, and research facilities must develop, document, and follow an appropriate plan for environment enhancement adequate to promote the psychological well-being of nonhuman primates." This is supposed to include provisions for social housing unless a nonhuman primate is aggressive, debilitated, or suspected of carrying a contagious disease or there are reasons set forth in the research proposal to be exempt from various forms of enrichment (such as social housing, perches, swings, mirrors, or foraging).[25]

Outside federally funded research labs, there are fewer protections for monkeys kept as pets and used in entertainment, as oversight by the USDA is very limited. Schuler and Abee note, "Nonhuman primates maintained in captivity have a valuable role in education and research. They are also occasionally used in entertainment. The scope of these activities can range from large, accredited zoos to small 'roadside' exhibits; from national primate research centers to small academic institutions with only a few monkeys; and from movie sets to street performers." Human use of other animal beings entails responsibilities to them, though. They continue, "Attached to these uses of primates comes an ethical responsibility to provide the animals with an environment that promotes their physical and behavioral health and well-being. Thus, an obligation is entailed that those individuals/institutions caring for captive primates should make every effort to ensure adequate veterinary care and husbandry are provided, that the animals are housed in appropriate facilities, and that as broad a range of species-typical behaviors are able to be expressed by the animals as is possible for the captive environment."[26] But there is little by way of enforcement of welfare standards in non-federally funded facilities. This means we need to rely on internalized ethical commitments of the humans involved with primates in these ways. And yet human exceptionalism remains deeply entrenched and prevents us from achieving anything close to ethical relationships with most great apes, much less the rest of the primates.

While some of the large-brained social mammals like apes, dolphins, whales, and elephants might break through into the circle even on the rights approach, this just draws the line in a different place and begs the question of what to make of the ingenious escapes by octopuses. How should we understand the ability of ravens to outsmart humans? If we are willing to deny the abilities of those animal beings most "like us," what is possible for our understanding of treatment of those animals seen as so different or "inferior"—for example, cattle, cats, coyotes, insects, mice, or snakes? And if we can continue to deny the social, emotional, and cognitive abilities of the whole range of animal beings, what does that say about our own species' social, emotional, cognitive, and moral capacity? Here, I tend to agree with Mary Anne Warren when she writes that while it is probably the case that other animal beings deserve to have certain kinds of rights recognized,

> [i]t is less important to maintain that other animals have moral rights than to maintain that we have moral obligations toward them. . . . If we reject the idea of obligations toward animals of other species, valuing them only instrumentally, then it is all but inevitable that our human psychology will prevent us from protecting them effectively. . . . The existence throughout the world of ancient moral traditions that accord moral status to animals, plants, and other parts of the natural world proves that human psychology does not preclude the acceptance of such obligations.[27]

Warren and Plumwood both encourage humans to decenter themselves when it comes to working out how best to form respectful relationships with other animal beings. Rather than focusing on finding enough evidence to make "them" enough like "us" to be worthy of rights, we should instead recognize and respect the vast continuities and differences among all life and realize that humans have moral obligations (different though they may be) in all of these relationships. Seeing value beyond commodification and self-interest is an important start, as is being willing to be seen as usable (and edible) by others.

Chapter Three

Horses and Cattle

This chapter is grounded in a discussion of *Black Beauty* in order to examine the lives of contemporary horses in cities, in competition, and at work on cattle ranches. While fewer horses in the United States are engaged in work in city streets than when *Black Beauty* was written, there are still contentious debates about using horses for carriage rides in cities. While the well-being of the horses is commonly the reason given for ending such activities, the result is a removal of horses from most people's lives. Those humans who do have sustained relationships with horses often compete with them, and in those activities, there are not infrequent occasions of abuse and harm. There are also frequent occasions for real bonding between horse and human, though. In contrast to the money- and prize-driven worlds of showing and the rodeo, horses are still frequently used on working ranches. In fact, those who resist the industrial model of concentrated animal feeding operations (CAFOs) for raising cattle are quite likely to use horses as working partners as they move cattle from pasture to pasture. Ranch horses' lives connect to the lives of cattle, and grazing cattle are often in competition with "wild" horses in the United States. These overlapping lives result in complex situations where someone eating grass-fed beef (perhaps in an effort to not participate in the animal suffering and environmental degradation caused by industrial farming) may unwittingly contribute to the death of wild horses. Instead of putting horses and cattle in competition with each other, though, contemporary cattle ranches might be a place to enhance the long-standing partnership between humans and horses and horses and cattle. This chapter explores that possibility through an ecofeminist lens based in the work of Charlotte

Perkins Gilman, Karen Warren, Carol Adams, A. Breeze Harper, and Val Plumwood.

HEARING THE HORSE

Present estimates suggest that in the United States less than 1 percent of people own a horse (though about 2 percent of the population is involved in the horse industry in one way or another).[1] A small number of people take riding lessons, rent horses for trail or carriage rides, or go to a petting zoo or circus that has horses. The most common uses of horses today are in horse racing, horse showing, and rodeos. These all raise ethical concerns as horses are pushed to physically perform in order for the humans around them to gain titles and money (money from prizes, training, and breeding). Used as an object in a business, many horses come to be seen as disposable. They are raced when they are injured, and many die in this line of work. Horses who are deemed to be no longer profitable are often sold to be slaughtered for their meat. While this practice is not confined to the racing industry, it is important to note that "of the 100,000 American horses transported in cramped trucks from the US to slaughterhouses in Canada and Mexico every year, more than 12,000 are thoroughbred racehorses. Others are shipped to Japan for racing and breeding, and they too will eventually become dog food."[2] While there are particular ethical issues connected to racing, showing, and rodeos,[3] the larger concern I want to raise here is the act of reducing horses to disposable objects and failing to see them as deserving of respect. This has been an issue for horses throughout their time with humans, though there are also plenty of counterexamples in which horses are seen as true partners with humans, or even as divine.

While horses were part of everyday life just one hundred years ago, they've all but disappeared from the lives of most people living in the United States today. Still, there are more than nine million horses in the United States today, and a romantic attachment remains.[4] For many, free bands of living horses represent the "wild frontier" of the west and are an icon of freedom. As an icon of freedom, though, the horse is a complicated figure. Horses helped bring white settlers west, and with them came ranching and farming and the removal of Native Americans and buffalo from their lands. Cattle (and sheep) came with the settlers, leading to the mythic cowboy and his horse. Some of those cowboys became legendary lawmen while others became notorious or celebrated outlaws, but (at least in the stories) they all were individuals who defied convention and law to act freely. While many had respect for the horses in their lives, life for their horses was generally one of hard use and early death. Ill-fitting saddles, improper shoeing, and bad riding and driving all made the horses' lives less than ideal. Overuse in pulling a plow could break down a horse's body. Use on a stagecoach line or as part of the Pony Express was only for the young and fit. Horses were usually seen as a tool, though a very valuable one (hence the practice of hanging horse thieves).

The horses' labor opened up possibilities for the settlers, and, in turn, many of these people developed breeding programs that still influence popular breeds, such as the quarter horse, Morgan, Appaloosa, and thoroughbred. Ironically, however, many of these breeding programs produced horses that could not perform the work of their ancestors. Bred for looks alone, some lines do not stay sound past the age of five, while others carry serious genetic disorders. The quarter horse alone has five genetic disorders that commonly impact individuals of that breed.[5] Hyperkalemic periodic paralysis (HYPP) is a condition that affects about 3 percent of the breed but 60 percent of halter horses. Halter horses are those bred to compete in conformation class. While good conformation should be the foundation for healthy horses, those with HYPP suffer from muscle tremors, cramping, paralysis, collapse, and even death.[6] Breeding for aesthetics alone, in order to gain titles, prize money, and breeding fees, has caused many horses to suffer. In such cases, the icon of freedom has become a prisoner of human aesthetics and greed.

At the same time that the horse was a tool of white settlers, the horse was also an important part of many Native American cultures and was used to great effect to defend their lands against the colonists and settlers. Ironically, in the dominant account of the history of horses in the Americas, Native Americans first got horses from the Spaniards who came to colonize the Americas. Native Americans then used the horse to become more mobile, hunt more buffalo, and resist colonization. The peoples of the North American Plains are especially known for their horse culture. Becoming expert horsepeople, many of today's cowboys are Native Americans who breed horses, work cattle by horseback, and successfully compete on the rodeo circuit.

Another emerging view argues that horses did not go extinct in the Americas and were here and part of native cultures long before the Spaniards and other colonists arrived. Yvette Running Horse Collins (a Lakota/Nakota/Cheyenne scholar) relies on oral histories and fossil evidence to make the case that horses were always in the Americas and not reintroduced by the Spaniards. She reports that many different native cultures, with different languages and creation stories, have accounts of receiving the horse from the creator and understand horses to be their own people or nation. This is supported by fossil evidence that can place horses in the Americas between the times of the supposed extinction and the reintroduction.[7] Either way, horses have been, and are, important to many native peoples.

One Blackfoot story, "The Orphan Boy and the Elk Dog," tells of a young orphaned boy who is turned out by his people because he cannot hear and seems dim witted. When he regains his hearing and returns to his people, one family takes him in, giving him the name Long Arrow. To thank his new family, he travels a great distance in search of the Elk Dogs (Pono-Kamita) of which his father has heard. While these animals are large and strong like an elk, they are friendly and loyal like a dog. Through Long Arrow's bravery, he is gifted a herd of horses and the magic to work with them.[8] Elsewhere, the story of "Bringer of the Mystery Dog" tells of the Sioux migration from the woods to the plains and their adaptation to a life following the buffalo. A young boy, Little Dog, who is very good at training dogs, wants to do something brave for his people and goes out tracking a Pawnee party. What he finds is an old, blind Pawnee man on a horse. His people had heard of these mystery dogs (Sunka Wak'an) but had not believed in their existence. Now the boy returns with a horse, and he is given a new name: Bringer of the Mystery Dog.[9] The lives of the people are changed by the presence of the horse, and in both stories there is respect accorded to horses and the people who work with them. This respect did not mean no use, though. Among Native Americans, horses were sometimes used as food and sometimes for transportation. They were used in these ways even while they also held spiritual value. They were used so effectively in resisting the U.S. government that on September 28, 1874, when the U.S. Army attacked a Comanche stronghold, they slaughtered more than one thousand horses.[10] Horses have been subject to this kind of danger throughout their history with humans.

Horses have a long history of military use around the world. In the United States alone, their service in the cavalry—at home and abroad—is extensive. Roughly one to three million horses and mules died in the American Civil War,[11] while about 1,325,000 U.S. horses were used in World War I.[12] In these roles, the horse appears to some as a liberator and to others as an oppressor. They have defended freedom and been a tool of imperialistic expansion. The same can be said of their work in mounted police patrols.

Now in decline, mounted police patrols have been an effective form of crowd control and community outreach for the police. But they have also been used to intimidate and harm protesters.

This brief account of the long and complicated history of horses in the United States demonstrates some of the impacts horses have had on the social and political development of the country. Given the importance of the horse in the past, it is essential to carefully consider their present and future place and treatment. The story of *Black Beauty* can be a helpful guide here. Written by Anna Sewell in England in 1877, *Black Beauty* did much to change hearts and laws regarding the treatment of working horses. The book also contains critiques of war, drinking, cruelty, and thoughtlessness. It was written at a time when campaigns for women's suffrage were strong, along with the temperance and anti-vivisection movements. In the United States, these overlapped with abolitionism, which called for the end of slavery (the Civil War had ended just about a decade before the book's publication). Women were quite active in all of these social reform endeavors even though they themselves did not yet have the vote. Women's voices are central in the story of *Black Beauty*, as are the voices of the horses themselves. This makes it an early example of ecofeminism.

Male cruelty and thoughtlessness is remarked upon throughout the book—boys throwing stones at horses to make them run, young men running horses too hard, men risking the lives of horses jumping during a hunt (fox hunting—as in *Dr. Dolittle*—is also condemned in the novel as cruel to the fox), and men overloading and whipping horses. Women are not portrayed as cruel, but their thoughtlessness is condemned. Those women who don't think about the horses and men waiting in the snow while they are shopping or dancing at a party show a failure of sympathy. Black Beauty says, "I wonder if the beautiful ladies ever think of the weary cabman waiting on his box, and his patient beast standing till his legs get stiff with cold."[13] There is also a general concern with fashion, for which both men and women are chastised. Wanting horses to travel with a high head and arched neck resulted in practices that forced the horses into this position, often making it difficult for them to breathe properly or to pull. This was done with a bearing rein, or overcheck, which is a strap that prevents horses from lowering their heads. The use of the bearing rein is addressed numerous times in the novel, but the argument against its use gets its full expression from a woman:

"Is it not better," she said, "to lead a good fashion than to follow a bad one? A great many gentlemen do not use bearing reins now. My carriage horses have not worn them for fifteen years, and work with much less fatigue than those who have them. Besides," she added in a very serious tone, "we have no right to distress any of God's creatures without a very good reason. We call them dumb animals, and so they are, for they cannot tell us how they feel, but they do not suffer less because they have no words."[14]

This statement is not unlike what Charlotte Perkins Gilman wrote in her short story "When I Was a Witch" in 1909. In this story, the narrator finds her wishes coming true as she wishes to end the suffering of the animals in the city. While she wishes for cats and dogs to die peacefully, and so escape the pain and indignity of their lives, for horses she wishes "that every person who strikes or otherwise hurts a horse unnecessarily shall feel the pain intended—and the horse not feel it!"[15] She then sees this very thing happen with the horse pulling the garbage cart, with teamsters hauling a load, and with a boy driving a wagon.

CHARLOTTE PERKINS GILMAN AND *BLACK BEAUTY*

Gilman was an early ecofeminist pragmatist philosopher. Writing and speaking throughout the United States and Europe in the late 1800s and early 1900s, Gilman argued against the dependence of women on men (patriarchy) and the dependence of animals on humans. As with the pragmatist thinkers discussed in chapter 1, she was writing at a time when evolutionary theory was in the air. She thought that male selection among humans had resulted in smaller and weaker females with exaggerated sexual characteristics, like large breasts. Smaller bodies actually made it harder for women to survive pregnancy and childbirth. She saw the same thing happening with domesticated animals (especially smaller dogs) who require human assistance to procreate. She also noted the physical difficulties many domesticated animals face as a result of inbreeding (such as genetic diseases like HYPP in quarter horses).

Not only was such dependence a problem physically, but it also created ethical and political issues. This dependence was accompanied by dominance and control. Gilman understood that the patriarchal system was not conducive to democracy and turned women and other-than-human animals into artificial and dependent creatures who suffered at the whim of powerful men. With this power, these men lost their sense of justice. She writes that "the conditions of slavery, of ownership, of authority, with the dependence and submission of the owned, check the growth of ethics completely. This dominance underlies the despotism of officer, priest, and king, and still finds expression in the attitude of our 'captains of industry.'"[16] For Gilman, ethical and just political relationships required an end of submission and dependence, an understanding of our interrelatedness, and a focus on our mutual happiness and improvement. In her view, improving the status of one group by oppressing another does not work.

Gilman argued that women needed to understand that their own oppression went hand in hand with the oppression of other animals, and she urged women to stop wearing hats with feathers (birds were being hunted to extinction for fashion), to stop wearing fur (animals were being trapped and confined for fur coats and accessories), and to stop wearing corsets (made of whale bone). Not only did the corsets result in the death of numerous whales (discussed in chapter 5), but they also limited and harmed women's bodies. In her novels, she both critiqued the systems of industrial farming and slaughter that were then emerging and painted a picture of a possible vegetarian alternative in *Herland* and one with less meat in *Moving the Mountain*: "A proper proportion of edible animals are raised under good conditions— nice, healthy, happy beasts; killed so that they don't know it!—and never kept beyond a certain time limit."[17]

In Gilman's narrative, Herland is an isolated society of women who can procreate without men (as do many species) and so have evolved without the artifices of gendered expectations. The women are strong, intelligent people with a cooperative social arrangement. The women of Herland also demonstrate a sympathetic understanding of the plight of animals. There are no domesticated animals except for some cats (who don't eat birds). The women explain that raising animals for meat or milk is cruel and would overtax their environment. When the male visitors to Herland ask how they do without milk, the women point out that they have plenty of milk of their own. The women grow distressed when they hear about dairies in the United States: "'Has the cow no child? . . . Is there milk for the calf and you, too?' It took some time to make clear to those three sweet-faced women the process which robs the cow of her calf, and the calf of its true food; and the talk led us into a further discussion of the meat business. They heard it out, looking very white, and presently begged to be excused."[18]

Gilman developed this idea of common cause between women and other animal beings, which is also expressed in *Black Beauty*. Sewell writes that the world has gotten into a bad state because people are too concerned with themselves and "won't trouble themselves to stand up for the oppressed." This character continues, "My doctrine is this, if we see cruelty or wrong that we have the power to stop, and do nothing, we make ourselves sharers in the guilt."[19] There is no neutral position when it comes to defending the weak and oppressed, and we are all implicated in a number of unjust and cruel practices regarding the treatment of horses and humans alike. Sewell's novel also portrays the kindness and generosity of those in the working class in comparison to the selfish behavior of many in the upper classes, and it advocates for strikes and the reform of working conditions for humans and horses alike.[20] Gilman, too, saw this connection as she called for a shift from an individualistic ethic to a social ethic that sees the interlocking systems of oppression and develops a social consciousness that can take up the women's movement, the labor movement, and the animal movement.

The story of *Black Beauty* can be read with the horses as a stand-in for various human groups who suffer similar cruelty, neglect, and overuse. But it is clear that Sewell (and Gilman) takes such treatment of horses and humans together and argues that both need to stop. Sewell points out that economic and political systems create problems and stand in the way of ameliorating those same problems. For instance, the system of cab fairs in London incentivized drivers to overwork their horses, and yet those same drivers did not have the political power to get the system changed. As a result, the drivers and the horses continued to suffer. Some of Sewell's insights come from her own experience. An injury in her youth caused her to be unable to walk, so she relied on horse-powered transportation, and she observed a great deal about the horses' treatment. A skilled driver herself, she clearly developed sympathy for the horses on whom she relied. She observed that most humans ignored, took for granted, and/or harmed the horses who aided their work and lives.

Sewell's sympathetic attachment to horses made (and makes) some critics dismissive of her work. She is also often accused of anthropomorphizing the horses in the story. Anthropomorphizing is attributing human characteristics to nonhuman animals, and many argue that this practice both distorts our understanding of the animals themselves and causes misplaced concern about some specific ways humans treat these animals. It is important to note that, in *Black Beauty*, the horses do not talk with humans with spoken English. The horses do develop a way of communicating with humans who pay attention—a nuzzle, a spook, a nicker, a turned ear—and they read and understand humans very well. Black Beauty often remarks on the character of the individual humans he encounters and makes judgments about the kind of people with whom he'd rather be working. The horses in the book do talk with each other, but that is not necessarily anthropomorphizing. We know horses communicate with humans and other horses through body language and vocalization. Horses also learn from one another. If horses and humans (both social mammals) share these traits, it is not anthropomorphizing to recognize and honor these traits in horses.

When Black Beauty is getting ready to be weaned and leave his mother, she advises him about getting on in the world—"do your best wherever it is, and keep up your good name"—and hopes that he will "fall into good hands."[21] We don't know whether dams actually give their foals this kind of advice, but we do know that horses learn tasks simply from observing other horses perform them. Horses have complex social systems that help them form alliances for protection, maintain bonds despite conflict, and share learning. They copy the behavior of other horses, especially "higher-ranking, older horses in their social group."[22] So it is not much of a stretch to think that Black Beauty, at least in part, accepted the harness and training because he'd observed his mother being driven. He doesn't like the bridle at first, but he observes, "I know my mother always wore one when she went out, and all horses did when they were grown up."[23] Sewell gave voice to the horses and allowed horses to see and think about the world from their own embodied perspective.

There were elements of class prejudice and elitism present in late nineteenth-century England (and the United States) that make their way into the book. The book makes much of being well bred, and Black Beauty's "good breeding" is continually recognized by discerning humans who see beyond the injuries he has sustained through poor treatment. There may also be some sense of hierarchy among the animals. While there is recognition that dogs often suffer as horses do (having their tails docked, for instance), Black Beauty does on one occasion say that a groom did not properly care for his feed and "thought no more of that than if I had been a cow."[24] This could simply be a recognition of the different needs of cows and horses, but it also falls into the social habit of treating horses very differently from other animals considered livestock. In the United States, different laws govern the transport and slaughter of horses than those governing the same for other livestock. The recent ban on horse slaughter in the United States makes the hierarchy humans impose upon livestock species quite clear (more on this in chapter 4 on pigs and poultry). Horses get special protections even though other livestock animals suffer in similar ways. Cattle are a case in point.

CONVERSING WITH CATTLE

There is no reason to think that mares and foals are more attached to each other than are cows and calves. There is no reason to think that the social structures in horse herds are any more important or complex than those in a herd of cattle. Watching a cutting horse work cattle, one can see the meeting of two species' (three if one counts the human) minds. Both species suffer physical and psychological harm from many of the ways humans treat and kill them. And yet, in the United States, the enforcement of humane standards for horses far exceeds the rules and enforcement for cattle.

Horse shows are required to have technical delegates to ensure that rules and welfare standards are followed. There are rules limiting the kinds of bits that can be used, and a competitor can be disqualified if there are signs of the overuse of spurs or whips. Equestrians can be barred from showing for overworking a horse or using excessive corrections. Competitors cannot show a lame horse, and random drug tests are conducted to limit the practice of using drugs to mask a horse's pain.[25] Horses may not be transported in double-decker trailers, and the United States now bans their slaughter for human consumption. At the same time, however, there are very few welfare regulations regarding other livestock animals and very limited enforcement of those that do exist.

In the feedlot system of meat production, calves spend a short amount of time out on grass with their mothers. Then they are shipped, in all kinds of weather, tightly packed and stacked in a double-decker trailer to a feedlot where they are crowded together and forced to live in their own waste while they gorge on food that makes them sick. Fed various antibiotics and other medications to keep them alive long enough to reach slaughter weight (which is now much younger than in the past), they are then moved to a slaughter facility where they face further suffering as they are processed in a fast-moving automated slaughter facility that can result in them being conscious while hanging in the air by one leg, bleeding, and being de-hided. While there are welfare rules in place to govern the slaughtering process, there is little to no enforcement of these standards, and the industry is left to govern itself. There is no honoring the nature of cattle in this system, much less any recognition of the individual cattle. While one hundred thousand horses may be shipped out of the United States each year for slaughter, almost three million cattle are slaughtered in the United States.

Life is not really better for dairy cows. As cows are social mammals, calves normally would stay with their mothers until they are around ten months old. However, most U.S. dairies are large confinement dairies. Here calves are removed from their mothers almost immediately so that the cows can be milked, and this early removal is stressful for both cow and calf. Young, and without well-developed immune systems, most calves are housed alone in an attempt to keep them healthy. Most of the young females will be kept to join the milking herd, while most male calves will go into veal production. Long the poster child for animal cruelty within the livestock industry, veal calves in the United States are kept confined so they don't develop their muscles and are denied roughage so they don't get iron. Kept on iron-deficient diets to keep the meat white, they are not in good health, and their lives are short. Calves are slaughtered between four and six months of age; yet veal is still a highly prized meat by many. All dairy products— milk, cheese, and butter—are part of the veal industry, as all dairies need to constantly breed cows in order to get milk and then need a profitable way of dealing with the male calves who are born.

However, it doesn't have to be this way. Thinking back to the concerns raised by Gilman in her novels, the women of Herland were appalled to learn that calves are separated from their mothers and the milk taken for human consumption. One possibility is to give up consuming dairy products. This is what the women of Herland did, primarily because they didn't have enough land to graze the animals. They found it an inefficient use of resources to feed animals to get food from them (milk or meat) compared to feeding people directly. They also found it a cruel practice and, as mothers themselves, sympathized with the cows. Gilman was also critical of how human breeding had impacted the life and nature of the cows themselves. Similar to her critique that men selecting women based on their physical appearance had weakened women's bodies and resulted in oversized breasts, she saw in her own time that dairy cows found it hard to walk because of their large udders.

She compares the wild cow and a modern dairy cow to make her point that females and males share equally in their species life unless distorted by male human desires. "The wild cow is a female. She has healthy calves, and milk enough for them; and that is all the femininity she needs. Otherwise than that she is bovine rather than feminine. She is a light, strong, swift, sinewy creature, able to run, jump, and fight, if necessary." In other words, without human intervention, cows have more in common with bulls than differences from them. But humans' desires have changed the nature and bodies of cows: "We, for economic uses, have artificially developed the cow's capacity for procuring milk. She has become a walking milk-machine, bred and tended to that express end, her value measured in quarts. The cow is over-sexed."[26] This situation has only been exaggerated more with modern breeding and hormones. Modern dairy cows find it difficult to walk due to the size of their udders, which is then used as a reason to keep them confined.

ECOFEMINISM AND ECOWOMANISM

Gilman's ecofeminist insight that human women were in much the same position as the milk cows of her time is reminiscent of Carol Adams's position on dairy cows and her insight that cattle and horses are not really different. Adams tells of the horror and deep sadness she felt when her pony, Jimmy, was shot and killed. That same night, when she took a bite of a hamburger, she saw her pony. "I was thinking about one dead animal yet eating another dead animal. What was the difference between this dead cow and the dead pony whom I would be burying the next day? I could summon no ethical defense for a favoritism that would exclude the cow from my concern because I had not known her."[27] Adams, in this moment, rejected the hierarchy that placed horses above cows and was able to extend her sympathy and moral concern to beings with whom she has no personal relationship. This is why she became a vegetarian. Her road to veganism rests on many of the same connections Gilman observed and critiqued.

Adams argues that feminists should be vegans in order to avoid being complicit in the exploitation of livestock animals. She sees that eggs and dairy products are especially problematic because they are "feminized protein," which require humans to control other female animals' reproductive choices and then to remove (and often slaughter) their offspring. In contemporary U.S. society, laws governing reproductive rights and access to birth control often have similar consequences. Some women are virtually forced into reproduction (mostly white women) while others have had that right denied (forced sterilizations of women of color).

To better understand this ecofeminist perspective, though, let's back up a bit. While there were many women writing during Gilman and Sewell's time who understood the linked experiences and interests of women and other animals, not all feminists agreed that this insight provided a path to liberation. When Mary Wollstonecraft wrote *A Vindication of the Rights of Woman* in 1792, one of the responses to her work was to trivialize it by asking what was next: *The Vindication of the Rights of Beasts*? In fact, Wollstonecraft had been careful to separate human women from other animals and to argue that, as humans, women had the capacity to reason and deserved the right to an equal education and the right to vote. This separation of women from the rest of nature has been taken up by most feminists since that time, whether they are liberal feminists, socialist feminists, Marxist feminists, or radical feminists. Ecofeminists, though, reject this line and argue that trying to fight oppression for one group by oppressing another group fails to address the logic of domination that makes oppression possible in the first place.

Ecofeminist philosopher Karen Warren points out that much of Western philosophy divides the world into binaries or dualisms such as reason/emotion, culture/nature, male/female, white/black, light/dark, and human/animal. Dividing the world in this way requires drastic oversimplification, as we know, for instance, that in human brains our rational and emotional capacities are connected and that there are more than two distinct sexes. But such binaries serve the purpose of being able to rank humans and other beings, as humans tend to attach greater value to one half of these dualisms. Such value hierarchies would include the views that men are superior or more valuable than women, that white people are superior or more valuable than people of color, and that human beings are superior or more valuable than other animal beings. Once such views are in place, Warren argues, the logic of domination can flourish, as men are seen as justified in dominating and oppressing women, white people are seen as justified in dominating and oppressing people of color, and human beings are seen as justified in dominating and oppressing other animal beings. On this account, it doesn't work to liberate humans from racial or gender oppression by arguing that they are fully human or like white men because they are superior to other animal beings. Such a move leaves the logic of domination in place and only moves some pieces around (temporarily). Ecofeminists called for intersectional analysis and politics long before that was a word and ran into resistance from many quarters, including other feminists.

Many ecofeminists and ecowomanists call on all people, but especially women and those working for social justice, to follow a vegetarian or vegan diet. They argue that given the interlocking systems of oppression that are supported by the logic of domination, to continue to participate in the oppression of other-than-human animals is to be complicit in one's own oppression as a woman. Some feminists resist this call by appealing to women's autonomy, the freedom of choice, and respect for cultural variation. These are all core principles of feminist theory (at least liberal feminism), but they tend to rest on the same dualisms, value hierarchies, and logic of domination that ecofeminists seek to change. Carol Adams's response to such positions is to ask how one's freedom can rest on the oppression and death of others. She used this position in her 1994 book, *Neither Beast nor Man*, when she argued that all women's and gender studies conferences should be vegan spaces. She argued that given the shared logic of domination operating within sexist, racist, and speciesist theories and practices, one can't work to undo one "ism" while consciously promoting another.

Alice Walker makes a similar case. In her story "Am I Blue" (mentioned in chapter 1), Alice Walker tells about a horse, Blue, who lived alone in a field near where she was living. While she was feeding him apples, she realized Blue was lonely. She had forgotten what it was like to communicate with a horse. She writes, "If we are brought up around animals as children we take this for granted. By the time we are adults we no longer remember. However, the animals have not changed. . . . [I]t is their nature to express themselves. What else are they going to express? And they do. And, generally speaking, they are ignored." She then relates this concept to the experiences of various humans who are not fully seen or heard: black women, Asian women, Native Americans, and youth.[28]

Walker draws connections between the disrespectful way humans treat livestock, the institution and lived experience of slavery, and the removal of Native Americans. She notes that, in one town, one company slaughters twenty-seven million hogs each year.

> Beings who are treated with such disrespect and cruelty that it is amazing that any of us can bear knowing what is going on. This must be the same blind heart and unseeing gaze that was turned on the slave trade, during its four horrendous centuries, when black people coming to America on slave ships were treated as cruelly as these hogs, their lives often eaten up by forced labor within as little as seven years. What have we turned off in ourselves to be able to bear the mistreatment of the precious other animals that inhabit the planet with us? The carnage, in this one case, is so bad that the countryside around the facility is completely, densely polluted, and the people who live there are sick. The freeing of animals, the returning of land and habitat to them, must become part of what it means to be human. Part of what it means to be animal.

Without the other animals the land is dead in spirit, as it is dead in spirit when indigenous human life is removed from it. [29]

As Melanie Harris notes, Walker points to the parallel oppressions that are suffered by the earth, plants, animals, women, and especially women of color. [30] Walker makes one such connection when she points out that "society's treatment of [unwed mothers] reflects the abandonment and neglect of that other scorned and unprotected mother of us all: Mother Earth. And see how angry and disgusted She has become with us." [31] In another instance, she calls on menopausal women to get their estrogen from plant sources because "[t]o imprison pregnant mares in order to use their urine to make Premarin, an estrogen-replacement drug for menopausal women, is an outrage against nature and beauty that will inevitably be felt by the women to whom this drug is administered." She writes that a human life cannot be improved because a mother's child was sold to become dog food and she was imprisoned. [32]

A. Breeze Harper builds on this view to make an ecowomanist argument that women of color are especially well placed to understand how women and other animals are linked under the logic of domination: "For example, many of us black female vegans realize that much of how non-human animals are treated in the USA frighteningly parallels the way black females were treated during chattel slavery." [33] Harper believes there should be the same outrage about human and nonhuman slavery. In Harper's book *Sistah Vegan: Black Female Vegans Speak on Food, Identity, Health, and Society*, Delicia Dunham notes that, like black women under slavery, animals "are given no choice of mate; they are forced to engage in sexual activity with one another while their 'master' watches, to live in separate quarters from loved ones and to give birth to beings who are promptly taken away and sold to other plantations. They are forced to suckle beings not their own for the benefit of others." [34] This statement echoes Adams's concerns noted earlier. Harper also notes that many people are addicted to fast food, sugar, and meat, and thus they are slaves to food that harms them, as well as other animal beings:

Who and what are we hurting, deceiving, and stealing from to bring us our powdered-sugar donut, that Coolatta, or that ham, egg, and cheese English muffin? Recent research shows that we're hurting ourselves and exploiting and enslaving others—nonhuman animals and humans—in a way that is similar to colonialism; similar to when many of our African ancestors were torn from

their communities and shipped to the Caribbean and Americas to chop cane for
the production of sucrose and rum for addicted Europeans.

She says, "we must extend our antiracist and antipoverty belief to all people,
nonhuman animals, and Mother Gaia."[35]

Adams and Harper (and many other ecofeminists and ecowomanists)
draw from these connections between women and other animal beings and
call on women to follow a vegan diet. Ecofeminist philosopher Val Plumwood understands these strong connections, but she reaches a different conclusion. Some of Plumwood's views were discussed in chapter 2, but here I
focus on her critique of Adams's argument. I want to be clear, however, that
Adams and Plumwood share the analysis of the logic of domination (presented earlier) and the belief that factory farming is unethical.[36] Plumwood
writes that "the ruthless, reductionistic . . . treatment of animals as replaceable and tradeable items of property characteristic of the commodity form
and a capitalist economic rationality" is an outcome of the logic of domination and needs to be changed.[37] At the same time, though, she worries that
the call for veganism falls into the dualistic, value hierarchical way of thinking that supports the logic of domination. For her, it reifies a mind/body
dualism, as some forms of veganism reject humans' ecological embodiment.
Humans do have bodies, and these bodies can serve as food for other animal
beings just as the bodies of other animals can serve as food for human beings.
She writes, "We cannot give up using one another, but we can give up the
use/respect dualism, which means working toward ethical, respectful and
constrained forms of use."[38] In the context of *Black Beauty*, as well as the
current conditions faced by cattle in the United States, Plumwood's position
makes a great deal of sense. While some animal rights advocates today want
to end all use of horses, this was not Sewell's position. She also called for
"ethical, respectful and constrained forms of use," and her novel did much to
improve the lives (and deaths) of horses.

Calls to ban all consumption and use of horses and cattle may not be as
respectful as they first appear. Plumwood worries that the call for veganism
reifies an animal/plant dualism. While she avoids any attempt to see all life
as the same, she does think all life is interdependent and worthy of respect. In
"Animals and Ecology: Toward a Better Integration," Plumwood argues for
what she calls "Ecological Animalism," which entails "a dialogical ethics of
sharing and negotiation or partnership between humans and animals, while
undertaking a re-evaluation of human identity that affirms inclusion in ani-

mal and ecological spheres. The theory I shall develop is a context-sensitive semi-vegetarian position." Plumwood calls for contextual eating that respects animals and plants as individuals in their own right as well as in relationship with humans. This can include a vegan diet, but this is not a universal prescription. To situate humans ecologically, she argues, humans must rethink the category of edible to include themselves and realize they exist in "an ecological universe of mutual use" that "sees humans and animals as mutually available for respectful use in conditions of equality."[39] Plumwood's position shares much in common with American pragmatism, which was introduced in chapter 1 and will be more fully developed in the next chapter. At this point, though, it is important to note that her approach does not result in universal or absolutist positions, but it calls on all of us to thoughtfully consider the well-being of other beings and so change many individual and social practices to ameliorate (improve) our own lives and the lives of others and live with "respect and gratitude . . . opposing factory farming and . . . minimizing the use of sensitive beings for food."[40]

POSSIBLE ALTERNATIVES

How might the lives of horses and cattle be ameliorated? How might it be possible to combine respect and use? First, it would be necessary to overcome the human/animal binary and realize that human and other animal beings are in complex interdependent relationships with one another. Following a pragmatist ecofeminist approach challenges humans to understand their being as on a continuum with the rest of life and to understand that humans are in various relationships of interdependence. Rather than reducing other animal beings to objects of use, this recognition of interdependence should call out respect and gratitude. Humans would not be who and what they are without the transformational power—both physical and cultural—of horses and cattle. We should respect and honor them.

Second, it would be necessary to rethink current rates of consumption and kinds of use. It is not possible to consume meat and dairy products at the current rates in the United States without reducing livestock animals to objects of use. Denying cattle's subjectivity is required for CAFOs and centralized high-speed slaughter operations to produce cheap (if unsafe) meat and dairy products. As of January 2020, the USDA reported an annual production of 28,748 million tons of beef and veal meat, 49,161 million tons of poultry meat, and 23,315 million tons of pork meat. This comes to about 33,004,000 cattle, 9,160,910,000 chickens, 236,860,000 turkeys, and 124,436,000 pigs.[41] There is no way to show respect and gratitude, much less develop relationships, when feeding and slaughtering on this scale. Similarly with horses, uses that reduce them to work that provides money and power to humans, and throws them away when they are no longer profitable, fails to respect their individual needs and desires and prevents true partnership.

Third, it would be necessary to overcome human-held value hierarchies that operate within our views of, and relationships with, other animal beings. Giving up human exceptionalism is an important step, but we also need to rethink human hierarchies concerning other animal beings. For instance, while in the United States the horse holds a privileged position over cattle, there are cultures in which the cow is held in the more esteemed position. There is nothing that different between horses and cattle to justify such hierarchies, and counterexamples help make this point. The Hindu culture of present-day India and the Maasai culture of Africa are two examples. Cattle have long been seen as useful sources of food, fiber, and fuel, but in India they are also seen as sacred. Writing about the domestication of animals in India, Clutton-Brock notes, "From ancient times, zebu cattle have been used throughout the subcontinent as draft oxen and for milk products, and the dung is very important for use as a fertilizer and as a fuel and building material. Today, beef is eaten in some communities, but the cow has always been a sacred animal in the Hindu religion and is never killed." In addition, Gaur are a forest cattle who roam freely but are managed by the provisioning of salt for the cattle by tribes in eastern India, Bangladesh, and Myanmar (Burma) who occasionally kill them in ritual sacrifice.[42]

Cattle are eaten in India, and India has one of the largest tanning industries in the world, with more than two thousand tanneries.[43] Further, cattle and oxen are still regularly used to haul heavy loads, farm, and move people. Veterinary care is limited, and many of these animals suffer in the same ways the horses in the story of *Black Beauty* suffered. Horses, donkeys, and burros also are still used in these ways in India (and many parts of the world).[44] The honoring of the cow, though, does make it easier for some to intervene to improve the lives and deaths of cattle in India, and there are now legal limits on the weight they can carry. It is harder to raise the same concern in the United States, where cattle are seen primarily as objects of use. India, in fact, has constitutional protections for other animal beings. In spring 2019, a judge in India ruled that all animals have "a 'distinct legal persona with corresponding rights, duties, and liabilities of a living person' and that 'all the citizens throughout the State of Haryana are hereby declared persons in loco parentis as the human face for the welfare/protection of animals,' implying that citizens have legal responsibilities and functions similar to those of a parent vis-à-vis minor children for the welfare and protection of animals."[45]

The Maasai provide another interesting example of how reverence and use can coexist. The Maasai understand themselves to have been entrusted with the care of all cattle by their god—Ngai (meaning sky)—when the earth and sky separated. (This is similar to the relationships some Native Americans have with buffalo—*iinnii*. The Blackfeet reintroduced buffalo to tribal land in 2016.)[46] Traditionally the Maasai did not plow the ground to farm (though now there are Maasai farmers), as that would disturb the grass on which cattle rely. The Maasai also herd goats whom they keep for meat. However, they rarely eat their cattle (that is usually reserved for special rituals) but live off the milk and blood of their cattle. In order to do this, they keep large quantities of cattle so none are harmed by the taking of milk and blood. They honor both the cattle and the grass (land) on which they and the cattle depend. When they had the ability to move around and follow the water, this worked well. Colonial rule and appropriation of land, however, have greatly changed the conditions under which the Maasai live, and they now find themselves trying to survive on degraded land and face competition from wildlife such as elephants. Since their entire culture is built around the use and value of cattle, it is clear in this case that cattle have shaped people as much as people have shaped cattle. The Maasai use cattle dung to build houses, urine to sterilize dishes, and hides to make clothes, and the cattle themselves are a form of currency and wealth. The Maasai relationships with their environment are complex, but here my focus is on how they honor cattle.[47]

By honoring the cattle in these ways, the larger environments are also able to maintain their integrity. The grasslands are kept healthy by the grazing cattle with whom they have co-evolved. In the past, in what is now the United States, this ecological role was filled by bison (more commonly referred to as buffalo). The Lakota understand this relationship between the buffalo and the land and see them as sacred. They are sacred because "it is their role to provide food and other practical benefits for the people. In return for their role as providers for the people, however, they deserve respect."[48] While there are some efforts to reintroduce buffalo, today healthy ecosystems (including other wildlife) can be maintained with some amount of pasture-based cattle ranching. Grass-fed beef is gaining in popularity, but it can't meet the current demand for beef. With changes in consumption practices, though, this way of raising cattle for meat and dairy products is a viable option. It is an option that *can* entail respect for the cattle, the land, and the horses who are often used in this kind of ranching.

Plumwood's approach to such issues would not be to call for a ban on using horses, donkeys, burros, cattle, or oxen in all ways. Instead, it would call for context-specific analysis and approaches for ameliorating the lives of these various animal beings (and the human beings with whom they live and work). A version of this kind of respectful use can increasingly be found in the United States on some small-scale, grass-fed cattle ranches. Just to provide one example, Salmon Creek Meats, run by Joe and Sona Markholt, was one of the grass-fed cattle operations I featured in my book *Livestock: Food, Fiber, and Friends*. They raise breeds of cattle that can do well on pasture and protect their young from predators. The cattle are not dehorned. They are gradually weaned when they are six months old. The cattle spend their lives out on pasture. Any hay they eat is grown by Joe. Joe and his family move the cattle among several pastures, and during the summer "they go up the mountain." Joe uses horses to move his cattle and to go up to check on them. They currently have eight horses who are partners in the work of the ranch. He said that's more than they probably should have, but "once you start working with them they become your buddy."[49]

Joe helped his uncle Lee train and race quarter horses, and his daughter Uriah competes in barrel racing and roping. But there is a different relationship that develops between horse and human when working together on the ranch. Joe talked about how the quiet and careful work to move cattle up the mountain has a different energy than the timed competitive events. The humans and the horses "get jacked up and excited" in competition. This can be one reason some choose not to use competition horses for ranch work. Another is that a competition horse can win money, and it doesn't make sense to injure such horses by working cattle over uneven terrain. That said, Joe thinks it does the competition horses good to get out and work cattle or go on camping trips. It gives their minds something more to do.

Part of the different relationship with ranch horses may also be related to how they are bred. Breeding horses for ranch work rather than for competition in halter classes, or to compete in highly specialized sports such as cutting or reining, results in horses that are sound in body and mind. They are flexible in body and mind and usually interested in learning to do their work.[50] Joe said they always try to cross foundation stock on the sire's side with racing speed on the dam's side. This way they get well-built horses who can move but who also have a mind and who "watch a cow." Even when breeding for racing (which they don't do anymore, as quarter horse racing is shrinking in the Pacific Northwest), they bred with an eye for work the horse could do after racing. He said fewer retired quarter horses end up as meat after their racing career than do thoroughbred horses because they are more versatile and not overspecialized. Quarter horses bred for racing do require an experienced person, as they are hotter than the more typical quarter horse. They can still make good working horses, though, so they help create different possibilities for humans, cattle, and wildlife.

Grass-fed dairy farms and grass-fed beef can both be approached in ways that mitigate many of the environmental concerns connected to raising livestock animals. While this in no way settles the questions surrounding the ethics of using and consuming other animal beings in this way in the first place, this approach can ameliorate some of the issues. With regard to the animals themselves, they can live a life more in keeping with their species' needs and desires (something that confinement frustrates). With regard to the environment, while CAFOs produce concentrated waste that often pollutes the air and waterways (killing fish and other aquatic life), well-managed grazing can improve the fertility of the land and increase water retention. Grazed land also provides better habitat for other wildlife than does developed or farmed land.[51] Much of this wildlife is welcomed—birds, butterflies, and smaller mammals. Some are more controversial. Grazed land not only improves the grasses on which cattle graze but also can improve the land for other grazers such as deer and elk. This situation also means grazing can provide an improved ecosystem for bears, mountain lions, coyotes, and wolves. While some ranchers work with such potential livestock predators, others seek their removal.

Since the cattle at Salmon Creek are not in a barn, predation is a risk, but one of the reasons Joe has the cattle he does is that they can and will protect their young. Mountain lions and coyotes are known to be in the area, and wolves are moving closer. With a herd, the risk of loss is limited. The elk share the pastures with cattle—coming and going as they please. He noted that "it takes a lot of time and money to build a fence to deter elk, and they have a right to be out there too." He enjoys seeing them. "It's all about balance. A few wolves can be a good thing—they keep the elk numbers down." He does worry that government regulations sometimes go too far, though, and "too many wolves gets out of balance, too." Joe is glad he's been able to share this life with his daughter, as "this type of farming is the only way to go. It's a lot of work—haying, fencing, butchering—but it's good work."[52]

On this ranch, the humans, the horses, the cattle, the elk, and the coyotes (and perhaps, in the future, wolves) live in a beautiful place and exist in relationships of mutual dependence and respect. This is only possible if the humans involved can enter into respectful relationships with the land, wildlife, and livestock animals. It also requires that the humans value these respectful relationships as much as, or more than, profit. As we will see in chapters 6 and 7, though, many ranchers do not want to accept the risk of predation and so seek to eliminate potential predators such as mountain lions, coyotes, and wolves. This approach fails to respect the mountain lions, coyotes, and wolves and, once again, returns to the mind-set that sees cattle (or sheep or goats or chickens) purely as a source of profit. Pasture-based systems of raising livestock have to look to the ethics of the human relationships with the livestock, as well as to the relationships with all the wildlife that might share their space.

Chapter Four

Pigs and Poultry

This chapter examines the conditions of pigs and poultry in contemporary industrial farming, as well as the emerging alternatives of pasture-based agriculture, through a discussion of *Babe* (1995) and *Chicken Run* (2000). The work of ecofeminists Carol Adams and Val Plumwood is again integrated in this discussion, and the work of Alice Walker is developed. The work of John Dewey is then combined with these ecofeminist perspectives in order to develop a pragmatist ecofeminist ethic of respectful use. Together, these theorists point to the importance of using a pragmatist approach to discuss and evaluate what these different systems mean for the animals themselves, for the environment, for farmers, and for consumers.

INDUSTRIAL PRODUCTION

While cattle production has become increasingly industrialized, many cattle do still spend some of their lives grazing on grass. The changes to cattle's lives are the result of producers (they really are no longer ranchers or farmers) who are trying to replicate what they see as the success of pig and poultry production. Pigs and poultry spend their entire lives (unnaturally short though many of these lives are) in confinement. Poultry emerge from the egg in hatcheries (never having a mother in their lives), are shipped through the mail, and then are placed in barns with twenty-five thousand other chicks if they are to be "broilers" or placed in cages with one hundred thousand to one million hens per barn if they are to be "layers."[1] Those layers who end up in a "cage-free" operation find themselves with more room to move and some perches and nest boxes, but they are still in a very unnatural flock size of thirty thousand or more.[2] None of these conditions allow for the chickens to express their natural behaviors and egg-laying cycles. Further, the concentration of so many birds creates serious problems with air pollution, and their accumulated excrement is too strong to be safely used as fertilizer.

Pigs, too, are born in confinement. They have their mother to nurse from until they are only a few weeks old (most pigs would wean their offspring when they are eight to ten weeks old), but she cannot really nurture them as she is in a farrowing crate and can't move. The young pigs are removed and placed in crates or pens to be "finished" by the age of six months when they are sent to slaughter.[3] This kind of system is not in line with the needs and desires of the species. As one study found, pigs regularly foraged, built nests, nuzzled, and "formed complex social bonds: females from the same litter tended to stick together long after weaning, and piglets maintained bonds with their mother even after she'd given birth to her next litter."[4] These behaviors and bonds are not available to pigs in industrial livestock production systems. As with chickens, being raised in such concentrated numbers results in air pollution, and their accumulated waste is frequently a source of water pollution as manure lagoons leak or are flooded in storms.

This industrial model is what makes it possible to produce the large amounts of meat produced and consumed in the United States. As mentioned in the previous chapter, this means 49,161 million tons of poultry meat and 23,315 million tons of pork meat, or 9,160,910,000 chickens, 236,860,000 turkeys, and 124,436,000 pigs.[5] On this scale, there is no respect for the individual animals, the humans who work in the industry, the humans who consume the meat and eggs (often being recalled for safety issues), or the environment.

BABE

We actually see some of this kind of industrial pig operation in the opening scenes of the movie *Babe: A Little Pig Goes a Long Way*. Babe's mother is in a crate that doesn't really allow her to move so the piglets can have constant access to her milk and grow faster. It is clearly an industrial production model, with metal and concrete instead of dirt and straw. It is a bright and loud environment. Then a truck arrives and abruptly removes the babies from the mother. The scale of the operation is seen as countless rows of similarly situated sows are shown calling to their young. The impact of this trauma is made evident when Babe (who was saved from moving to an industrial feeding operation in order to be raffled off as a prize at a fair) recounts the story to other animals. His sadness and loneliness tug at the heart of Fly, the female border collie who is raising her own puppies when Babe arrives at the Hoggett farm. When those puppies are weaned and sold to other farmers, Fly also experiences a loss, and she begins to teach Babe how to herd just as she had taught her own offspring.

The movie is based on the 1983 book *Babe: The Gallant Pig*, which was originally published under the title *Sheep Pig*. While the basics of the story in the book and the movie are the same—Babe learns to herd sheep in order to save himself from becoming dinner—there are a number of interesting and important differences. One difference is that, in the movie, Fly has a male border collie companion named Rex. Rex is in charge, and he disapproves of Fly taking care of Babe. At one point, Rex attacks Fly and injures her (reminiscent of human scenes of domestic violence). In the book, Fly is the only dog in the story, and she is the one who teaches Babe to herd. In both the movie and the book, Babe's success at herding is made possible through the cooperation of the sheep. He first meets the ewe Maa when she is brought into the barn to heal and rest. Babe is kind to her, and they become friends. When she is back with the flock, she tells the other sheep to trust him. The sheep like Babe because he asks them politely to do things rather than scaring and dominating them as the dogs do.

Babe's life in the book and the movie is one that few pigs today have the chance to experience. He has straw in which to nest, he is fed the humans' leftovers, and he roams freely. In the past, dairies would often raise a few pigs on the byproducts of milking. The pigs might also root in the orchard, cleaning out plants like blackberries and turning (and fertilizing) the soil. It was once more common to fence animals out of areas like gardens than it was to confine the animals. So historically pigs had a great deal of freedom to roam and eat as they could. Simon Fairlie refers to pigs and poultry as "default livestock" because they can be raised without major inputs of water and grain. They live on what humans leave behind.[6]

Pigs are known to be quite intelligent and highly social. They sleep together, play, communicate, mark territory, and dream.[7] This of course raises questions about using them as food, and it definitely calls into question the practices of modern industrial pig farming. These pigs are kept on concrete and have no nesting materials. The flooring and their speedy weight gain often cause them to be lame. Lack of movement (they have about six to eight square feet of space) makes them weak. They have nothing to do since they don't need to forage for food or build nests.[8] The crowding does result in fights, so many producers cut their teeth and tails. There are smaller-scale pig farms raising pastured pigs who do move around, forage for food, build nests, and form social bonds with other pigs and with humans. But these pigs generally take longer to "finish," and so the meat that comes from their slaughter is more expensive.[9] But it is meat that comes from animals who lived lives that allowed them to fulfill many of their natural needs and desires.

Not all pigs are destined to become dinner. While Babe's job of herding sheep is unusual, pigs are trained to hunt truffles and are valued for their sense of smell. Some pigs are used as therapy animals. Many pigs are kept as pets. They are known to be good problem solvers. The sociality and intelligence of pigs that makes them useful to humans in these nonlethal ways also deserves respect when the pigs are being raised to become meat. That means people have to be willing to pay more so farmers can return pigs to settings where they can roam, forage, and build relationships. Babe forms relationships with Fly and Maa, and in the movie he has an important friendship with Ferdinand.

Ferdinand, a significant character in the movie who was not in the book, is a duck. In the movie, Ferdinand and Babe are friends, and it is Ferdinand who gets the idea of making himself useful so as not to become dinner. He tries to be an alarm clock like the rooster. This results in annoying the humans and the privileged house cat. When the cat chases Ferdinand, they make a mess of the house. Ferdinand must leave the farm or face immediate death.

Making Babe and Ferdinand friends carries a great deal of meaning as confined pig production closely followed the model of confined poultry production. Chickens were the first livestock animal to move to the large-scale industrial model of confinement and fast growth. That model is also used for ducks and geese. Ferdinand's story could have been one of being born in a hatchery, shipped in the mail, and then housed indoors with six thousand to one hundred thousand other ducks.[10] He would be slaughtered at about seven to eight weeks old,[11] never going outside, never going in water, never flying, and never nesting. While the ducks on the Hoggett farm don't have that life, they are still slaughtered and eaten. This gives Ferdinand and Babe common cause in trying to find ways to make themselves useful and so not be seen as food. A complicating factor that the movie does make prominent is that Babe is saved from being Christmas dinner because a duck was put on the plate instead. Ferdinand and Babe look in through a window to see a duck carcass in the center of the dinner table. This duck is not someone the movie audience gets to know, though. Probably thinking that knowing that duck would have been too much for the audience to handle, the duck remains an "absent referent" (in Carol Adams's terms).

CAROL ADAMS AND VAL PLUMWOOD ON THE LOGIC OF DOMINATION IN *BABE*

The work of Carol Adams was briefly mentioned in the previous chapter when discussing dairy cows and Adams's idea of feminized protein. As mentioned, Adams builds on the work of ecofeminist philosopher Karen Warren, who argues that women and other marginalized communities of humans find themselves operating as oppressed groups within a logic of domination. So, too, does the rest of nature, as well as other-than-human animals. This logic rests on a practice of dividing the world up. A common way to do this sorting and categorizing is to use what are taken to be mutually exclusive binaries: male/female, human/nonhuman, reason/emotion, white/black, rich/poor, culture/nature—and the list can go on. Then one side of the binary is judged to be superior or more important in some way, and the binary builds into a value hierarchy. For example, in the history of Western philosophy, humans' rational capacity (often connected to the capacity for language) was what was seen to separate humans from the rest of the animals (and nature as a whole). Further, to be male was to be more fully human than being female, since men were seen as more rational than women, who were seen as ruled by emotion. For most of these philosophers, being Greek or European also entailed being more rational, and so more "civilized," than being any of a number of "others." From here, it is a small step to the logic of domination (also referred to by Plumwood as the logic of colonization), which uses these value hierarchies to justify European colonization and rule, white supremacy, sex discrimination, and the virtually unlimited use of other-than-human animals and the rest of nature.

There are many problems with the logic of domination. For one, even if the differences suggested by the binaries existed, the value hierarchies that follow are not justified. Being different does not, on its own, result in superiority and inferiority. A particular difference may be better or worse for particular purposes, or in particular contexts, but not universally. A further problem with the logic of domination, though, is that the binaries do not hold. There are few (if any) completely mutually exclusive categories other than in the human mind. Male and female may represent convenient place holders at either end of a spectrum of sex and gender characteristics, but they are not clear-cut biological or social categories. Race, ethnicity, and nationality do not serve as clean markers for divisions as their meanings are contingent. Further, people have had sex across these perceived lines (forced and voluntary), and most humans living today demonstrate in their living bodies that the binaries do not hold. Similarly, human and nonhuman can be hard to make sense of when one examines the genetic material shared across species or the microbiome that is necessary for human survival. [12]

Dismantling the binaries and/or the value hierarchies that human cultures have built up over time challenges the logic of domination. This kind of deep change in thinking, though, is difficult and entails changing many human institutions as well as individuals. This way of thinking has informed (and been informed by) family structures, political systems, religions, and science. As a consequence, many find it easier to tinker with the categories but leave the overall structure of the logic of domination in place. For instance, women working for equal rights often appeal to the fact that as humans they share in the capacity for reason (and language), unlike other-than-human animals, and so they should be political, social, and moral equals with men. While Mary Wollstonecraft (see chapter 3) famously made such an argument in her 1792 *Vindication of the Rights of Woman*, this strategy is still seen today when ecofeminists are criticized by other feminists for connecting women with nature (or emotions) or for suggesting that speciesism is connected with sexism and racism. Many feminists see such connections as trivializing human women's "real" problems. The problem with this common strategy of reinforcing one binary to dismantle another is that this process is one of gaining inclusion on the valued side of a binary, but it does not dismantle the binaries, the value hierarchies, or the logic of domination. [13] Because the logic remained in place in the late nineteenth century, it made sense to some white suffrage activists in the United States to use their "whiteness" to argue that they were more fit to vote than black men. These are strategies that pit the oppressed against each other, and by which one group gains more privileges only by being sure there is an "other" who can remain disempowered and exploitable.

The desire that Babe and Ferdinand express to become useful animals so as not to become food for humans buys into the binary of useful/useless animals, which was also expressed in the story as smart animals as opposed to stupid animals. When the puppies ask Fly what a pig is for, she says they are to eat. Worried that they, too, might be eaten, Fly assures the puppies that humans don't eat smart animals such as dogs. They eat sheep, cows, ducks, and chickens—stupid animals.[14] The dogs are seen as smart and useful animals, while pigs, ducks, and sheep are seen as stupid and useless in terms of doing any work on the farm. While they are used as food, it is their status as "useless" that allows them to be seen as food in a way that the dogs are not. While the movie offers a subtle critique of this way of seeing the animals, it also reinforces it by requiring Ferdinand and Babe to become useful and not to be seen as food.

Ecofeminist philosopher Val Plumwood provides an interesting account of the book and movie *Babe*. In "'Babe': The Tale of the Speaking Meat," she writes, "Because the main theme of *Babe* turns around the refusal of communicative status to animals, the film is of considerable moral interest for philosophical accounts of human-animal relations. . . . *Babe* repeatedly problematises the kind of prejudice that relegates the other to a sphere of radical otherness marked by rational deficiency, mechanistic reduction and exclusion from communicative status." She argues that the story is about much more than problematizing meat; "it also poses ethical and political questions, analogous to some of those arising in post-colonial theory, about the distinction between meat and non-meat animals and about the role of the human contract with those special and more privileged 'pet' animals who can never be 'meat.'"[15] Plumwood notes, however, that many people saw the movie mostly as a story about how hard work and determination can enable people to overcome obstacles and make something of themselves. On such a view, the movie is not really about pigs, sheep, dogs, and ducks. The humans viewing the movie can thereby avoid the sorrow and shame that Plumwood herself felt with regard to our "complicity in the dominant cultural tradition of rational human mastery over animals and nature—as well as everything else considered beneath the master realm of reason."[16]

For Plumwood, allowing the "meat animal" to speak was a violation of the norms of distancing and mechanization present in meat production that help reinforce divides such as us/them, mind/body, and process/product. A speaking pig suggests continuity with human embodiment and emotions rather than a sharp divide, and Babe's birth and weaning connect the product of meat to the violent process put in place by humans. These put before the audience some important ethical concerns not usually confronted in daily life due to the sequestering of meat production in contemporary industrialized societies. Further, she thinks the movie makes the audience confront the possibility that if the body of the pig (which is seen by many as nothing more than meat) is connected to a feeling, thinking, and communicative mind, then the human body might also be seen as meat. To avoid confronting this possibility, humans have constructed hierarchies of animal beings, with humans on top. Some animals, such as the large-brained social mammals and those considered pets, get a status closer to humans, but those animals considered livestock are toward the bottom of the hierarchy.

In *Babe*, for instance, we see the special status afforded to dogs and cats that is denied to pigs, sheep, and ducks. Babe's (and possibly Maa's and Ferdinand's) presence disrupts this view. As mentioned before, this arrangement poses ethical and political questions about hierarchies of all kinds, but especially about the distinction between meat and non-meat animals. Key to this hierarchy is seeing that it is being arranged from more to less intelligent, and from more to less communicative. This matches with more and less morally considerable. *Babe* suggests that acknowledging the communicative capacities of livestock animals could change farming from the norm of institutionalized violence to a communicative ethic. As Plumwood writes, "Communicative relationships open up new moral possibilities for organizing life in ways that can negotiate conflicts of interests, build agreement, trust and mutuality, and avoid instrumentalism and the imposition of the will of one party on the other by force." Such a communicative ethic has to acknowledge and deal with inequalities of power and tendencies toward various kinds of centrism (anthropocentrism, androcentrism, Eurocentrism), so it needs "to be part of a plural set of grounds for valuation . . . and to be sensitive to communicative capacities within species as well as to their capacities for communication with humans."[17]

As long as only exceptional ducks and pigs escape the fate of being seen as "useless," and so available to be used as food for humans and their pets, the logic of human domination remains in place and unchallenged. Livestock animals are still, in Adams's words, ontologized as edible. That is, their very being is to exist as food for humans (and human pets). As Plumwood points out, one can be seen not only as edible but also as having other purposes and desires (see chapter 3). When a being is ontologized solely as edible, though, industrial systems of animal agriculture can start to make sense. The animals are seen to have no needs and desires of their own. They exist solely to become food as quickly and efficiently as possible.

Further, reducing these animals to simply their function as food removes the idea of individuality and individual personality. The animals function as categories—as beef and pork—rather than as individual cows or pigs. This is what Adams refers to as "mass terms." When one uses the mass term *beef*, the individual living cows who had to exist to create that beef disappear from sight and thought. They become what Adams calls an absent referent. The cows are a necessary referent since one can't have beef for dinner unless there were once living individual cows, but the term *beef* has made them absent. For many people, it is easier to eat other animals when mechanisms such as mass terms are in place and when there is distance between them and the animals whom they are eating. Once an animal gains status as an individual, many people have a harder time seeing them as appropriate food. When an animal escapes on the way to slaughter, for instance, many confirmed meat eaters will root for that individual animal, sympathize with that individual animal, and support the idea of that individual living out their natural life span at a farm animal sanctuary. That individual escapes the consequences of the logic of domination, but the logic remains, as few go on to question the system from which the animal escaped.

The movie *Babe*, even as it reinforced certain value hierarchies, did do much to reinstate the individuality of some animals who are usually ontologized solely as edible. As a result, it got many people thinking about their choice to eat these animals at all. The lead actor in the movie, James Cromwell, who played Farmer Hoggett, had been a vegetarian before making the movie. This initial change in diet had been inspired when he rode his motorcycle through cattle feedlots in Texas. He became a vegan after making the movie *Babe*. He is also an animal activist who narrated *Farm to Fridge* and is "adamant that *Babe* is not a kids' movie, and also that animals have unalienable rights that humans need to recognize." For him, an important part of what keeps people from really thinking about how humans use other animals is "the corporate mentality bred by a financial and economic system that puts profits before people, and creates—in the people that work for them—the very narrow, limited, inhumane routine. And that they are stuck in it." He is optimistic about the spread of vegan options, though, and thinks this development marks a change in consciousness.[18]

POULTRY

The move to vegetarianism is seen by many as an important step toward dismantling the logic of domination. Carol Adams, though, sees it as another example of gaining recognition for some by further oppressing others and calls for veganism.[19] This was already discussed in the previous chapter in connection with dairy cows. Here it comes up in relation to eggs. While ducks and geese have not yet become profitable in large-scale egg production, chickens have become egg-laying machines. One thing that allowed the move to large-scale, confined production of chicken was the increasing specialization of the birds. While "broilers" were bred to grow quickly and to grow more breast meat (which is why most broiler chickens can't walk, or even stand, by the time they are six weeks old), "layers" were bred to produce more and more eggs. While the hope was for an egg a day, most commercial hens lay 250 eggs a year.[20] This far exceeds the previous norm of 153 and the more natural range of 10–15 eggs a year for wild birds.

Having reduced these chickens to their food functions with the mass terms of *broiler* and *layer*, their needs and desires have been set aside to focus on production. "Broilers" live in crowded and filthy conditions. Since they will be killed within six weeks, no effort is made to clean the barns in which 25,000 or more chickens are housed. These chickens grow so big so fast that their legs can't keep up with their weight, so they are lame or crippled at the time they are "snatched" and put in boxes for transport to slaughter. This process of capture and transport causes more injuries and stress. Chicken slaughter is a highly mechanized process, but it is not clean or stress free for the chickens or the humans involved.[21] Many who find this kind of life and death inhumane and unethical choose to stop eating meat and become vegetarians.

While egg production may seem more humane, there may be more suffering and death involved in industrial egg production systems than in meat production. This is why some argue that ending one's egg and milk consumption would do more for animal welfare than not eating meat. Most eggs in the United States come from confinement operations. Given the specialized breeds, the male chicks born in hatcheries producing laying hens have no value and are sorted and killed as soon as they hatch. They are gassed, suffocated, or ground up alive. Then the female chicks are sent through the mail without food and water, and many die before reaching their destination. Some may be lucky enough to land at a well-run backyard hen house or small farm, but most end up in barns with five hundred thousand or more other birds. Most are still in cage systems in which the hens have their beaks trimmed to prevent injury and don't have enough space to extend their wings. Each hen has sixty-seven square inches and lives in a stack of cages with accumulating manure, which causes lung and eye problems. While there is a push to move to cage-free production, there is no call to decrease the number of birds being housed together, so fighting is likely. These birds will have more space (two hundred square inches per bird), perches they can use, and some version of a nest box for laying. Free range doesn't really differ from cage free in industrial production. There are no requirements about the size and quality of the outdoor space provided, and no requirement that the hens ever go outside. They may not even have access to the outdoor area much of the year due to concerns about weather and disease. [22] Even with these alternatives becoming more common, it is important to note that 90 percent of the eggs purchased in the United States come from caged production systems. [23]

Whatever the production model, the hens lay so many eggs that their calcium is depleted and their legs give out. Their lungs and eyes are also damaged from the ammonia that accumulates in the barns (even those barns that do remove waste by conveyor belts). All hens' egg production decreases as they age, but given the high rate of production in commercial operations, hens are considered "spent" before they are two years old. At that time, all the hens in a given barn will be killed, the barn cleaned out, and new chicks brought in to start the process all over again.

The assumption in these egg and meat production systems is that chickens are mindless beings who do not suffer, or whose suffering does not matter. But chickens are highly social, caring, and intelligent animals. Hens build nests, sit on clutches, and are very protective of their brood. They use a complex system of communication that includes more than thirty distinct calls. Various experiments have demonstrated that while their brains differ from human brains, chickens have long memories, can recognize faces, subtract and add, and feel empathy. [24]

CHICKEN RUN

The 2000 movie *Chicken Run* challenged the idea of ontologizing chickens as just egg producers or just meat. In this movie, the Tweedy egg "farm" is portrayed much like a prisoner-of-war camp. The hens are in huts like barracks. Unlike most egg-producing chickens in the United States, these hens do get to move between the huts and the yard at will, and each has an individual nesting box. The yard is bare dirt, no grass. While male chicks are typically ground up at birth, there is an old rooster living with these hens. His name is Fowler. The perimeter of the yard is strung with barbed wire, and two menacing dogs join Mr. Tweedy and his rifle on regular patrols around the yard. One hen in particular, Ginger, spearheads numerous escape attempts. She is aided in this endeavor by Mac, who is a good engineer. Since Ginger is always the first to get out, she repeatedly gets caught by Mr. Tweedy and thrown in solitary confinement in a coal bin. This treatment does not deter Ginger, though, who dreams of a better place with grass and no fences, no dogs, and no farmer. When the other hens lose faith in her vision, Ginger notes that they have internalized their oppression: "the fence is in your head, not just around the farm."

Mrs. Tweedy has a chart on which each hen is listed by number (though the chickens refer to each other by names), and each hen's egg production is tracked. In the movie, when a particular hen's production level falls off, Mrs. Tweedy marches out in the style of a Nazi commandant—a stiff-legged march in tall black boots. She points to the offending hen, who is then taken to the shed and has her head cut off with a hatchet. The hen's name is Edwina. The next time we see Edwina, all that is visible are her bones on a plate in the middle of the dining room table (though in reality laying hens are not used for meat, as they don't have much "meat on their bones"). All the hens' egg production drops as the days get shorter, and they begin to molt. Molting is when chickens lose their feathers and begin to grow new ones. This time off from laying also allows the hens to replenish nutrients. It is common practice to keep hens under lights to keep egg production going and forestall molting. This situation means the hens deplete nutrients like calcium, and their bones become brittle and break. When it makes financial sense to keep hens in production as long as possible, egg producers resort to forced molting. In the past, this process entailed withholding food for five to fourteen days to get the hens to stop egg production quickly and then get back into egg production. Forced molting is still practiced, but protests over starving birds have modified the practice, and a low-protein and low-energy diet (combined with lighting changes) has the same result. Overall, though, forced molting is less common now, as the industry finds it more profitable just to kill all the hens in a barn before they are two years old (and can no longer stand on their brittle legs) and start again, since all hens will produce fewer eggs as they age.[25]

The hens in *Chicken Run* look out for each other, and those producing abundantly try to share their eggs with those who are not producing at any given time. While this practice offers some protection to particular individuals, they can't hide the overall drop in egg production charted by Mrs. Tweedy. Seeing her profits fall, she refers to the hens as worthless and stupid. She then sees a poultry production magazine (the movie does not hide behind the idea that this is farming) with an ad for a machine to make chicken meat pies. The ad copy focuses on the greater profitability of meat over egg production, making it clear that money is Mrs. Tweedy's main motivation. The arrival of the pie machine makes it clear to everyone that there is no escaping Edwina's fate unless they escape the farm.

By this time, Rocky the Flying Rooster has arrived at the "farm." Shot out of a cannon at a nearby circus, he appears to fly into the yard. Ginger agrees to hide Rocky from the circus manager if he teaches the hens to fly so they can escape. Rocky lets the hens believe he can do this and has them start getting into shape. These efforts are frustrated when Mrs. Tweedy orders more food for the chickens to fatten them up for the pie machine. While Ginger begs them not to eat the food, most of the hens eat themselves sick. Once the machine has been assembled, Mrs. Tweedy asks for a bird to use to test the machine. Mr. Tweedy, who has suspicions that the hens are organizing and plotting against him, is only too happy to bring the ringleader Ginger for the test. Ginger is shackled upside down by her feet and starts down the line. She calls out that she doesn't want to be made into a pie—she doesn't want to be a pie. With her cry, she is challenging the ontology of the production system. Rocky hears her and swoops in. The two manage to escape the worst of the machine and return to the yard.

While this act of heroism renews everyone's faith in Rocky, the urgent need to escape makes him realize he can no longer delay revealing that he can't fly. He packs up and leaves, leaving behind the rest of his promotion poster that makes it clear to the hens that he can't fly without the aid of a cannon. While this discovery is initially disappointing, it does give Mac some new ideas about how to propel the hens up and over the fence. Although these efforts are not very successful, they lead to the realization that Fowler had been in the air force. The chickens enlist the rats, Nick and Fetcher, to help get them the materials they need to build a plane. The rats are paid with eggs. The chickens also steal parts from the pie machine. Rocky returns just in time to help get the plane off the ground. During the escape, the rats allow "their" eggs to be thrown at the Tweedys, and Ginger cuts the line dangling from the plane, causing Mrs. Tweedy to fall from the sky into the pie machine.

We next see the chickens at a chicken sanctuary. There are trees and grass, and baby chicks have been hatched. The chickens are enjoying their physical freedom and social lives. The two rats are also there, discussing the possibility of starting their own egg farm, though they can't decide whether they first need a chicken or an egg. This exchange shows that the logic of the production model remains a threat. That it is transferred from humans to rats is interesting, and this idea will be discussed more in chapter 6.

PRAGMATIST-INFORMED ECOFEMINISM

One of the ironic aspects of the industrial production of pigs and poultry is that these are animals who have lived in close contact with humans for thousands of years. The smaller size of chickens often meant they were kept close to the house, and even today backyard chickens are common. This arrangement allows humans to develop relationships with individual chickens. Pigs, too, were often near the house, as they were fed on human leftovers. Not that long ago, pigs wandered human settlements freely to provide waste management services, as they can eat human garbage and feces. This cleaning service was needed to enable increasing numbers of humans to settle in one spot and not die of disease.[26]

Interestingly, being kept near the house meant that pigs and poultry were often cared for by women. In *Babe*, Mrs. Hoggett ontologizes Babe as edible. She likes the idea of feeding up a pig for Christmas dinner and starts listing what his body will yield: hams, bacon, pork chops, kidneys, liver, chitterlings, trotters, and blood for black pudding.[27] In *Chicken Run*, Mrs. Tweedy likewise ontologizes the chickens as edible. Dissatisfied with the yields from egg production, she invests in a machine that will turn the chickens into chicken pot pies.

Like most livestock animals, the women in these stories do not have names and identities of their own. They have no name or identity other than their status as married women. They are known only as Mrs. Hoggett and Mrs. Tweedy. Farmer Hoggett is known by his occupation, but not Mrs. Tweedy. There are gendered stereotypes operating in both stories, as well as challenges to some gender stereotypes. The two women represent two different female stereotypes. Mrs. Hoggett is portrayed as not very smart or observant but generally kind and nurturing. She is always talking and thinks her husband is too soft hearted. Mrs. Tweedy is mean and miserly. She dominates her husband. She calls Mr. Tweedy an idiot and kicks him hard enough to leave a mark on his behind. While Farmer Hoggett breaks with male stereotypes by showing compassion for the other animals and understanding them as intelligent individuals, Mr. Tweedy remains antagonistic toward the hens as a defense against his domineering wife. The gender stereotypes apply to the other-than-human animals in both films as well. Rex dominates Fly in the movie version of *Babe*, and Rocky plays the role of the womanizer and keeps calling Ginger "dollface" and a "crazy chick," even as she insists that he use her name. Ecofeminists would argue that these films offer some challenges to traditional notions of gender, though both are firmly in a heteronormative framework. More important, though, these stories subtly demonstrate that various forms of human-to-human oppression are wrapped up with the human oppression of other animal beings.

While theorists such as Adams, Harper, Walker, and Plumwood would agree that the gender and species oppressions presented in the stories of *Babe* and *Chicken Run* are intertwined and need to be addressed together, these theorists diverge on what they think that requires. As discussed earlier, Adams and Harper require a move to veganism, while Plumwood does not. Walker is more complicated here, as her position continues to evolve, but her views seem to closely align with those of Plumwood. While practicing vegetarian and vegan diets at some points in her life, at other times Walker is called by her place and her relationships with other humans to eat some animal-based foods. She describes herself as mostly vegetarian.

In the foreword to Marjorie Spiegel's book *The Dreaded Comparison: Human and Animal Slavery*, Alice Walker notes the discomfort many feel when faced with comparisons between human slavery and the treatment of other-than-human animals by humans. On the one hand, many find such comparisons demeaning for those humans who have been oppressed and brutalized by slavery. On the other hand, many find themselves stricken by guilt over their own complicity in such a system of oppression and brutalization. She writes,

> It is a comparison that, even for those of us who recognize its validity, is a difficult one to face. Especially so if we are the descendants of slaves. Or of slaveowners. Or of both. Especially so if we are also responsible in some way for the present treatment of animals. Especially so if we, for instance, participate in or profit from animal research (what beings who loved life died for our lipstick, lotions, medicines, and so on?) or if we own animals or if we eat

animals or if we are content to know that animals are shut up "safely" in zoos. In short, if we are complicit in their enslavement and destruction, which is to say if we are, at this juncture in history, master.[28]

She says that while our first response is often to feel guilty and ashamed, we need to move to ask what we should do in order to live in a world where humans realize that "[t]he animals of the world exist for their own reasons. They were not made for humans any more than black people were made for whites or women for men."[29] Importantly here, Walker sits with the discomfort that we are all implicated in the oppression of animals rather than advocating for any particular changes in habits that can be seen as exonerating us. We are all, in fact, responsible in some way for the present (and past) treatment of animals.

Here a return to pragmatism and Plumwood is useful. A pragmatist approach to philosophy is not one that seeks absolute or universalizable principles. As mentioned in chapter 1, pragmatism works with situated knowledge to arrive at situationally influenced ethical and political responses to whatever is currently perceived as a problematic situation. For a pragmatist ethics, an action or institution will be judged on how it makes things better or worse, seeking to improve (ameliorate) the situation for as many as possible in the long run. Rather than arriving at a set of moral or political principles, it arrives at guidelines for action, within particular sets of circumstances, through deliberation about an array of considerations connected to a variety of possible futures.

On this approach, better and worse is not reduced to utilitarian principles of seeking pleasure and avoiding pain (physical and/or intellectual), though this is considered. Especially important would be considering the long-term improvement of the material, social, and psychological (emotional) well-being of all the beings involved in a situation. As with many utilitarian views, any being who can experience better and worse material, social, and psychological (emotional) states needs to be considered in assessing possible future action. This needs to be done with an eye to future as well as present circumstances. Dewey's notion of dress rehearsals becomes an important tool for testing one's hypothesis about what to do without yet taking action. In one's imagination, various scenarios can be played out into possible futures so one can assess the various consequences of any particular action. One has to be aware that how things play out in the real world will not match such imagined scenarios (and every solution will give rise to new problems), but this step in inquiry is important for eliminating some avenues of action. A pragmatist approach also has to consider more than those consequences, which can be measured along utilitarian lines, though.

Better or worse is not arrived at by universal principles such as Kant's categorical imperative, though such principles may provide some insight to include in one's inquiry. The categorical imperative asks people to consider whether the intention of their action could be universalized without contradiction. A specified subset of this imperative is the call to treat all rational beings as ends in themselves and never merely as a means. For the pragmatist approach, Kant's consideration of the universalizability of one's intention really boils down to a specific kind of dramatic rehearsal, which can provide important information about how particular actions might play out. A pragmatist would not think that intentions alone provide the moral judgment of what one should do, but since means and ends must be consistent with each other for a pragmatist, this aspect of inquiry is an important element in one's larger deliberation. For instance, one does not develop an environment of trust by means of lying, and one does not achieve a community of care and generosity through self-interest alone. In fact, Kant's examples of how to inquire about the morality of specific intentions largely play out as dress rehearsals along the lines of a consequentialist approach to ethics. They do ask the actor to consider more than material and psychological well-being, though, and to overtly pay attention to actions that would help maintain stable social and political relationships that allow for human flourishing. Treating other rational beings as ends in themselves, and never merely as means, requires acting in ways so as to maintain the trust and stability of the community even in the midst of changes to the status quo. One should not completely ignore the needs and desires of any such beings, even if one disagrees with their choices and actions.

While this particular version of a deontological ethic is clear that other-than-human animals do not directly count in such moral consideration, some have tried to use this approach with those large-brained social mammals deemed to be rational, and others have modified the criteria to include all beings with an interest in life. A recent example of a revised deontological approach can be found in Christine M. Korsgaard's *Fellow Creatures: Our Obligations to Other Animals*. She argues that other creatures have things they value and that they, and their life worlds, should be respected. This entails not treating other creatures as mere means. To make her case, though, she has to make many adjustments to Kant's theory.[30] Such attempts are cumbersome and inadequate to the project of providing full moral consideration to other-than-human animals, but on a pragmatist approach such a theory does not need to do that work all on its own. Combining utilitarian and deontological insights, though, provides useful guidance for taking in a fuller array of considerations in one's deliberation. Adding still other approaches such as virtue and care ethics helps even more.

While better or worse will not just be a matter of the character of the person or institution acting, it is an important aspect of any ongoing situation and community. So, too, is paying attention to what circumstances will help build healthy and flexible relationships among beings, communities, and institutions. Virtue ethics generally focuses on enabling individuals (as well as their communities) to create habits of deliberation and action that avoid the risks of either/or thinking, which sees ways of acting as always required or never allowed. Instead, as with an ethics of care, attention should be paid to what works to provide for well-being and flourishing within a network of relationships (which can include other-than-human animals). Maintaining these relationships is as important to deliberation as are measures of pleasure and pain, or considerations of intention.

With regard to other-than-human animals, all of these approaches have been used to argue that humans *do not* need to take other animals into account in their moral considerations, and all have been used to argue that humans *do* need to consider other animals. The best-known examples of using these theories in ways that take other animals into account include Peter Singer's use of utilitarianism to argue for animal welfare, Tom Regan and Gary Francione's use of a deontological ethic to argue for animal rights, Martha Nussbaum's use of virtue ethics to argue for a capabilities approach to animal well-being, and Carol Adams and Josephine Donovan's use of care ethics to argue for different relationships among humans and other animal beings. While all of these approaches provide useful insights into what is at stake in human relationships with other animal beings, none of them on their own can arrive at an all-encompassing directive for such relationships despite their claims to do so.

On a pragmatist approach, all of these moral theories (and the political theories connected to each general kind of moral theory) are tools in a fuller moral deliberation. They are not in and of themselves the way to arrive at "the" answer about "the" right thing to do. Further, whatever judgment is reached by this pluralistic, deliberative pragmatist inquiry should still be understood as a hypothesis to be more fully tested and revised when played out in actual experience. Actions should always be subject to further inquiry and ongoing revision. With regard to pigs and poultry in particular, a pragmatist approach provides possibilities for the ongoing amelioration of the long-standing relationships humans have had with these beings.

For example, in *Livestock: Food, Fiber, and Friends* I give an account of how humans moved from intimate relationships with these species to a distanced and industrialized production process for meat and eggs. While pigs and poultry lived in relative freedom and close proximity with humans for thousands of years, and were generally known as individuals with individual personalities, they are now raised in highly confined and concealed spaces in such numbers as to mask any hint of individuality. Each move along the way to this dramatic shift can be justified by means of appeals to improving some aspect of the animals' welfare, satisfying the intention to provide affordable meat to all humans, promoting human and wildlife flourishing by lowering the human demand for hunted wildlife, and promoting relationships of care among humans and a widening group of other-than-human animals who rely on meat in their diet.

While generally more attention has been paid to animal welfare over the last 150 years, most of that concern has been focused on wildlife and has left livestock animals out of consideration. As livestock animals, pigs are not covered by the Animal Welfare Act of 1966, and all birds are exempt from this act. It covered dogs, cats, monkeys, rabbits, hamsters, and guinea pigs. An amendment in 1970 extended the act to cover all warm-bodied mammals but then specifically exempted mice, rats, birds, and farm animals (making sure that horses and poultry, along with cattle, sheep, and pigs, remained in the category of farm animals). While there is increasing concern and oversight for those animal beings used in scientific research, this really just turns out to be a concern over nonhuman primates—doing little to challenge the binaries supporting the logic of domination.

While many push to create meaningful welfare standards for animals being raised and killed for food, exemptions continue to be made for any practice that is standard in the industry—such as the cutting of pigs' tails and trimming chickens' beaks. The rise of "ag gag" laws makes it difficult and illegal to gain access to assess the conditions of the lives and deaths of those animals used for food. Most people seem more willing to embrace the idea that animals are conscious, complex beings worthy of respect if they are not animals they see as food.

But given the earlier discussion of pragmatism in chapter 1, such a line makes no sense. There are no sharp breaks in the continuity of animal life.

This ontological realization of relatedness is important to a pragmatist perspective, and it is something often missing from the other more standard approaches to ethics. It is also missing from some ecofeminist calls for veganism. As discussed in chapter 3, Plumwood worried that ontological veganism fails to respect the more radical continuity of humans with other animal life and so tries to move animals into the category of nonedible and unusable (along with humans). This act both fails to respect plants as belonging on this continuum of life and fails to understand humans as embodied beings who can serve as food for other beings. Instead, given the continuity, connectedness, and interdependence of all life, Plumwood follows a pragmatist lead and argues for respectful use and respectful eating along largely pluralistic and fallibilistic (not universally or dogmatically required) lines. This is possible only when humans enter into dialogical relations with other life, though, and give up the idea that humans are the only truly conscious and communicative beings (as Walker did when she communicated with Blue).

Plumwood's statement of the ethics she seeks to foster provides a nice summary of an ecofeminist pragmatist ethic: "[W]e might expect an appropriate methodology for dealing with difference and translation indeterminacy in the non-human case to be one which could hold relatively open expectations, noting the presence of uncertainty and adopting a tentative stance which explored a range of alternatives and attempted to imagine and situate concept formation in terms of different forms of life." This idea mirrors pragmatist understandings of fallibility and holding views as hypotheses rather than fixed and final truths. It requires being open to the different embodied experiences of various animal beings, but not finding them so foreign as to be unrelatable. She continues, "Both human and non-human cases require openness to the other and careful, sensitive, and above all, self-critical observation which admitted and slowed for perspectival and 'centric' bias." As with the pragmatists, Plumwood acknowledges that all knowledge and value judgments are rooted in one's locatedness and experience, but by being conscious of this limitation, greater understanding can be achieved. This is true for communication among humans, as well as among humans and other animal beings. According to Plumwood, "The problems in representing another species' speech or subjectivity in human terms are real, but they do not rule out such representation in any general way, and they pale before the difficulties of failing to represent them at all, or before the enormity of representing communicative and intentional beings as beings lacking all communicative and mental capacity. That is a much greater inaccuracy and injustice than any anthropomorphism."[31]

This larger kind of change in perspective is necessary because it does not work to simply extend the consideration given to pets to livestock since that contract itself is based on exclusion and complicity. Plumwood suggests that a bargain was struck with some wolves that they would never be meat if they would help humans imprison and oppress other animals that humans would use as meat for themselves and wolves' dog descendants.[32] This contract establishes the special status of dogs, but it requires their complicity in the continued oppression of other animals: "To the extent that it is an exclusionary contract, in which some make a living by complicity in instrumentalizing, imprisoning and oppressing others, the contract of colonization cannot be extended to provide liberty for all. Such a contract cannot be made liberatory for all by being extended to all, one at a time, and the attempt to do so merely re-erects the moral dualist barrier in a new place."[33]

Instead, Plumwood argues, we need "to break down this residual contract and associated dualisms if we are to overcome the taboo against recognizing the subjectivity of the meat animal as well as the general failure to recognize animal subjectivity."[34] This does not necessarily mean that all farming would be unethical or that one must end all consumption of meat. Plumwood turns to Native American and other indigenous philosophies for guidance here: "For most or all American Indians food (plant as well as animal) is kin. Relationship to plants and animals as, on the one hand, food and, on the other hand, kin creates a tension which is dealt with mythically, ritually, and ceremonially, but which is never denied. It is this refusal to deny the dilemma in which we are implicated in this life, a refusal to take the way of bad faith, moral supremacy, or self-deception which constitutes a radical challenge to our relationship to our food." Plumwood argues that this is a challenge the industrialized countries must face: "The American Indian view that considerability goes 'all the way down' requires a response considerably more sophisticated than those we have seen in the West, which consist either in drawing lines of moral considerability in order to create an out-group, or in constructing hierarchies of considerability creating de-facto out-groups in particular cases."[35] An approach based on the notions of considerability and use will be explored further in chapter 7.

Chapter Five

Whales and Fishes

This chapter focuses on whales and fishes and moves from a discussion of *Moby-Dick* to examine the increased critical attention focused on keeping dolphins and whales in captivity and using them in entertainment. Humans have long and complicated relationships with the animals of the oceans. The eating of various fishes is common across most cultures. Fishing and aquaculture have long histories (a million years of fishing in the wild and five thousand years of aquaculture).[1] The rise of industrial fishing practices and industrial fish farming, though, has changed these relationships. Fishes have increasingly come to be seen simply as a resource. Overfishing has caused fisheries to collapse, and the wasted bycatch means less food in the oceans for other sea creatures. Orca whales in the Pacific Northwest, for instance, have been found dead from starvation. According to an article in the *New York Times*, "Listed as endangered since 2005, the orcas are essentially starving, as their primary prey, the Chinook, or king salmon, are dying off."[2] The human relationships with the mammals of the ocean have also changed. Not so long ago whales and dolphins were seen as resources for food and oil, but now many see them as intelligent, sentient creatures and object to hunting them or keeping them in captivity. Films such as *The Cove* (2009) and *Blackfish* (2013) highlight growing concerns over the use of whales and dolphins in entertainment and as food. While *Blackfish* focuses on orca whales and purports to show abusive conditions in marine parks, *The Cove* focuses on bottlenose dolphins and discusses problems with captivity as well as the hunting practices that accompany the capture of dolphins for marine parks. Both films received a great deal of public attention, and *Blackfish*

resulted in many boycotting Sea World and Marineland. The public response
to the films demonstrates a growing concern for sea mammals and a growing
respect for their intelligence and their cultures. I will use the critical pragmatism of Alain L. Locke to argue for the possibility of understanding an
exchange among human and other animal cultures. The native philosophies
of Vine Deloria Jr. and Robin Wall Kimmerer will be introduced to begin an
examination of more inclusive ways of understanding human relationships
with other animal (and plant) beings.

WHALES AND WHALING

Dolphins and whales have long been considered among the most intelligent
mammals (along with apes and elephants). They, too, have passed the mirror
recognition test and have complex forms of species communication or language. Dolphins have been used in language research involving sign language and have demonstrated that they understand not only signs for objects
but also word order. For instance, they know the difference between being
asked to bring the ball to the basket and being asked to bring the basket to the
ball. Whales and dolphins enjoy learning and are capable of producing novel
actions as well. In one experiment, two dolphins were asked to do something
new—to "create." They communicated with each other and then simultaneously performed a sequence of actions they had never done before.[3] As with
other large-brained social mammals, whales and dolphins have long natural
life spans and long childhoods in which they learn from their family and
community.

Whales are some of the longest-living mammals in existence. Their
strength and intelligence has made them one of the challenging big-game
animals. Hunting whales has always been dangerous. Many indigenous peoples hunted whales as a means of subsistence, eating their meat and blubber
and using their bones. Some still do so today. In Canada, after a century of
the whales being nearly extinct, the Inuit fought for their treaty rights to
whale and successfully hunted a bowhead whale in 2014. In the United
States, the Makah tribe in the state of Washington continues to try to revive
their practice of hunting the gray whale. A successful hunt in 1999 was
followed by a request for a waiver from the Marine Mammal Protection Act
in 2005. In 2015, National Oceanic and Atmospheric Association (NOAA)
Fisheries issued a Draft Environmental Impact Statement (DEIS) on the
waiver request. As of February 2020, NOAA Fisheries is in the process of

preparing a supplement to the DEIS, and no decision on the waiver has yet been made.[4] Many are outraged by this hunting and are trying to have it stopped. There are ethical concerns related to hunting an intelligent and self-conscious creature. There are also concerns about the protection of various species of whales, many of which have gone extinct or are now endangered. The irony, of course, is that it was not indigenous hunters who overhunted whales. It was commercial whale hunts that did the damage. Whales were hunted for oil to burn in lamps and to use as a lubricant for gears in the increasingly mechanized and industrialized world, and their bones were also used for corsets and fashion accessories (as Gilman problematized in chapter 3). While the Inuit were hunting whales up to eight thousand years ago, Norway has been a whaling country for four thousand years, and Japan probably as long. The Basque entered commercial whaling in the tenth or eleventh century.[5] Historically, the whaling industry was a global concern. Norway, Japan, England, Spain, France, the Netherlands, Greenland, and the United States were all big players. Today Japan and Norway remain major whaling countries and resist the pressure of the International Whaling Commission (IWC), which regulates whale hunting. Japan pulled out of the IWC in July 2019 in order to resume commercial whaling without restriction.

In his book *Among Whales*, Roger Payne combines his scientific knowledge of whales with a call to learn from whales and rethink the model of human domination represented in commercial whaling. He notes that the right whales (so named because they were the right whale to hunt—right kind of oil and didn't sink) were the first to be pushed near extinction, as they could be harpooned from the shore. The right whale, the bow whale, and the gray whale gained some protection in 1937, while the blue whale gained protection in 1960; however, enforcement was limited.[6] World War II gave the whales a bit of a rest, as whaling boats were sunk or put to other uses. The Convention for Regulation of Whaling was written in 1946, but it did little to protect whales until the 1970s. Public pressure, often focused on the discovery of the song of the humpback whale, moved the IWC to do more to take up the protection of whales. But any country has ninety days to declare that they will not be bound by a regulation the IWC passes. Norway and Japan have used this tactic regularly. Iceland (which left the IWC in 1992), Norway, and Japan also use "scientific whaling" to procure whale meat. Claiming that they need to survey and study whale populations, they kill whales to see what they are eating.[7] The former Soviet Union killed seven thousand humpback whales right after they were protected. The 1986 moratorium on commercial whaling was helpful, as was the declaration of eleven million square miles of Antarctic ocean as a sanctuary in 1994.[8] These efforts have resulted in reducing the hunting of whales to about one thousand a year. There have also been efforts to make the killing of whales more humane. In the past, the harpooning of the whale was not what ultimately killed the whale. The harpoon allowed the boats to stay with the whale until the animal was exhausted. Then the work of killing the whale with lances and knives could begin. The whale eventually bled out—a slow, painful death. Other methods of killing have included plugging their nostrils, exploding harpoons, shooting with guns, and electrocution.[9] Given their size and complexity, there is no easy or pain-free way to kill a whale.

MOBY-DICK

The classic whaling story, of course, is *Moby-Dick* by Herman Melville. Published in 1851, *Moby-Dick* is a complicated story that reveals complex and conflicted ideas about gender, race, and species. Here, I am reading the book with a sole focus on the account of whales it provides. Melville is at pains to describe the strength and intelligence of whales and thereby elevate the standing of whalers within society. He argues that whalers are braver than soldiers, and, while they are butchers of a sort, they are expert butchers who maintain high standards of cleanliness.[10] Seen as dangerous and disreputable work, Melville pointed out the hypocrisy of people who denigrate the whaling profession while relying on the products of the whaling trade. He writes, "But, though the world scouts at us whale hunters, yet does it unwittingly pay us the profoundest homage: yea, an all-abounding adoration for almost all the tapers, lamps, and candles that burn round the globe, burn, as before so many shrines, to our glory!"[11] The large profits of the whaling industry supported this worldwide dependence on the trade. Melville reports that the U.S. trade alone was worth $7 million—that would be more than $200 million today. Money is what lured men to the trade even though men regularly died and were injured in pursuing their quarry. The story of Moby-Dick is, in part, the story of Captain Ahab seeking to kill Moby-Dick as revenge for the whale biting off his leg. Many whalers were missing fingers and limbs. "For God's sake, be economical with your lamps and candles! not a gallon you burn, but at least one drop of man's blood was spilled for it."[12]

While Starbuck (the first mate) disapproves of taking vengeance on a "dumb brute," Ahab sees strength and malice in Moby-Dick. Ishmael (the narrator) calls him a "murdering monster" who would seem to flee but then turn around and attack.[13] "The Sperm whale is in some cases sufficiently powerful knowing, and judiciously malicious, as with direct aforethought to stave in, utterly destroy, and sink a large ship; and what is more, the Sperm whale has done it." When they are hit by big boats, they swim off uninjured. They pull big boats when caught on lines. Melville notes that this type of whale acts "not so often with blind rage, as with willful, deliberate designs of destruction to his pursuers; nor is it without conveying some eloquent indication of his character, that upon being attacked he will frequently open his mouth, and retain it in that dread expansion for several consecutive minutes."[14] Melville's language continuously points to the intelligence and agency of the whales. They are described as cunning and deceitful.[15] Melville describes the action of a hunted whale: "All alive to his jeopardy, he was going to 'head out.'" Once harpooned, Melville notes the "agonizing spouts," the "tormented body," and labored breathing as the whale dies, and the whaler "for a moment, stood thoughtfully eyeing the vast corpse he had made."[16] While the whaler kills whales, he also expresses admiration for his prey. Melville notes the "appalling beauty of the vast milky mass" when describing Moby-Dick.[17] These descriptions stand in tension with terms used to hide the individuality, intelligence, and pain of the whales—*spouter, blubber boiler, lamp feeder, hundred barreler*.[18] These are more examples of the kind of mass terms Carol Adams believes foster human distance from other animal beings and encourage human use and consumption of these beings. Such terms hide the reality of the human killing of other animal beings and harden hearts.

Melville, too, was worried that the world's appetite for whale oil was deadening human connection with these ancient creatures. When the crew of the *Pequod* encounters an old and injured whale, they have no pity and begin the hunt. Melville writes, "For all his old age, and his one arm, and blind eyes, he must die the death and be murdered in order to light the gay bridals and other merry-makings of men, and also to illuminate the solemn churches that preach unconditional inoffensiveness by all to all."[19] When the old whale is butchered, they find in him a stone lance from before the European "discovery" of America. Part of Melville's respect for whales rests on the fact that they have been around since ancient times. Much older than humans as a species, and long-lived as individuals, Melville sees whales as containing ancient wisdom.

Melville does ask whether whales can endure all the hunting or whether they will "be exterminated." While seemingly plentiful at the time of *Moby-Dick*, Melville wonders "may it not be, that since Adam's time they have degenerated?" and ponders the possibility that they will go the way of the buffalo in the United States. [20] He concludes that the whale is "immortal in his species, however perishable in his individuality. He swam the seas before the continents broke water. . . . In Noah's flood he despised Noah's ark; and if ever the world is to be again flooded . . . then the eternal whale will still survive, and rearing upon the top-most crest of the equatorial flood, spot his frothed defiance to the skies." [21] Melville's confidence rests on the fact that even when whales are found in groups, humans can only kill a few at a time. But separate from the fact that changes in technology made it possible to kill and capture more whales than could a boat like the *Pequod*, Melville's own account includes a scene of mass devastation. He notes that the pressure of the whaling industry had caused the whales to begin to herd for their own safety (an example of human action modifying the lives of other animal beings). Whaling ships took advantage of this and gathered around big herds of whales and "gallied" them. That is, they frightened them into a panic. Once some are shot with harpoons they become mad with pain. What had been controlled circling to protect the young becomes unrestrained dashing about that kills other whales. More injuries occur as the lines cut and encircle fins and tails. Untold numbers are injured and may later die. Many whales die and are unrecovered, though some are later found floating (called waifs) and are taken as fair game by any passing ship. Not only does such hunting of a herd directly result in the deaths of numerous whales, but orphaned calves will also die, and social systems will be disrupted and destabilized. [22] Nonetheless, Melville remains confident that whales will endure and thrive.

He is confident in the whales' intelligence, as he notes they move around to elude their human hunters, and they can always go to the ice. He then compares whales to elephants, who have been hunted in great numbers but still thrive. We now know, of course, that his confidence was misplaced. The human appetite for ivory has decimated elephant populations. There are now only roughly four hundred thousand African elephants and forty thousand Asian elephants, and their ranges have dramatically decreased. Many elephants also find themselves in captivity in zoos and circuses (which are being phased out in the United States) and working in the logging and tourist industries. Similarly, whale numbers dramatically declined in the mid-1800s, due to the human appetite for whale oil, and then faced new pressures as

humans captured whales and dolphins for captivity and entertainment purposes in the mid-1900s. For those remaining, the ocean habitat has been
degraded by overfishing, pollution, and climate change.

The whaling industry was not separated from the livestock industry,
which has been the focus of the last two chapters. Whaling ships kept livestock on board as food. Melville notes the presence of live pigs on board in
passing.[23] While whale meat is eaten by indigenous peoples (Melville gives
the example of the "Exquimaux"), it is not as frequently consumed as other
animals by those deemed "civilized."[24] Even whalers often didn't eat whale
meat. But there is a scene in *Moby-Dick* in which Stubb (the second mate)
orders the cook to prepare him a whale steak. Not only was the ship itself
fueled by the fat of whale bodies, but the whale was also cooked by his own
oil ("the whale supplies his own fuel and burns by his own body"[25]) and then
eaten by the light of whale oil burning in a lamp. "That mortal man should
feed upon the creature that feeds his lamp, and like Stubb, eat him by his own
light, as you may say; this seems so outlandish a thing."[26] But Melville
points out that all meat-eating humans are doing something similar. He notes
that many will cut up roast beef with a knife that has a handle made of the
bones of the same animal they are eating and will pick their teeth with the
feather of the bird they've just eaten. He writes,

> But no doubt the first man that ever murdered an ox was regarded as a murder-
> er . . . if he had been put on his trial by oxen, he certainly would have been. . . .
> Go to the meat-market of a Saturday night and see the crowds of live bipeds
> staring up at the long rows of dead quadrupeds. Does not that sight take a tooth
> out of the cannibal's jaw? Cannibals? who is not a cannibal? I tell you it will
> be more tolerable for the Fejee that salted down a lean missionary in his cellar
> against a coming famine . . . in the day of judgment, than for thee, civilized
> and enlightened gourmand, who nailest geese to the ground and feastest on
> their bloated livers in thy paté-de-foie-gras.[27]

Melville is pointing out the hypocrisy of those humans who see eating whale
meat as ethically wrong but see no issues with eating other animals, such as
force-fed geese. The latter issue is still common today. For instance, many
who protest the Makah hunting up to two gray whales a year give little or no
thought to the lives and yearly deaths of the millions of pigs, cattle, and
chickens consumed in the United States alone.

In an extreme irony, Melville also points out that the Society for the
Suppression of Cruelty to Ganders uses quills to write out their pleas for

compassion. It proves difficult to escape our reliance on the lives and deaths of other beings, but some give it little thought and find themselves involved in practices that are quite contradictory. Similarly, people who refused to eat whale meat in the 1800s would have carried umbrellas and whips made from whale bone, not to mention having their bodies encased in whale bone corsets and hoops. Whale by-products were also commonly found in perfumes, paints, hair powders, and claret. Up until the post–World War II era, their oil was used to make margarine.[28]

While *Moby-Dick* is focused on the sperm whale, Melville gives accounts of right whales, narwhals, fin-back whales (shy and solitary), killer whales, and others. Melville not only notes the differences among various species of whales but also makes the case for seeing them as mammals and not as fish. Pointing to their lungs and the need to breathe out of the water, their horizontal tail, their warm-bloodedness, and the fact that they lactate, he agrees with the then growing consensus that whales are mammals. He also details different classifications of whales, including porpoises (or dolphins) as one of the smallest kinds.

FLIPPER AND DOLPHIN CULTURE

The whale most people in the United States are familiar with is the bottlenose dolphin. This is a consequence of the television show *Flipper* (following the Flipper movies of 1963 and 1964), which ran from 1964 to 1967. This show is considered a dolphin version of *Lassie*, and it introduced the viewing public to the ecosystem of the Florida coral reefs and to the idea that dolphins are intelligent, problem-solving language users. Bottlenose dolphins are found in marine parks around the world and serve as a major entertainment attraction.

They are also the most studied of all whales, both in the "wild" and in captivity. Most work on marine mammal communication has been done with bottlenose dolphins. This work focuses on their vocalizations and their use of echolocation. Each dolphin has an individual call that appears to function as a name. They have regional dialects, and they seem to communicate about food, danger, location, and plans for a hunt. They also use vocalization as a way to learn things. Experiments have shown that an individual dolphin who is given an instruction by a human can tell another dolphin what to do. Many scientists think vocal learning is something only humans, whales (including dolphins), elephants, birds, and maybe bats do.[29] Such social learning is one thing that makes the transmission of culture possible. Long life histories also make culture development and transmission more possible. The long infant dependency and juvenile period are times of learning. The long life of dolphins and whales (with females living past menopause) means there are elders around to teach and demonstrate for the young. For many, this is an important reason to focus on protecting whales and dolphins. When individuals die, pieces of a culture may die with them. When whole groups are killed, an entire culture (and possibly language) may disappear.[30] Today, many scientists are comfortable attributing culture to most species of whales and dolphins. Some groups of dolphins have learned group-specific behaviors that require planning and deliberation. Some examples include bubble play, putting sponges on their nose to help catch fish, creating mud rings around prey, barrier fishing, and chasing fish to the shore and temporarily stranding themselves in order to catch the fish. These techniques are not hardwired into the species but are instead learned. They demonstrate flexible behaviors and the ability to cooperate with others.[31] Dolphins and other whales are also known to cooperate with other species.

Some examples include the toothed whales. The best known include bottlenose dolphins and orcas (also known as killer whales). Melville's Moby-Dick, a sperm whale, is another toothed whale with echolocation abilities that surpass those of the bottlenose dolphin and orca whale. They also have complex social structures and cultures that rival these more commonly recognized species. Bottlenose dolphins demonstrate variability in habitats, social patterns, and foraging patterns. For instance, some drive fish to shore and go up on the beach to eat them; some hit fish with their tails, while others use sponges on their noses to scoop up prey. In some cases, hunting techniques require sequenced and coordinated actions, and they divide the labor within the group. The use of a mud ring and the tactic of driving prey to waiting community members are just two examples. Dolphins also hunt cooperatively with humans. In one example in Brazil, some human fishers call dolphins by slapping the water. The dolphins then herd fish toward them. When the dolphins dive in a particular way, the human fishers know to throw their nets.[32]

Orcas are proficient predators. This is in large part because "they are social, clever, and cultural." Orcas in the Pacific Northwest fall into different ecotypes that may share the same waters but eat different prey. The resident pods eat salmon, the transient pods eat marine mammals, and the offshore pods eat deepwater fish such as sharks. These groups are genetically distinct and seem to learn their eating patterns from their group. Some salmon-eating whales have a marked preference for particular salmon species.[33] Each kind of orca is successful because of their "highly sophisticated *communal* intelligence. . . . They learn from each other and work with each other."[34] They have complex community structures with specific dialects, which allows them to cooperate to appraise a situation and decide on a method of attack. They may use a wash wave, ball and stun fish, or go on shore to capture seals or sea lions. They have also been known to cooperate with human whalers by herding humpbacks toward a boat and helping to harass and tire the harpooned whale. In return, the whales got first dibs on the carcass, primarily eating the tongue and lips. This cooperation with humans was limited to specific individuals and died out when increasingly efficient whaling ended their lives.[35]

Defining culture as socially learned and transmitted behavior patterns that are shared by a group, most whale and dolphin researchers agree that whales and dolphins have cultures. They also agree the heavy whaling of the past, and the current threats to whales, contribute to cultural disruptions and to the loss of cultures. More than an individual whale is lost when one is killed. All the knowledge and learned behaviors of that whale are no longer resources for other whales. Cultural traits build up over time and result in behaviors that no single individual would have arrived at on their own.[36] Long lives, strong social bonds, communication, decision-making systems, and the capacity to learn (parental care) allow these mammals to accumulate and pass on behaviors.[37] The song of the humpback whale is a well-known example. These songs are highly structured, containing themes and phrases, and can change rapidly when one group of whales encounters another group's song.[38] Bowheads, blues, minkes, and fin whales also sing. The bowhead's song is not as complex as the humpback's, but an individual may sing more than one song, and the songs change completely from year to year (clearly relying on cultural transmission). Over the last thirty years, blue whale songs have been getting lower in pitch in a coordinated way. "This high conformity and change in unison over weeks and years among whales that can hear one another, at least within oceans, means that social learning has to have a role, as with the humpback songs."[39] Migratory patterns and hunting and feeding tactics also demonstrate coordinated, learned behaviors. For instance, humpback whales corral herring using several different techniques—blowing bubbles, slapping their flippers, or using sounds. The whales decide on which tactic to use, and different whales specialize in different roles. Humpbacks also show quite a range of bubble formation (for example, bubble columns, bubble clouds, and bubble curtains). [40]

The evidence for culture in whales and dolphins is strong, and this raises questions about the ethics of killing them. By the time a species is numerically or genetically endangered, it is already culturally impoverished. That loss is harder to recover from. Culture is a large part of what makes it possible for these various species to survive. "The evidence for cetacean culture is multifaceted, spanning foraging behavior, vocalizations, movements, social behavior, and play. . . . Cetacean cultures are transmitted both vertically, from parent to offspring, as well as horizontally between peers. There are highly stable cultural features, probably lasting generations, as well as transitory fads. So there is much to the culture of whales and dolphins." [41]

THE CRITICAL PRAGMATISM OF ALAIN L. LOCKE

In discussing culture among other-than-human animals, it is interesting to turn to the pragmatist philosophy of Alain L. Locke. While Locke wrote about how human cultures meet and shape each other, much of what he wrote seems applicable to what we see in culture among apes, elephants, and marine mammals such as whales (and probably many more species). Values, for Locke, are guided by emotion as well as concrete consequences, and different culture groups came to value different things. Despite these different values, different cultural groups could recognize each other's values. Locke argued that many values that differed from culture to culture had cultural equivalencies in that they performed similar functions in their respective cultures. This allows for limited cultural convertibility wherein an object or value belief of one culture can be taken up and used somewhat differently by another culture. Exchanges among different cultural groups allow for mutual modification of cultures, which Locke terms cultural reciprocity. Cultural diversity then becomes an important precondition of cultural change, adaptability, and growth. "Variation is at the root of cultural change, and cultural diversity is conducive to it." [42] He argues for an ethics and politics rooted in respect and reciprocity that does not seek conformity to any particular way of being, that practices nonaggression and nondisparagement. On this view, there is no place to claim that certain beings or certain practices are ultimately superior or inferior. Any such judgments are limited by time and context. Those who fail to practice this equal respect usually seek to dominate those who are perceived as different. They are unable or unwilling to see things from a perspective different from their own, and such people are, for Locke, threats to peaceful coexistence and constructive mutual dependence.

While Locke was focused on contact among various human cultures, his view provides important guidance for human understanding of, and contact with, the different animal cultures as well. While he argues that "[p]olitical and culture dogmatism, in the form of culture bias, nation worship, and racism still stands in the way and must first be invalidated and abandoned,"[43] one could add speciesism to the list of obstacles. One thing that all these obstacles have in common is a failure to recognize one's own limits and fallibility. For Locke, value judgments and judgments of other cultures should always be understood to be tentative and revisable. He calls this critical pragmatism. Such an approach allows for new information to be encountered in an open-ended process of inquiry that permits a certain kind of cultural relativism allowing for greater mutual understanding.

One important point for the discussion here is that this tolerance of, and even interest in, others does not require finding some kind of identity with oneself. It can allow for radical incommensurability alongside some cultural equivalence. In other words, other animal beings do not have to have brains identical to human beings in order to be recognized as having intelligence, memory, or emotions. One would just need to find equivalent functions in brains or behaviors. Given the continuity of human and other animal beings, it would be surprising if no such functional similarities were found. In *Natural Relations: Ecology, Animal Rights, and Social Justice*, Ted Benton points out some aspects of a general framework that humans share with other mammals, as well as many other animal beings. These include being born and developing over time, dying, sexual reproduction, social cooperation, and at least temporary social stability and the possibility of social integration.[44] It seems we may share these and more with dolphins and whales.

Dolphins and whales who have been studied in captivity (mostly bottlenose dolphins and orcas) demonstrate self-recognition by passing the mirror recognition test. Given that they live in complex fission-fusion societies, recognition of other individuals and social intelligence are also required.[45] They generally have a school, group, or pod that consists of those with whom they regularly swim. Sometimes these contain individuals from other species. In these groups, they pay attention to each other and coordinate activities.[46] They form alliances, demonstrate empathy, and participate in active social learning. While there is a complex interaction among habitat, types of foraging, social behavior, and societal structure, these same traits are also taken as indicative of consciousness. The brains of whales and dolphins are large for their body size and have complex cortical folding.[47] "Modern cetacean brains are among the largest of all mammals both in absolute mass and in relation to body size." While the brain-to-body-size measure (also known as the Encephalization Quotient or EQ) is the most common comparison made, some argue that absolute brain size might be a better measure to consider. The EQ privileges human brains, while in absolute size the sperm whale (for example) has a brain 60 percent larger than that of an elephant and six times that of a human. Bigger brains require reorganization. For instance, bigger brains show more modules and cortical adjacency. The syrificational index measures the neocortical surface area compared to brain weight. In humans that is 1.75, while in toothed whales such as dolphins and orcas it is 2.4–2.7.[48] But size alone doesn't tell the whole story. Dolphins evolved to have less of the brain focused on smell and more focused on hearing. Their brains also integrate hearing with cognition in novel ways and show a "hyperproliferation and reorganization of the cerebral hemisphere" and the "development of unique neocortical architecture." Selection for echolocation may be the reason for these changes.[49]

Brain comparisons are complicated as different brains are adapted to different environments, different bodies, and different activities. For instance, while the decreased focus on smell is accompanied by a smaller hippocampus (emotions, memory, and special navigation), it is also accompanied by a very large amygdala (emotions and memory), and a highly developed cortical limbic lobe (memory, learning, and behavior) and entorhinal region (focused on memory, navigation, and time). The regions for attention, judgment, and social awareness (cingulate and insular cortices) are extra developed in dolphins.[50] There is experimental evidence for dolphins having good sensory perception, a long attention span, good working memory, good long-term memory (tested up to twenty years), the ability to form and generalize concepts and update representations, and the ability to learn how to learn (show flexibility, judgment, and the ability to generalize rules beyond a specific problem). They can create novel behaviors, understand presence and absence, have a sense of self and others, reason and make decisions, and understand semantically (attach a sound or symbol to a thing) and syntactically (understand different meanings in different word order).[51]

Given the social complexity, intelligence, communication, and emotions found in whales and dolphins, many today argue that they should not be killed for food. If they are to be killed, the methods of killing them should take into account their individual and social suffering. Most methods of killing dolphins and whales take repeated blows, cuts, and spearing, and the animal takes minutes or hours to die. Distress calls in dolphins have been identified as connected to physical pain, and these calls are heard during the infamous killing of dolphins in Taiji, Japan. Since the Japanese do not understand the term *whale* to include small toothed whales, they did not consider themselves bound by the IWC in hunting dolphins even when they were a member.[52] This annual "hunt" was shown in the movie *The Cove* in 2009. Interestingly, this film returns us to the television show *Flipper*. While most of the dolphins driven into the cove are killed, a few are sold to marine parks for training. Ric O'Bary was the main trainer for the dolphins who starred in *Flipper*, and he now regrets his participation in the capture and captivity of dolphins. He has become an activist and seeks to end the keeping of dolphins in captivity and their use in entertainment. This effort is tied to ending their use as meat (primarily in commercial whaling practices, but some activists include Aboriginal hunting of whales as well). Other human-caused dangers that whales face include ship strikes, military sonar testing, pollution, and getting caught in fishing line and fish nets.

Pollution, and its contribution to climate change, may be the biggest shared danger we face with whales. Given that whales have a lot of fat, they accumulate toxins. Organic halogens such as fluorine, chlorine, bromine, and iodine don't dissolve in salt water, but they do accumulate in sea creatures. Pesticides, fungicides, herbicides, and insecticides (used to produce food for humans and livestock animals) are some of the main sources of these toxins. These substances mimic female hormones that can affect the development of organisms, alter gene activation, impact fertility, and contribute to cancer. There are high levels of bioaccumulation of polychlorinated biphenyls (PCBs) from all the plastic (and other things) humans produce. Even though PCBs are now banned in the United States, they persist in the environment. Apex predators, such as orcas and sperm whales, get all the toxins that have accumulated in the various layers of the food chain. Orcas and beluga whales have been found with concentrations of PCBs that are much higher than what would require toxic cleanup procedures if found outside an animal's body.[53]

While whales and dolphins often get to join the small circle of beings that humans consider worthy of moral consideration, it is important to note how much they share with other mammals (including their land-based ancestors) who often don't make it onto that list. Whales' genetic ancestry ties them to land-based even-toed ungulates, such as sheep, goats, cows, pigs, deer, and camels.[54] The hippopotamus is their closest land-living relative. Whales made the move from land to sea in less than ten million years, and they've been fully in the water for more than forty million years. With eighty species today (and six hundred species already extinct), they are the most diverse marine mammal group.[55] Given their size, long lives, and complex intelligence, whales capture the human imagination and bring attention to human-caused problems such as hunting, pollution, and climate change that affect not just individual whales but also entire systems on which all living creatures depend. Those who are apex predators rely on the health of each layer of the system and so demonstrate the many ways the lives and deaths of all beings interact, intersect, and interlock.[56] Interdependence is one of the lessons humans can learn from whales.

We don't even know all the ways that the loss of whales from human activity impacts the ocean ecosystems. The nutrients distributed from the death of one whale can reach to the depths of the ocean floor. While a whale carcass would probably first provide food for orcas and sharks, the bulk of the carcass sinks. Various creatures feed on the body all the way down until what's left comes to rest on the ocean floor to be fully recycled by sleeper sharks, eel-like hagfish, rattail fish, stone crabs, and small crustaceans called amphipods. Then bacteria move in on the bones (breaking down the fat inside the bones), with limpets and snails in turn feeding on the bacteria. Polychete worms cover the carcass and reach densities of forty thousand per square meter, and Osedax (zombie worms) tunnel into the bones where their symbiotic bacteria feed on the fat, which is then absorbed by the worm.[57] "More than four hundred species of macrofauna (this category excludes bacteria) have been identified in whale falls, with at least a hundred at any one carcass. Tens of thousands of individual animals of many kinds may be at work decomposing a single skeleton at any one time." This recycling takes at least ten years, perhaps a hundred.[58] A humpback whale can be fifty feet long. In 1920, a Norwegian ship killed some blue whales that were more than one hundred feet long. These baleen whales have jaws the size of telephone poles.[59] Such large creatures both feed on and feed many other living organisms, including humans, in a complex cycle.

An Inuit-Inupiaq story, "The Gift of the Whale," tells that the Great Spirit created the land, sun, moon, stars, oceans, fishes, birds, seals, walruses, bears, and then the Inupiaq. The Great Spirit taught the Inupiaq to use and respect their environment. Then the Great Spirit provided the best gift—the bowhead whale. This whale was beautiful and lived in perfect balance with the world, but the Inupiaq needed to use the whale to live. They could be fed on its meat and use its bones to make homes. So the Great Spirit made a time each spring when the whales opened a "whale road" where they would surface and wait to be struck by harpoons. As long as the Inupiaq respected the whale, and only took the few that they needed, the whales would continue to offer themselves in this way. But the Great Spirit didn't want to watch this killing, so at this same time in spring heavy clouds hang over the water. [60]

How much less would the Great Spirit want to watch the practices of industrialized whaling? As we saw in *Moby-Dick*, whaling became a global commercial enterprise that respected no limits on how many whales should be killed. Now many species of whales are endangered. Things get out of balance when desire is put above need. "Using hunting technologies that are so efficient that a species can be wiped out entirely, hunting and fishing industries are frequently dipping into the pool that populations need to reproduce and maintain their numbers for the sake of survival." [61]

FISHES AND NATIVE AMERICAN PHILOSOPHY

We don't know why the whale's ancestors returned to the water more than fifty million years ago, nor exactly why some of them evolved into the biggest creatures to ever inhabit the earth. [62] The studies humans have done are on a few select species of whales (and a few select individuals of those species). The amount we don't know about whales is immense, and since humans have pushed some to extinction and others to the brink of extinction, there will always be much that we can never know. The same holds true for much of the rest of sea life: "Two-thirds of the world's fish stocks are either fished at their limit or over fished. The UN food and agriculture organisation (FAO) has estimated that 70 percent of the fish population is fully used, overused or in crisis. Plummeting numbers of fish have led some fisheries organisations, and some countries, to see whales as competitors for dwindling fish stocks." [63] Rather than face the consequences of humans' fishing in unsustainable ways, some actually suggest culling whales and other ocean predators as a way of increasing the stock of fish. Sea lions, labeled as pests or nuisance animals, are already killed and relocated for preying on salmon. Declaring relocation efforts to have failed, Oregon just returned to the practice of killing sea lions to protect steelhead salmon in the Willamette River. The state continues (along with Washington) to kill sea lions in the Columbia River to protect endangered salmon. [64]

As fishing becomes unsustainable, humans have begun to study fishes in order to farm them. As with whales, we know the most about those we hunt. Fish farming has been part of human cultures since at least the time of ancient Egypt—a tomb from 2500 BCE depicts a tilapia pond.[65] Aquaculture was a way to stabilize the availability of fishes that were often only available on a seasonal basis and to make more fresh fish available for consumption. Fish flesh tends to spoil quickly due to its oil content, so most fish was dried, salted, or pickled. Fish ponds allowed for the harvesting of fishes at the time of consumption, before refrigeration made it possible to get fresh fish onto people's tables. At first, humans simply created barriers to corral fishes and eels into areas where they were naturally found. Over time, they created technologies to build structures and to aerate the water. They also placed pens near channels that provided water circulation. Early guidance on fish farming suggested creating a habitat that mimicked what the fishes were accustomed to so they would not be too stressed by captivity.[66] This insight also helped narrow the range of fishes raised in captivity to those who could handle higher stocking densities without undue stress, aggression, or disease. Today the most commonly farmed sea life include Atlantic salmon, tilapia, catfish, carp, shrimps, oysters, mussels, and clams.

Some fishes, though, are not suitable for farming. Some of the most desired fishes include Pacific salmon and tuna, and neither is yet farmed. Unlike their Atlantic cousins, Pacific salmon have not adapted to confinement. This means that fish farms in the Pacific Northwest are usually stocked with Atlantic salmon, who pose a risk to native fishes in the area. They are kept in net pens in the ocean. This kind of farming runs the risk of spreading lice and disease from the farmed salmon to wild salmon who share the same water. Waste can accumulate near the net pens and impact the rest of the life in the area. Fish do escape from these nets and then present competition for food that the already endangered wild salmon need. It is estimated that salmon are now extinct in 40 percent of their range and at risk in much of the rest.[67] Salmon numbers were put under pressure with the advent of canning, which resulted in unsustainable takes by the mid-to-late 1800s. This situation, combined with the degradation of river habitat by logging, mining, dams, and livestock, pushed them to their endangered status and the eventual protection of some salmon by the Endangered Species Act.

While salmon had long been eaten by Native Americans (at least as long as eight thousand years ago[68]), the salmon had been respected as integral to the ecosystem and to human cultures. Those who came to exploit the salmon for money did not share this outlook. "Salmon were no longer citizens in the same community with humans. Instead they were reduced to a commodity that had value only when put in a can and converted to cash."[69] For many Native Americans, salmon are an especially important creature. The story of "Salmon Boy" from the Haida shows the need to respect the Salmon People, even as humans rely on salmon for food. The boy in the story does not respect the salmon, wasting their meat and bodies. One day he is pulled under the water, and the Salmon People take him out into the ocean. Once back in their home, the salmon are very much like human beings, with a village similar to the boy's. He is taught that when he catches and eats a salmon, he needs to return the bones and other uneaten parts of the body to the water so the salmon can come back to life. When the salmon return to the rivers, the boy goes with them and is caught by his mother, who recognizes his copper necklace. She holds him until his fish skin is shed and he is human again. Salmon Boy then teaches his people what he has learned. When the time comes for the dead salmon's bodies to float toward the ocean, he sees the body of an old, worn-out salmon and knows it is his own soul. He spears the body and dies. His people then place his body in the river, where it sinks and returns to the ocean with the Salmon People.[70]

In this story, the humans relate to the salmon as people who deserve respect and gratitude from humans. The salmon are also shown to have not only power over the humans but also a willingness to teach the humans. The relationship of interdependence provides food for humans if they in turn provide prayer, reverence, and material support for the salmon. This relationship also helped develop the notion of the gift economy found among many native peoples: "The sustainable relationship between the Pacific salmon and Native Americans derived . . . from an economy based on the age-old concept of the gift and a belief system that treated all parts of the earth—plants, animal, rocks—as equal members of a community." Giving a gift establishes a certain kind of credit, while accepting a gift creates obligations or a kind of debt.[71] This kind of relationship exists among humans and between humans and other animal beings. So hunters assume obligations to the animals they kill, as that killing is a gift on the part of the other animal.

Fish of all kinds gave the basic gift of life to humans in that "fish are the common ancestors of all land vertebrates, animals with backbones, going back hundreds of millions of years."[72] These same fish continue to give humans the gift of life by providing food for humans. But that gift has not continued to be repaid, and fish stocks are dwindling. Modern fishing is not respectful; it generally does not honor the need to let young fish grow and breeding fish breed. Instead, trawlers scoop and kill everything in their path. Dams prevent salmon from returning to their spawning ground (or their young returning to the ocean), and pollution threatens fish in the ocean, lakes, and rivers.

As with salmon, tunas have been hunted for thousands of years. Early on they were only hunted seasonally and from the shore. Humans had to know their habits in order to find and kill them. Sound was often used to steer fish in a particular direction, or fire was used to attract them. Once corralled, "the tuna panic and swim frantically, charging the sides of the net, even wounding one another. . . . The tuna that remain enmeshed in the net are hauled in to the boats with gaffs, many of them already half dead from their experience in the death chamber."[73] Japan especially pursued tuna as they moved to the offshore, and year-round pursuit of tuna developed in the 1920s. One way to find tuna in the deep sea is to follow dolphins. When the nets are deployed to catch the tuna, though, many other sea creatures (including dolphins) get caught and killed. Public outrage resulted in calls to end this practice and to require labeling for dolphin-safe tuna. There are other dark sides to tuna fishing. Thailand is known to fill out crews by means of human trafficking. Chicken of the Sea's parent company recently committed to "overhaul[ing] its practices in an effort to 'tackle illegal fishing and overfishing, as well as improve the livelihoods of hundreds of thousands of workers throughout [the company's] supply chains.'" This includes shifting away from bottom trawling and employing third-party audits to ensure humane working conditions.[74]

Industrial fishing methods brought on a collapse in tuna stock in the 1960s.[75] There had been a response to declining numbers with the Tuna Conventions Act in 1950, which limited the methods of fishing in order to protect stocks and limit bycatch. Concerns about dolphin safety also resulted in some changes in fishing practices in 1990. Despite all this, tuna numbers remain vulnerable: "As the methods of catching tuna have advanced over the years, the conservation and management of tuna has not evolved as quickly. According to the United Nations Food and Agriculture Organization, most tuna stocks are fully exploited (meaning there is no room for fishery expansion) and some are already overexploited (there is a risk of stock collapse)."[76]

Tuna feed on other fishes and so can only be healthy and abundant when the ocean ecosystem is healthy.[77] Given overfishing, pollution, and climate change, few marine fisheries remain healthy today. The push to aquaculture, seen by many as a way to help save marine fisheries, also contributes to the decline of wild populations of fishes and marine mammals (discussed earlier). As long as some fish refuse to be farmed, and as long as ocean and river systems are able to sustain them, humans will continue to fish. The lives and deaths of tunas and dolphins will remain enmeshed with each other and the nets within which they die.

PRAGMATISM AND INDIGENOUS PHILOSOPHY: VINE DELORIA JR. AND ROBIN WALL KIMMERER

From the Native American perspective, not only dolphins but also whales, apes, and elephants are candidates for being persons and having culture. In his foreword to the book *Keepers of the Animals: Native American Stories and Wildlife Activities for Children*, Vine Deloria Jr. (Standing Rock Sioux) writes, "Native North Americans saw themselves as participants in a great natural order of life, related in some fundamental manner to every other living species. It was said that each species had a particular knowledge of the universe and specific skills for living in it." The story "Salmon Boy" (described earlier in this chapter) comes from this same book, and Deloria thinks such stories are an important way for children to learn about better relationships with other-than-human animals. Since humans are younger than other animal species, they need to respect and learn from other animal beings. Native Americans followed animal trails, watched what animals ate to determine what was edible, and gathered information about where possible prey might be gathered from observing other predators. "Many of the social systems of tribes were patterned after their observations of the birds and animals, and in those tribes that organized themselves in clans, every effort was made to follow the behavior of the clan totem animal or birds."[78] Religious ceremonies honor these relationships, and over time, some relationships have become particularly close. Some of those (discussed in this book) include relationships with salmon, whales, buffalos, horses, and wolves. In all of these relationships, the animals are seen not only as similar to humans but also as their own unique selves. "[O]ther creatures do have thought processes, emotions, personal relationships and many of the experiences that we have in our lives. We must carefully accord these other creatures the respect that they deserve and the right to live without unnecessary harm. Wanton killings of different animals by some hunters and sportsmen are completely outside the traditional way that native people have treated other species."[79]

As with Plumwood, this approach does not result in an ethic of nonuse or simply leaving alone. Instead, it calls for difficult and complex relationships of giving and taking. Guidance for navigating such relationships can be found in native philosophies.

Robin Wall Kimmerer (Potawatomi) notes, "Indigenous peoples are the stewards of fully 4 percent of the land area of the United States and represent some 700 distinct communities possessing detailed knowledge of the biota of their homelands. Globally, indigenous peoples inhabit areas with some of the highest remaining biodiversity on the planet."[80] Traditional ecological knowledge (TEK) is rooted in long-term, intimate relationships with places and understands other-than-human life as being in reciprocal relationships with humans. Ignoring such a knowledge base limits our possibilities for the future. She continues, "TEK is laden with associated values, while the scientific community prides itself on data that are 'value free.' TEK includes an ethic of reciprocal respect and obligations between humans and the nonhuman world. In indigenous science, nature is subject, not object."[81] This situation changes both ethical relationships and knowledge in ways that resonate with ecofeminist as well as pragmatist philosophies: "In indigenous epistemology, a thing is understood only when it is understood with all aspects of human experience, that is, the mind, body, emotion, and spirit."[82]

In his book *Native Pragmatism: Rethinking the Roots of American Philosophy*, Scott L. Pratt argues that pragmatism is rooted in commitments shared with "ways of thinking indigenous to North America" due to the complex cultural interactions that occurred during colonization.[83] According to Pratt, much of what is central to pragmatism is found in older indigenous traditions, and there are enough examples of cultural contact to warrant the claim that these commitments have their roots in indigenous philosophies. These commitments include "the principles of interaction, pluralism, community, and growth," and these provide for "a philosophical attitude, well established in Native traditions, that will sustain diversity and growth."[84] Respect for others is central to this attitude. The native influence not only helped shape "a distinctive conception of pluralist democratic society" but also shaped "a distinctive approach to American science" that is "framed by a conception of experimental science grounded in community and a community grounded in the practices of freedom and democracy."[85] Kimmerer seems to be in agreement when she writes that "TEK is highly rational, empirical, and pragmatic, while simultaneously integrating cultural values and moral perspectives. With its worldview of respect, responsibility, and reciprocity with nature, TEK does not compete with science or detract from its power but extends the scope of science into human interactions with the natural world."[86]

Kimmerer also notes that language shapes the relationships we see as possible: "Our toddlers speak of plants and animals as if they were people, extending to them self and intention and compassion—until we teach them not to." We have to train children into the supposedly objective language of human exceptionalism. "When we tell them that the tree is not a who, but an it, we make that maple an object, we put a barrier between us, absolving ourselves of moral responsibility and opening the door to exploitation. Saying it makes a living land into 'natural resources.' If a maple is an it, we can take up the chain saw. If a maple is a her, we think twice." Kimmerer suggests that different language is an important step in helping us rethink our relations. As with Plumwood, part of the need for different language is to find ways to recognize the multiplicity of minds and persons found in the world: "Maybe a grammar of animacy could lead us to whole new ways of living in the world, other species a sovereign people, a world with a democracy of species, not a tyranny of one; with moral responsibility to water and wolves, and with a legal system that recognizes the standing of other species." As an example, she speaks of the gift of berries, noting that the berries thrive with human care and humans thrive with the berries: "We are bound in a covenant of reciprocity, a pact of mutual responsibility to sustain those who sustain us." Forgetting this lesson, though, humans develop habits of taking that diminish possibilities for the future.[87] New language might help make new ways of thinking and action more possible. In the Potawatomi language, "Birds, bugs, and berries are spoken of with the same respectful grammar as humans are, as if we were all members of the same family. Because we are. There is no *it* for nature. Living beings are referred to as subjects, never as objects, and personhood is extended to all who breathe and some who don't."[88]

The language enables a different way of thinking and creates the possibility of paying attention to the languages of other-than-human animals. This way of thinking enriches the possibilities of the world. Kimmerer writes,

> Imagine walking through a richly inhabited world of birch people, bear people, rock people, beings we think of and therefore speak of as persons worthy of our respect, of inclusion in a peopled world. We Americans are reluctant to learn a foreign language of our own species, let alone another species. But imagine the possibilities. Imagine the access we would have to different per-

spectives, the things we might see through other eyes, the wisdom that surrounds us. We do not have to figure out everything by ourselves: there are intelligences other than our own, teachers all around us. Imagine how much less lonely the world would be. [89]

This recognition of other intelligences and teachers opens up new ways of understanding, and it provides the ground for a variety of moral obligations. Animals have to eat to survive. This entails taking other life—plant and animal. Rather than see this necessity as granting permission to consume without restraint, though, the recognition that one is consuming beings worthy of respect sets limits on how much one consumes and with what attitude: "We have no choice but to consume, but we can choose to consume a plant or animal in a way that honors the life that is given and the life that flourishes as a consequence. Instead of avoiding ethical jeopardy by creating distance, we can embrace and reconcile that tension." One way to do that is to "acknowledge food plants and animals as fellow beings and through sophisticated practices of reciprocity demonstrate respect for the sacred exchange of life among relatives."[90] Traditional ecological knowledge and the grammar of animacy need to inform how we live with animals (and the rest of nature).

Chapter Six

Pests

This chapter examines human relationships with animals commonly considered to be pests. While these relationships are often antagonistic and lethal for the other-than-human animals, such an approach fails to appreciate human interdependence, with those animal beings seen as pests, and often results in creating further problems and perceived divides. The philosophy of Rachel Carson is discussed to critique the model of trying to dominate and control nature (especially in the form of insects), and Lori Gruen's view of entangled empathy is used and critiqued in an attempt to develop a more inclusive ethics. Using the story of *Charlotte's Web*, special attention is focused on spiders in order to ask whether an ethic of empathy can be used to gain a greater understanding of "pests" such as insects, spiders, prairie dogs, and coyotes. Depending on where you live and what you do for a living, different animals may fall into the category that humans label as pests. In some parts of the world, feral dogs and cats may be considered pests; in others, rabbits, kangaroos, or sea lions might be considered pests. In most places, mice and rats (and other "vermin") are considered pests, as well as most spiders, flies, mosquitoes, and snakes. In some cases, "pest" applies to animals who might be seen as dangerous, but any animal who causes perceived economic losses or causes a nuisance of some kind can be seen as a pest. So, while prairie dogs might be seen as cute and harmless by some people in some places, many ranchers in Montana, South Dakota, and Wyoming consider them a nuisance. Once an animal is labeled as a pest, humans generally feel justified in killing individuals of that species rather than looking for ways to coexist (throughout human history the same can generally be

107

said about groups of humans who get labeled as nuisances. Under this guise, the United States called for the extermination of wolves and continues a war with coyotes. While there is increasing research showing that such predators should be seen as integral to an ecosystem rather than as pests, there are fewer champions of the "pests" most of us encounter on a more regular basis: flies, mosquitoes, ants, mice, rats, spiders, and snakes.

INSECTS AND SPIDERS

Concerns about disease or poisonous bites are one way to make it onto this list of pests. But that does not encompass the whole life process of these beings, nor does it acknowledge their full role in various ecosystems. Flies, for instance, can be an important part of the natural processes of recycling. While some flies (like deer flies who feed on living creatures) are considered bothersome, others (like blow flies who feed on carcasses) provide an important ecological service. Fly larvae (maggots) can make quick work of a carcass. They also provide food for other creatures such as birds.[1] Many beetles also help break down trees and carcasses and so contribute to building healthy soil. There are roughly seven hundred species of dermestid beetles who come to a corpse after decomposition is complete and "eat the remaining wool, feathers, gristle, fur, and skin—everything except bare bone. . . . In a forest, rodents as well as deer would gnaw on them [the bones] to get their needed calcium."[2] Other beetles help dismantle dead and dying trees. In doing so, they create habitat for other insects and spiders who in turn attract those who prey on them.[3] This decaying matter also helps build healthy soil. "[I]nsects, molds, bacteria, and beavers have engineered the most amazingly foolproof, and most effective and intricate, cooperative system-solution to the death-into-life-cycle of trees."[4] In short, healthy ecosystems require an array of insects and spiders in order to remain healthy, and yet humans often try to remove these very creatures.

To add more complexity, there are the cases where one "pest" may help control the population of another "pest" animal. Spiders, for instance, catch many insects in their webs, and snakes (and coyotes) eat mice and rats. To complicate matters further, many of those animals considered pests are animals who thrive because of human habits of storing food and accumulating garbage. We cause the conditions that bring the animals to live and thrive in proximity with us, but we then kill them rather than trying to create the conditions that would discourage them living among us or limit their populations.

In contrast to the notion of pest, though, many native cultures seek to understand and honor these other animal beings. For instance, instead of fearing potentially poisonous creatures, the Choctaw understand the poison of these creatures as a necessary strategy of self-defense that will not be used against others without warning. The story "How Poison Came into the World" tells of a very poisonous plant that sickened and killed many Choctaw people. This saddens the plant, who decides to give its poison away. The plant calls the small people of the swamps together—bees, wasps, and snakes—to ask them whether they would like the poison. Wasp agrees to take some poison in order to defend nests but promises to buzz as a warning before using the poison. Bee also agrees to take some poison in order to defend hives, but to ensure that they use it wisely, Bee stipulates that using the poison will kill a bee. Water Moccasin and Rattlesnake also take some poison. The white mouth of the Water Moccasin will warn people to stay away, while the noise of Rattlesnake will warn people of their presence. "From then on, only those who were foolish and did not heed the warnings of the small ones who took the vine's poison were hurt."[5] Rather than centering the human and blaming the other-than-human animal for any harm the humans may suffer, this story informs the humans about the nature of particular animals and expects the humans to honor and respect the ways of these creatures. This story understands humans as one of many beings, including the plant, who have unique ways of living and navigating potential harm from others in their environment. Understanding and respect, rather than fear, becomes the primary way of relating.

While spiders are not mentioned in the story about poison, they, too, are often stereotyped and feared. While only a few spiders are poisonous, this fear often colors human relationships with them. But again, this is not the only way of seeing spiders. The Hopi credit spiders with helping to create the world and ordering the clans. In "How Grandmother Spider Named the Clans," Grandmother Spider helps the Sky God make the earth. She stays with the animals and begins to order them into different nations and give them names. She then leads the people and the animals out of the underworld to the world above. Once there, she separates the humans into clans, each with an animal to lead them. This story places spiders at the center of the web of life and creates human dependence on the spider for their very existence and social order. In the Osage story "How the Spider Symbol Came to the

People," we see spiders as potential teachers and companions. When a chief is searching the forest for a powerful animal who can teach him a lesson and become a symbol for his people, he runs into a spider web. It's a large web that covers his eyes, and he falls. In his anger, he strikes at the spider. The spider speaks to the man, chastising him for running through the woods looking at the ground. When he says he was focused on finding a powerful symbol for his people, the spider says she can be that symbol. The man is scornful, noting the small size of the spider. She replies, "I am patient. I watch and I wait. Then all things come to me. If your people learn this, they will be strong indeed."[6] This story counters that common reaction of fear or disgust and presents another way of seeing and honoring spiders for their strengths and purposes. Spiderwebs are commonly used as a way to symbolize complex interconnections and strength. Spiders' silk is put to many uses beyond the web. They use it to make egg sacs, to wrap prey, as a lifeline to escape predators, as a dragline for moving prey, and for ballooning (as we'll see in *Charlotte's Web*). Spiders are great hunters and engineers who have inspired human art and design.[7]

GOING TO WAR WITH PESTS: RACHEL CARSON

Many of the more lethal forms of pest control turn out to cause a fair amount of environmental damage. Many humans see crop production as entailing a war with nature, as crops can be at the mercy of weather, insects, and molds. The war with insects, in particular, has unleashed a barrage of chemicals into the world, contaminating water and killing soil. Rachel Carson sounded the alarm on this approach to insect control in her 1962 book *Silent Spring*. She was concerned that this approach was based on an attempt to master and control nature. She thought that while it was important to gain scientific knowledge about the rest of nature, it was as important to feel with and respect the rest of nature. When doing her drawings of ocean creatures, she was careful to release them in the same spot where she had found them. As humans are one among many predators, Carson thought that humans should work to sustain healthy ecosystems rather than enter a war with nature. The use of chemicals like DDT, which emerged during the two world wars, represented the approach of a war with nature. While DDT was credited with controlling mosquitoes and lice during World War II, after the war it was used to do battle with the "hordes of insects" that presented a perceived threat to U.S. agricultural production. While Carson did not think this indiscriminate use of potent chemicals was the best approach to limiting crop damage by insects, she also grew increasingly alarmed by the unintended deaths of fishes, birds, and domesticated animals caused by the spraying of such chemicals. In addition, she worried about the long-term impacts on human health. While humans did not immediately die from exposure to most of the chemicals being used in agriculture (though some were potent enough for people to get sick or die on contact), they did present long-term health concerns.

In addition to her apprehension about the impacts of the chemicals themselves, Carson was concerned that the mind-set of mastering nature was being extended into the social and political realms of human society. She was writing during the Cold War and saw a related mind-set in the desire to root out and remove communists and others perceived to be dissidents. Connections between the war on communism and the war on insects can be found in campaigns that referred to fire ants as "red foreign invaders" and called for an all-out assault to remove the threat they posed. She also saw an authoritarian, undemocratic approach to the use of the chemicals. She asks, "Who has made the decision that sets in motion these chains of poisoning, this ever-widening wave of death that spreads out, like ripples when a pebble is dropped into a still pond? Who has placed in one pan of the scales the leaves that might have been eaten by the beetles and in the other the pitiful heaps of many-hued feathers, the lifeless remains of the birds that fell before the unselective bludgeon of insecticidal poisons?" Her answer is that it is the "authoritarian temporarily entrusted with power."[8] In other words, it is politicians: politicians working without the informed consent of the people they are supposed to represent. Individual landowners were not asked to give consent to such spraying. Further, given the methods of spraying, it was difficult (if not impossible) to protect one's land or animals from drift, if not from direct spraying itself.

These concerns remain with us today. While some chemicals have been banned from use in agriculture in the United States, a wide array of insecticides, pesticides, and chemical fertilizers remain in use in industrial agriculture production. The view of insects is still primarily of a pest to be eliminated. While some working within organic agriculture try to work with natural cycles of insect consumption and predation to control damage to their crops, the mind-set that worried Carson—one that seeks to control nature—is the one that continues to dominate the agricultural industry. She writes, "The 'control of nature' is a phrase conceived in arrogance, born of the Neanderthal age of biology and philosophy, when it was supposed that nature exists for the convenience of man."[9] Working with the rest of nature, rather than seeking to eliminate or control any one part of it (in this case, insects), made more sense to her.

LORI GRUEN AND *CHARLOTTE'S WEB*

This does not mean one is never justified in killing an insect or a mouse, but when killing is the first or only possible response to a particular species, things usually get out of balance pretty quickly. It is not as easy to generate interest in, and sympathy for, those animals considered pests, though. In her book *Entangled Empathy: An Alternative Ethics for Our Relationships with Animals*, ecofeminist philosopher Lori Gruen argues for an ethic of respect and responsiveness to other animal beings. She defines entangled empathy as "[a] type of caring perception focused on attending to another's experience of well being. As an experiential process involving a blend of emotion and cognition in which we recognize we are in relationships with others and are called upon to be responsive and responsible in these relationships by attending to another's needs, interests, desires, vulnerabilities, hopes, and sensitivities."[10] The ethics she develops is an important addition to the more traditional utilitarian and deontological approaches to animal ethics. It requires that humans pay attention to particularities of other animal beings rather than seek universal rules that try to encompass the myriad relationships in which humans find themselves. She is at pains to argue that while humans are embedded with other creatures, there are differences among these creatures and between humans and most other creatures. Care and concern for the other need to be developed without projecting human needs and desires onto other creatures, or reducing this care and concern to some instrumental value humans attach to another creature. This is fully in line with the pragmatist ecofeminist approach being presented in this book.

In describing this ethic of care that Gruen promotes, I have used the language of other animal or creature. Importantly, throughout the book, Gruen uses the word *organism*. I am sympathetic with this word, as it is the word preferred by John Dewey, a pragmatist philosopher, when he explored human relationships with the rest of nature (see chapter 4). He talked about the transactions (mutually influencing activities) between an organism and its environment (social, cultural, and natural). It is a capacious word that belies any sense of hierarchy even while acknowledging differences. This makes

Gruen's move to exclude bugs and bacteria—two types of beings often seen as "pests"—from her ethic a puzzling one. She argues that entangled empathy is limited to "sentient beings who have experiences" similar to animals.[11] While other approaches to ethics might help us improve human actions in relation to mountains, rivers, glaciers, or ecosystems, Gruen does not think empathy can work with regard to what many humans consider the nonsentient world. But she doesn't stop there. As mentioned earlier, she also excludes bacteria and bugs.

She writes, "I can't connect with microbes (even those that are part of me) and although I'm developing a more generous perception of bugs, my connection to them remains thin. I am not moved to act for their sakes if there are other conflicting values in play. I won't harm them and will try to move them to safety insofar as I understand where that might be, but I can't say I am acting from empathy when I do so." Here Gruen creates a hierarchy among living creatures based on how much she can or cannot attend to the other creatures' experiences and respect their needs and desires. While she doesn't want to do bugs harm, she does not feel empathy for them or concern for them in and of themselves. She seems unable to imaginatively connect with bugs in the same way that she is unable to muster direct concern for trees or rivers. "I feel a deep sense of grief when humans fell old trees or pave meadows or dump toxics in wetlands. This grief is largely driven by concern for the creatures that made their lives and their homes in these places, by my one-sided projection of connection, and perhaps by my feeling of 'species shame.' . . . My relationship to the meadow or the wetland or the insects that inhabit them are profoundly different from the relationships I can be in with the animals, fish, and birds who make their homes there." What is not completely clear is why Gruen moves from the duly noted difference she has in relationships with living animals and those she has with a meadow to conclude that humans cannot have empathetic relations with ecosystems or creatures who differ significantly from humans in how they inhabit their bodies and environments. "It isn't possible to be in *empathetic* relation to ecosystems or organisms that exist in ways that I can't imagine, beyond metaphor or projection, what it is like to be like."[12]

To be clear, Gruen is not saying that humans can't behave in ways that are ethically irresponsible and wrong with regard to actions that impact insects, wetlands, and trees. She just doesn't think empathy (as she's defined it) is helpful in understanding what is ethically wrong. Leaving aside, for now, the question of the other-than-animal entities she sets aside here, how is it that she can imagine what it is like to be like a fish but not what it is like to be like a spider, a mosquito, or a cockroach? Fish live in an entirely different medium and environment while terrestrial bugs share an environment with us. Why are "bugs" excluded while mice and rats are included? Mice and rats also experience the world quite differently from humans despite sharing a basic mammalian nature.

Searching for information on the life span and behavior of mice and rats demonstrates the main ways humans relate to these creatures. The information comes from exterminators and scientists using them to research human health. Mice are quite varied in size but generally live about a year. They prefer to burrow to stay protected from predators, are territorial, and are active during the night. They are very social and can have litters of four to twelve babies about every three weeks. While scientists use mice to study human health and behavior because there is overlap in their physical and mental processes with that of humans, mice hear and make ultrasonic sounds, feel changes in temperature through their whiskers, have a heartbeat six times faster than that of a human, and can shed their tail if caught by a predator.[13] Rats, while bigger than mice, are also nocturnal and highly social (with pack leaders), and they have high rates of reproduction (two thousand offspring in a year). They generally live longer than mice, with a life span of two to three years.[14] Some researchers question the use of mice and rats as a model for humans because of these differences. "Mice and rats are valuable model organisms thanks to their small size, short life spans and fast reproduction. However, when the goal is to further extend the already long human life span, studying fast aging species may not provide all the answers."[15] All of this suggests a very different life experience than that of humans, and yet we can relate. Many people keep mice and rats as pets, noting their distinct personalities and strong social bonds.

I think we can develop sympathy or empathy for creatures very different from ourselves.[16] This is one reason E. B. White's books *Charlotte's Web* (about a spider) and *Stuart Little* (about a mouse) are such interesting examples. These books work to make mice, rats, spiders, and pigs all relatable and sympathetic characters. In *Stuart Little*, this effort requires what would be considered inappropriate anthropomorphism, as Stuart Little dresses in suits and drives a car. In *Charlotte's Web*, however, other than having the animals speak (and write) in English, most of the story is driven by behaviors the various animal beings might exhibit in the course of living their lives.

Many people might refer to *Charlotte's Web* when writing about pigs since they read the story as one about seeing pigs (Wilbur in this case) as something more than food. But the story can also be read as a sympathetic account of the lives and deaths of spiders. In the story, a young girl named Fern saves a young pig from being killed by her father and raises him at her uncle's farm. The pig's name is Wilbur and, like Babe (discussed in chapter 4), Wilbur is a bit naive about his eventual purpose as food. In the 2006 live-action version of the movie, Fern eats bacon while she feeds Wilbur his bottle, and later Templeton the rat tells Wilbur his fate will be bacon, sausage, or a football. When Wilbur comments that humans love pigs, Templeton's retort is that they love pork. While Babe was befriended by Maa the sheep and Fly the dog, Wilbur is befriended by Charlotte the spider. From the descriptions in the book, it is likely that Charlotte is a barn spider (*Araneus cavaticus*). In fact, her full name is Charlotte A. Cavatica.

Female barn spiders are nocturnal, and they spin a new web every night and await their prey. They immobilize their prey and wrap them in silk until they are ready to eat them. During the day, these spiders rest near their nest. The females lay eggs toward the end of fall. An egg sac, which can contain more than two hundred eggs, keeps the eggs warm over the winter. The young spiders emerge in the warmth of spring. They are thought to have a life span of about one year. This is all consistent with how Charlotte behaves in the story. She catches and drinks the blood of flies, bugs, grasshoppers, beetles, moths, butterflies, cockroaches, gnats, midges, centipedes, mosquitoes, and crickets. She says that's how she's made; her body is adapted to the work. She notes that spiders have been eating flies and bugs for thousands of years, and she understands her family's work as that of trappers. While Wilbur is dismayed by her blood thirst, Charlotte points out that without her eating them, bugs would exist in destructive numbers. Spiders play an important part in any ecosystem. Wilbur notes that nobody on the farm has a kind word for a fly, and Charlotte puts them to sleep before eating them. So all in all Charlotte's life and work start to make sense to him, and Wilbur grows to truly like Charlotte.[17]

With Fern busy at school, Wilbur is lonely and Charlotte becomes his new friend. While his first impression is that she is deceitful, dangerous, and deadly, he soon finds out that she is a true and loyal friend.[18] Wilbur has similar doubts about Templeton the rat. When the goslings hatch, there is one unhatched egg. The gander lets Templeton take the egg as long as he promises not to kill any of the goslings, noting that they all knew he would try if he thought he could get away with it. The other animals in the barn think of rats as having no moral limits, no moral feelings, and no social connections or obligations.[19] And yet, when Wilbur is most in need, Templeton is helpful (though he is still characterized as selfish and without scruples). But it is Charlotte who does the most for Wilbur.

The sheep inform Wilbur that the people aren't just being kind when they feed him—they are fattening him up so they can eat him. The sheep call it murder. Wilbur screams that he wants to live and stay in the barn with his friends. He likes being out in the sun, and he remarks that he likes being in the forest, using his nose to forage for nuts, truffles, and roots. Charlotte promises to help keep him alive. She has to spin a new web each day, and she starts to weave special messages in her web. In the first web, she spins the words "some pig."[20] While everyone takes this as a sign of Wilbur's special-ness, Mrs. Zuckerman notes that she thinks it is the spider who seems spe-cial.[21] (Interestingly, this observation is missing from the 2006 movie, mak-ing Charlotte less of an agent in the minds of the humans.) The next web says "terrific," and Templeton is enlisted to retrieve magazine clippings from the dump so Charlotte can come up with other words.[22] The next word is "radi-ant."[23] The words in the web do keep Wilbur alive, as visitors flock to the farm to see Wilbur, but no one takes any note of Charlotte. The one excep-tion is when Fern defends Charlotte from her brother, who tries to capture her. In that instance, Charlotte is actually saved by Templeton, as during the commotion the unhatched gosling egg he had stored breaks open, and Fern and her brother run from the barn to escape the smell.

The family decides to take Wilbur to the county fair that fall. Wilbur wants Charlotte to come with him to the fair, but she's not sure she will be able to go, as it's time for her to lay her eggs. In the end, both Charlotte and Templeton accompany Wilbur to the fair. Charlotte, though, is tired from preparing to lay her eggs. Wilbur is worried about his friend. She spins another web with the word "humble" in it, thanks again to Templeton retriev-ing papers for Charlotte.[24] Then she makes her egg sac and lays 514 eggs. Wilbur's excitement over the prospect of Charlotte's babies is dampened when he learns she won't live to meet them herself—she says she's feeling her age.[25] While Wilbur wins a special prize at the fair, Charlotte's role in Wilbur's fame is discounted by the humans. She takes pride in her work, though. Feeling tired but peaceful, she says that she takes Wilbur's success as, in part, her own success. She is happy that Wilbur will live out his life and takes pride in that accomplishment.[26] She then tells Wilbur she'll be dead in a day or two and can't return to the farm. Wilbur decides he must take her egg sac back home with him, but he can't get to it. He calls on Templeton to get it for him. Templeton hesitates, pointing out all the things he's already done to help. Templeton remarks that instead of thanks and appreciation, all he ever receives is abuse and disregard.[27] Wilbur promises Templeton that he can eat first at the trough from now on, so he climbs up to get the egg sac (not unlike the chickens promising the rats eggs in return for their help in *Chicken Run*). Wilbur holds the sac in his mouth as he is loaded in the truck, and the next day Charlotte dies alone at the fairgrounds.[28] Wilbur guards the egg sac through the winter and anxiously awaits the spring arrival of the baby spiders. They arrive and grow quickly. Then they create silk balloons and begin to float away to make their way in the world. Wilbur is bereft at their departure. But in the end, three of Charlotte's offspring decide to stay and become Wilbur's friends.

This book continues to be read by many, and it has been made into two films. The 1973 film was an animated version while the 2006 film was live action. The second film, while straying a bit from the original story, does more to build empathy for both Wilbur and Charlotte. The special effects help the viewers connect to the animals, as they can read emotions on the faces of the animals. Fern serves as an important opening, as the viewer can join with her in her easy companionship and communication with the other animal beings, even though (as in the book) the adults see this as a phase that she will outgrow. From a pragmatist ecofeminist position, rather than outgrowing empathy, humans should find ways to extend and prolong empathetic understanding of this kind and allow it to help guide our relationships.

Returning to Gruen, her notion of empathy does and should extend to Wilbur. In *Entangled Empathy*, she notes that humans find themselves already in myriad relationships with other animal beings and that humans need to recognize the particularity of these animal others and work to be responsive to their needs and desires. Empathy requires ongoing reflection and correction as we learn more about various needs and desires.[29] Relationships based on an exploitative instrumentalism are ruled out on her view, and she argues that it is inappropriate to see these other beings as consumable. She thinks that the raising and killing of any animals for food is exploitative and so, by definition, unethical. Whether this occurs in industrial animal operations or on small farms, it "violently instrumentalizes individuals in deeply troubling ways, obliterates their personalities and interests, and turns them into both real and metaphorical fodder."[30] The shortened lives of animals killed for food is, on this view, wrong. But she goes further to argue that they shouldn't be seen as food at all. In *Ethics and Animals*, she says that even when eating animals who die a natural death we fail to respect them as "'fellow creatures,' who, like us, do not belong in the category of the edible." She then quickly moves to equating this with "turning other animals from living subjects with lives of their own into commodities or consumable objects," and this means "we have erased their subjectivity and reduced them to things." She thinks that seeing another being as food "forecloses another way of seeing animals, as beings with whom we can empathize and learn to understand and respond to differences. When we identify non-human animals as worthy of our moral attention because they are beings with whom we can empathize, they can no longer be seen merely as food."[31]

The book and the films of *Charlotte's Web* achieve this subjectivity for Wilbur and engender empathy in the human audience. It is far from clear that this empathy extends to other pigs, though. As with the earlier discussion of the film *Babe*, some humans are profoundly impacted and change their eating habits, but many others fail to make the empathetic connection to actual pigs being raised and used for food. And there is very little reason to think that the audience comes away with more empathy for spiders. As we saw earlier, Gruen argues humans can't have empathy with spiders because they are too different from humans. Yet the book and the films seek to create such empathy for Charlotte. The failure here has many sources, but one might be fear.

A PRAGMATIST ECOFEMINIST TAKE ON SPIDERS AND *CHARLOTTE'S WEB*

Some spiders do present a danger to humans. Of all the species of spiders (more than forty thousand), only a few present any kind of threat to humans, though. The brown recluse (or violin spider) is the most dangerous spider in the United States, causing skin ulcers. Death occurs, but rarely, due to an infection of the ulcer. The black widow spider, while never causing a death in the United States, does present a real danger as their venom causes muscle pain, cramping, nausea, and difficulty breathing. Brown and red widow spiders are spreading but inject less venom when they bite and so present little danger to humans. The yellow sac spider is more commonly found in the Americas, but their bite usually causes nothing more than redness and swelling. Wolf spiders are found throughout the world, but their bite usually causes a small skin irritation and itchiness. Brazilian wandering spiders (or banana spiders) are considered the most dangerous, as their venom attacks the nervous system. Funnel-web and red-backed spiders also pose a real threat to humans, but mostly in Australia and New Zealand. All this means there are good reasons to be careful around some spiders. One difficulty is that, when human-spider encounters take place, it may not be easy for the human to tell whether this particular spider presents a threat. Usually, in the United States, however, encounters with venomous spiders are rare and non-threatening. It should be noted that these same spiders may pose more of a threat to other animals who often live with humans, such as cats and dogs.

A pragmatist ecofeminist response to creatures such as spiders should include empathy and respect. The story of *Charlotte's Web* functions as a pragmatist ecofeminist narrative, as it presents the various creatures (spiders, pigs, sheep, geese, horses, humans) in transactive relationships with each other and their environments. There is an acknowledgment that all these creatures are born, grow, develop over time (changing as they live), and then die. There are interdependent relationships among the various creatures, some of which include predation—Charlotte eats other insects, Templeton would eat a gosling if he could, and Fern eats bacon. We don't know everything that is in Wilbur's slop, but traditionally this would have included all the kitchen waste and so would include the flesh of other animals. While we can't have the embodied lived experience of other creatures, as Val Plumwood notes, it is problematic to assume that no understanding or communication is possible. The pragmatist approach assumes evolutionary continuity as well as difference and so makes room for appreciating the functions of various animals being in particular environments and appreciating their own unique life purposes. This perspective acknowledges the use value of various creatures (including humans) but does not reduce any creature to that value alone. It does not, as Gruen does, put most animals in a category of not edible. But it also doesn't see the whole life (and death) of any animal as only meant for the purpose of being food for another. It also doesn't see other creatures as simply obstacles to human purposes but understands the complex human dependence on other life forms.

This perspective needs to be extended to those animals usually considered pests in order to stop the unnecessary, and often counterproductive, killing of those animals. Failing to understand the interconnectedness and interdependence of human beings, other animal beings, and the rest of nature results in forms of agriculture that wage war on insects and microbes that are important for maintaining healthy soil. The chemicals used to kill "pests" have effects on other creatures in the environment. Some kill other animals directly (e.g., birds caught in the spraying of pesticides), while others slowly pollute waterways and contaminate, deform, and kill creatures living there and creatures feeding on those living there (e.g., frogs suffering from deformities and low reproduction rates and whales accumulating dangerous chemicals in their fat from eating creatures who ate fish who swam in polluted water). The use of agricultural chemicals also harms the health of human agricultural workers and the consumers of these foods. While much of the food is grown for animals in the livestock industry, who will be killed before they suffer serious consequences of eating food grown in this way, that is not the case for dogs and cats, who suffer from increasing rates of cancer, or for their human companions (especially children) who accumulate these chemicals in their bodies. Those humans working in the fields suffer the most. The agricultural war on insects sickens and kills agricultural workers as they handle chemicals without proper safety equipment and pick (and eat) crops that have been sprayed. That many of these agricultural workers (and slaughterhouse workers) in the United States are immigrants who are also often characterized as "pests" and "nuisances" is not a coincidence. The logic of domination does not stay confined by human exceptionalism and quickly reveals itself as a logic of colonization, as it ontologizes some bodies as disposable and, therefore, candidates for unlimited use without the constraints of respect and reciprocity. This has been a central point of ecofeminist analysis for at least a century.

MAMMALIAN PESTS

In addition to posing a real or perceived threat to human health, another way an animal can be labeled a pest by humans is if they are perceived as interfering with plant and animal agriculture. Many of the animals considered pests for plant agriculture are the already discussed insects and rodents. Prairie dogs, coyotes, and wolves are all also seen as pests from the perspective of many livestock ranchers. Prairie dogs once ranged from Mexico to Canada in the grassland prairies. Seen as sacred keepers of water by some Native Americans, today many Native American ranchers support lethal means of controlling their numbers. They are thought to damage the grasses with their burrowing, though studies show this process creates healthier and more diverse grasslands. While this can be good for grazing animals (domestic and wild), it does present challenges for ranchers who want to bale hay. Though the risk is small, many think that their burrows present a hazard to cattle, who might break a leg if they step in a prairie dog den.[32] Widespread use of poison began in the 1880s and gained governmental subsidies in 1915. This, combined with recreational shooting, urban sprawl, drought, and cultivation of land, has reduced their range by 99 percent. While the U.S. Fish and Wildlife Service agreed that prairie dogs met the criteria to be listed as threatened in 2000, they are still not listed, so lethal methods of control continue to be implemented. Many ranchers in the United States see them as competing with cattle and playing no important ecological role. They refer to them as "grass-eating pests." Others argue that prairie dogs are a keystone species whose well-being is linked with that of the black-footed ferret, ferruginous hawks, and burrowing owls.[33] Protection for prairie dogs, however, remains elusive. In 1998, the American Society of Mammalogists called for the end of subsidized killing of prairie dogs and for increased study of these animals, who are an integral part of the grassland ecosystems.[34] While the role of buffalo in maintaining healthy grasslands was discussed in chapter 3, it is also important to note the role of the prairie dog in the overall ecosystem: "About 140 vertebrate species are associated with prairie dog colonies, along with many invertebrate species. . . . [L]arge grazers prefer the constantly rejuvenating grasses in dog towns, and there is no nutritional drawback from grazing in prairie dog areas."[35]

This means that while some native ranchers see the prairie dog as a pest, other native peoples (those involved in the Intertribal Prairie Ecosystem Restoration Consortium) see them as integral to prairie restoration. The conflict within native cultures, and between Native American nations and the U.S. government, over the control and use of specific lands puts the prairie dog in the middle of a complex situation. Most scientists see the prairie dog as not only contributing to the health and diversity of the grasslands but also eating those grasses. Linda Black Elk, who is a Native American ethnobotanist and plant ecologist, argues, "It is first critical for researchers to understand that good rangeland management (according to Native science) requires recognition of ecological interrelatedness. This is perhaps best exemplified in the Lakota phrase *mitákuye oyás'iŋ*, which translates literally as 'all my relatives.' This phrase reflects the belief that we, as human beings, are related to everything and everyone—from huge cottonwood trees to the cool wind, and from barking prairie dogs to the fertile soil." Understanding such systems requires long-term observation and experimentation, both of which the traditions of indigenous peoples provide, though this fact is often ignored in setting up range and wildlife management plans.[36] It also requires respecting the complex interactions of any ecosystem. Discussing the Cheyenne River Sioux Reservation experiment with raising buffalo for meat, Fred DuBray states, "We're not interested in buffalo ranching if it's done in the way that cattle ranching is usually done. Many ranchers, for instance, might spend a lot of time killing off prairie dogs and coyotes—animals they see as pests. But the buffalo don't see them as pests and neither do we. We're working to restore the whole habitat."[37] This view is still more the exception than the rule, though.

Coyotes continue to be killed in large numbers, though their wolf cousins have gained some protections and are even being reintroduced in some states. The extermination of wolves (who are discussed more in the next chapter) began in Europe in the Middle Ages, and their numbers were in sharp decline by the 1800s. This mind-set and approach was carried over with immigrants to the United States.[38] Ironically, it appears that the removal of the wolf has allowed for larger numbers of coyotes to inhabit an increasing territory. Research by biologist Robert Crabtree "shows that the killing of coyotes does not reduce their number long-term or protect game animals or livestock. Having evolved in the presence of a bigger, stronger predator, the wolf, coyotes are amazingly resilient. Kill some every year—in a process wildlife management agencies call 'mowing the lawn'—and they just keep coming back."[39] Livestock ranchers have often seen those animals that might prey on their sheep or cattle as pests to eliminate. In addition to coyotes and wolves, big cats and bears are on this list. Even today, when their numbers are so low as to present very little threat, lethal means of control remain legal and popular. Coyote killing presents the most dramatic picture, as the number of their deaths remains high.

Writing about attempts to ban coyote-killing contests, Karen E. Lange notes, "Coyote and other fur-bearing nongame animals (those not killed by hunters to eat) have long been considered pests, with few if any restrictions on their killing." In addition to offering bounties, those in the United States Department of Agriculture Wildlife Services engage in killing coyotes themselves. The agency "started killing as many coyotes as possible in 1931 and currently uses aerial gunning and poisons to kill tens of thousands each year (68,913 in 2017). In 1957, the first documented wildlife killing contest took place, organized by ranchers in Chandler, Arizona."[40]

Scientists have shown that killing coyotes increases their rates of reproduction and increases the likelihood that immature animals, and animals from disrupted packs, will prey on domesticated animals.[41] Nonetheless, at least forty-two states still sponsor coyote-killing contests.[42] There is also pressure to return to the use of poisons such as Compound 1080 and sodium cyanide, despite the risks to other animals. Oregon recently banned the use of sodium cyanide after an Idaho boy was harmed and his dog killed when they stepped on a sodium cyanide bomb.[43] Even websites designed to instruct people on killing coyotes note the danger of these chemicals (and traps) for humans and other animals.

In what is now the United States, coyotes have lived in close proximity to humans for more than fifteen thousand years. Eating mice, rats, rabbits, and other small creatures attracted to human settlement, they have helped make such settlement possible. While closely enough related to domesticated dogs to breed with them, coyotes are not domesticated, and their presence continues to unnerve many humans. Of concern to many of those humans is the safety of the coyote's dog cousins and of domesticated cats. In the name of protecting pets, as well as livestock, coyotes continue to be killed in large numbers.

Just like the insects discussed at the beginning of this chapter, "[n]ative carnivores, such as coyotes, foxes and bobcats, play a vital role in healthy ecosystems. They remove sick, weak and injured animals from deer populations, control rodent populations and consume carrion and roadkill. In some places, packs of coyotes defending their territories have even been used to protect livestock from other predators."[44] Evidence of their role and place in the world can be seen in the fact that coyotes are central to many Native American stories. The coyote is portrayed as a great hunter and creator in some stories, and a coward, thief, or trickster in others. In all cases, the coyote is seen as teaching wisdom to humans. In the Miwok story "Silver Fox and Coyote Create the Earth," the coyote and the fox (both wild canids) dance and sing the world into being and then give shape to the mountains, rivers, lakes, trees, birds, and other animal people.[45] In the Jicarilla Apache story "Coyote Obtains Fire," a coyote patiently tricks fireflies into showing him how to enter their sacred place where they have fire. He has a plan for getting the fire and enlists other animals to help him get away with it. He ties a cedar torch to his tail, and once he has it on fire he runs back out into the world with it.[46] In these stories, the coyote deserves thanks and reverence. In other stories, his foolishness or greed often gets the better of him, but he is treated with patience and understanding, as he has a place in the world.

A pragmatist ecofeminist approach to issues around mammalian pests echoes that described earlier for insects. These animals, though, also gain inclusion in Gruen's approach of entangled empathy. And yet prairie dogs and coyotes continue to be shot for sport, and the government continues to use resources to kill and remove them, with no respect for the complex interconnections in our shared dynamic ecosystems. A pragmatist ecofeminist approach not only challenges the logic of domination present in these approaches but also calls for a greater understanding of human continuity with the rest of life that resembles the spirit of the Lakota phrase *mitákuye oyás'iŋ* ("all my relatives").

Chapter Seven

Cats and Canines

This chapter focuses on big cats and wild canines and includes discussion of *Born Free*, *The Lion King*, *The Jungle Book*, *The Call of the Wild*, *White Fang*, and *Julie of the Wolves* in order to examine how humans often respond to those animals who can kill and eat them. Not only are these predators seen as dangerous, but they also often fall in the pest or nuisance category when they are perceived to threaten the livestock animals that humans raise for food. In addition, they are seen by many as a threat to their domesticated cousins—the dogs and cats with whom we share our homes. The ecowoman-ist philosophy of Alice Walker (discussed in chapters 1 and 4) will be used to rethink relationships based on fear and domination, as well as to argue for respectful coexistence and honoring the sacred. The pragmatist philosophy of Jane Addams is also used as an example of how to address complex and controversial issues, such as wolf predation, in a productive manner.

SOME HISTORY

While coyotes continue to be seen by many as pests or nuisance animals to be killed (as discussed in chapter 6), things are now more complicated for their canine cousins such as the gray wolf, the Mexican gray wolf, and the red wolf. Their listing (and delisting) as an endangered species, along with programs to reintroduce wild-bred as well as captive-bred individuals to parts of their former territory, has created a tension-filled environment for wolves in the United States. They have both impassioned protectors and persecutors. Once one of the most wide-ranging animals in the world, wolves are now found in only a few areas, and yet they continue to be seen as a "problem" for livestock ranchers and sport hunters, despite their small numbers. Large cats, such as cougars, bobcats, and lynx, face similar fear and anger from humans who want to live, hike, or farm in the cats' shrinking territory. Bears, too, face conflicted feelings from humans. Humans seem to have respect and awe for large carnivores. For some, this turns into a desire to protect such species, while, for others, this becomes a reason to prize them as a hunting trophy. Others see them as competition for wild game animals, or as a threat to livestock, and so as a nuisance animal to be deterred or destroyed. Fear has been a dominant motif for many Western views of large predators ("Little Red Riding Hood" and "The Three Little Pigs" might come to mind), while indigenous cultures often view them as kin with whom they cooperate and as powerful totem animals. Practices of Western colonization commonly viewed both indigenous peoples and indigenous predators as threats to "civilization" and so though that they must be removed. We continue to live with these legacies today.

This kind of fear leads to killing. Wolf bounties were offered in 600 BCE in Greece, from the 1500s to the 1700s in Europe, and between 1630 and 1915 in the United States.[1] While wolves were mostly eliminated from the lower forty-eight states by the 1940s, in 1952 in Alaska 4,200 wolves were killed, along with 50,000 red foxes, 35,000 coyotes, 7,500 lynx, 1,850 bears, 500 skunks, and 164 cougars.[2] In 2014, USDA Wildlife Services spent more than $1 billion to kill 322 wolves, 61,702 coyotes, 580 black bears, 305 mountain lions, 769 bobcats, 454 river otters, 2,930 foxes, 1,330 hawks, and 22,496 beavers.[3] For wolves and big cats in particular, there is an added irony to their fraught relationships with humans. While they are hunted, poisoned, and trapped, many of their canine and feline cousins live pampered lives in the homes of humans. While the evolutionary history is not yet completely clear, there was a common ancestor of canines and felines sixty million years ago. These lines split about twenty million years ago. The canine line split about 2.3 million years ago to give rise to the gray wolf (*Canis lupus*) and the dire wolf (*Canis dirus*).[4] Dogs, who are thought to have shared a common ancestor with wolves twenty thousand to forty thousand years ago, are used to protect livestock animals from wolves and to tree big cats for hunters. Big cats and domesticated cats shared a common ancestor until probably about ten thousand years ago.[5]

CATS

Large cats such as tigers, lions, and panthers have been kept in captivity for a long time. They were prized by early animal collectors. Such menageries eventually gave rise to zoos. While today in the United States there are strict regulations for keeping such animals, there are many smaller, poorly regulated zoos around the country (and the world) where animals are kept in horrific conditions. Some include what they call educational shows, but they primarily serve as entertainment. In many cases, fear and intimidation are used to train and control the animals. Circuses regularly held shows featuring lions and tigers, with the lion tamer image (including whip and chair) becoming iconic. A famous example of such an act was the Las Vegas show of Siegfried and Roy, which ended when one of the white Bengal tigers mauled Roy Horn in 2003. Despite the dangers, many states still allow keeping a cougar as a pet. In 1997, Pennsylvania had 48 cougars registered as pets, and Massachusetts had 250. Many more are unregistered.[6]

The most common images that come to mind when thinking of the large cats of the world are those of African lions and Bengal tigers, though there are thirty-seven feline species worldwide.[7] These animals are often featured in nature programming and movies (and Broadway musicals), such as *The Lion King* and *The Jungle Book*, which cement a particular image of these creatures in many people's minds. In these stories, the animals largely function as stand-ins for humans and human values, but in both cases there is some attempt to also present aspects of the actual lives of the animals around whom the stories are built. *The Lion King* does present the tensions between lions and hyenas around food, for example, but even as the story sends the message that all life is interconnected and balanced among predators and prey (the circle of life), the hyenas are portrayed as greedy and out of balance with the rest of nature. This portrayal represents hyenas unfairly, and the fact that several of the most famous voices of the hyenas come from a black and a Hispanic actor (Whoopi Goldberg and Cheech Marin) reinforces problematic stereotypes.

The Jungle Book (the book and the movie) likewise reinforces a variety of racial and ethnic stereotypes, even as it also presents some accurate points about the lives of the animals involved. Mowgli is a human boy who is found in the jungle and raised by wolves. The life of the wolves is accurate in many respects: they hunt at night, they share their kills with jackals, and only weak or lazy wolves are "cattle killers." They face the dangers of wolf traps, fires, and human encroachment. At the same time, a male wolf, Akela, is the head of the pack. In reality, a breeding pair shares the leadership of a pack. Other characters include Baloo, the brown bear, and Bagheera, the black panther, who both help teach Mowgli how to navigate the jungle and speak with the other animals in order to keep him safe from Shere Khan, the tiger. In the book, Kipling is clear that Shere Khan is lame and that is why he kills cattle and becomes hated by the humans. While this aspect is missing from the Disney movie, the fact that humans hunt tigers is at the root of Shere Khan's desire to kill Mowgli before he grows up. In his mind, humans can't be trusted. Eventually Mowgli returns to the human world. In the book, he is expelled from the wolf pack at the urging of Shere Khan. As Mowgli leaves, he says, "The jungle is shut for me, and I must forget your talk and your companionship."[8] However, when Mowgli later kills Shere Khan by working with the wolves to run the tiger over with the cattle Mowgli is guarding, the other humans become scared of Mowgli's ability to talk to the wolves. Despite saving the cattle, he is kicked out of the human village. He is a human who violates the expected and accepted relationships among humans and other animals. Along the way, Kipling provides interesting accounts of the lives of a variety of animals. In contrast, there is little attention paid to the actual social structure of lion prides in *The Lion King*. Despite not being a very accurate depiction of the lives of African lions, the story of *The Lion King* continues to generate interest in, and sympathy for, lions from people living in the United States, as does the less accurate Disney version of Kipling's story.

Another famous lion story is worth taking note of as well. The book and then movie *Born Free* were quite popular in the 1960s. This story, with all of its insensitivities to the British colonization of Africa, did much to change how people viewed predators such as lions. The story of Elsa the lioness turned the tables a bit, as a small group of humans became her pride. The story begins when George Adamson (a senior game warden for the East African Game Department—living in Kenya) is sent to kill a "man-eating" lion. He doesn't like killing lions (or other wildlife) but notes that most "man-eaters" had some kind of infirmity that prevented them from successfully hunting wild prey. When they became accustomed to hunting humans or human livestock animals, they wouldn't stop. On this occasion, the hunting party accidentally kills a female lion with three cubs. He takes the cubs home to his wife, Joy. She cares for the three cubs, with the help of a Somali servant, Nuru, until the cubs are about six months old. At this point, two of the cubs are sent to a zoo in Holland, but one cub, Elsa, stays with the Adamsons in Africa.

Lion cubs typically stay with their mother for two years, learning to hunt. The mother first regurgitates food for them, until they are old enough to eat from a kill and then eventually help with the hunting. Caring for an orphaned lioness, the Adamsons and Nuru follow Elsa's nature more than they expect her to conform to human life. She comes and goes on her own schedule, rolls in elephant dung, and has several encounters with free-living lions. By paying attention to Elsa, her humans avoid several possibly lethal encounters with snakes. For her part, Elsa learns to not hit humans with her full weight and allows specific humans to share in her kills. They are part of each other's worlds. In the end, the Adamsons wean Elsa away from her human family so she can live on her own. This is not an easy task for either Elsa or the humans. The first attempt does not go well, in part because they choose a location with a climate different from Elsa's birthplace and she is vulnerable to diseases in the area. While this place is rich in game, it does not fit Elsa. Ultimately, they settle on a hotter region just "thirty-five miles from Elsa's birthplace" that "was the type of country that was natural to her."[9] Here she learns to hunt for herself (with George's help) and is eventually left on her own. When the Adamsons visit the area, though, Elsa still comes to greet them before returning to her own life. An important thing that *Born Free* did was explaining Elsa on her own terms. While the emotional attachment of the Adamsons and the reader is powerful, Elsa remains her own individual self and is not anthropomorphized in inappropriate ways. The commonalities between humans and lions are simply present as this unusual hybrid pride communicates and cooperates together.

From these stories people often gain a sense of respect for the predators that seems to override their fear. The stories inspire calls for conservation from many living at a great distance from these creatures, and they contributed to the kind of public outrage seen in the United States when a hunter from Idaho killed Cecil the lion in 2015. And yet when a hiker was killed by a cougar in Oregon in 2018, there was public outrage against the cougar, and the cougar was killed. It seems there is less tolerance for big cats who pose a perceived threat to humans closer to home. Another contributing factor is that the cats who live in territories within the United States don't have the same public image as African lions, even though they are closely related. The large cats of North America are more elusive and so are harder to find and study.[10]

The evolutionary history of felines is difficult to decipher since they are so much alike. The earliest known cat appeared thirty-four million years ago, while modern cats evolved in the last twelve million years. The biggest known cats went extinct about ten thousand years ago (American lions and saber-toothed tigers). Genetically, cheetahs are closely related to cougars, while lions and tigers are closely related to bobcats and lynx. It is not known which cats moved where and when, though. What we do know is that the modern cougar emerged in North America about three hundred thousand years ago, the bobcat six hundred thousand years ago, and the lynx two hundred thousand ago.[11]

The cougar (*Puma concolor*), also known as a mountain lion, had a range up and down the Americas from Chile to the Yukon. The name *cougar* is from an Amazonian Tupi word meaning "false deer." Their color helps them blend in and hunt deers, elks, hares, porcupines, raccoons, squirrels, rabbits, beavers, and muskrats. While there are ten subspecies in the United States and Canada, they generally live eight to eleven years and hunt over a territory that can range between eight and five hundred square miles. Males are typically eleven feet long and weigh 145–165 pounds, and females are eight feet long and weigh 75–100 pounds; cubs stay with their mothers for about two years to learn how to hunt. They are good swimmers and can jump higher than other big cats, allowing them to take on prey much bigger than themselves.[12] A one-hundred-pound cougar can kill an eight-hundred-pound elk.[13] Despite this, cougar attacks on humans are rare. A woman was killed in British Columbia in 1996. She was protecting her child, whom the cougar probably saw as prey. Adult humans do not generally present as prey for cougars.[14] In the last century, there were fifteen fatal and fifty nonfatal cougar encounters, making such an encounter a very unlikely occurrence.[15] In this century, California lists eight cougar attacks since 2000, one of which was fatal.[16] In addition to a handful of other attacks, though, two were highly publicized: the 2015 killing in Oregon already mentioned, and an attack on two cyclists (one of whom was killed) in Washington in 2018. Such stories tend to put people on edge, and they start to kill big cats preemptively. But this is their territory.

Relationships between cougars and Native Americans are also fraught. While many are thought to have scavenged from cougar kills, and some Southwest tribes revere the cougar (the Apaches used their skin in maternity belts), Pacific Northwest tribes did not like the cougar, and in the Yukon, the Tlinget believed the lynx to be a malevolent spirit. Overall, however, cougars and other cats figure in twenty times fewer indigenous stories than do wolves. In the 1500s in California, Jesuits offered a bull to tribes for every cougar killed. A 1695 law in South Carolina "forced every aboriginal to kill a cougar or a wolf or a bear or two bobcats each year or to endure a public flogging."[17]

There are an estimated twenty thousand cougars in North America. California has the largest population at fifty-five hundred. They are known to live in eleven western states, with Oregon's population the next highest at three thousand. They are also found in Texas, Florida, South Dakota, British Columbia, and Alberta. These estimates require a great deal of guesswork as the cougar is very secretive and is rarely seen. Despite the unknown numbers, their semi-protected status as game animals means that all the western states still allow hunting of cougar.[18] Oregon is trying to bring back the use of dogs in cougar hunting, and trapping is still allowed in Texas and New Mexico.

The bobcat (also known as a wildcat) has been described as the coyote of the feline world due to its flexible diet and successful adaptation to living among human populations. They are found in southern Canada and all the states except Delaware. They will eat just about anything, including an armadillo. There are an estimated 700,000 to 1.5 million in the lower forty-eight states, each requiring a range between one and forty-two square miles. They are most abundant in the southeast and southern California. They generally live twelve to fifteen years, are weaned in under a year, are about three feet in length, and weigh between fourteen and twenty pounds. They are still valued for their hides, and roughly ninety thousand are trapped each year.[19]

Less common is the lynx (*Lynx canadensis*), with an estimated population of seven hundred in the lower forty-eight states and an unknown number in Canada and Alaska. Lynx and bobcats look alike and coexist in Canada, Washington, Idaho, Maine, Minnesota, and Colorado. They are generally three feet in length and twenty to thirty-five pounds (half the size of European lynx). They specialize in eating hares, but they also eat deer, grouses, and squirrels and require a territory of 2.5 to 92 square miles. They can live as long as fifteen years and are weaned in under a year. In the Americas, they are found mostly in Alaska and Canada, where they share the woods with wolves. Their preferred prey—hares—prefer forests, usually five to fifty years after a fire, so our recent policies of fire suppression have hurt the lynx in the United States.[20] In Alaska, they are hunted with regularity. There have been only two known lynx attacks on humans, one in the early 1900s and the other in 1974. And yet fear remains. Recent stories of urban lynx in Alaska fuel the fear, as do wolf sightings.

WOLVES

In the Americas, wolves ranged across two-thirds of North America, but by the 1920s, they were eliminated everywhere except the upper Great Lakes and Alaska. In addition to hunting and trapping, mange was deliberately introduced in Montana in the early 1900s to sicken and kill coyotes and wolves.[21] By 1856, the eastern wolves were already mostly gone.[22] Wolves in North America preyed on buffalo. As settlers killed and displaced both native peoples and buffalo, wolves also declined. They turned to livestock animals being brought into their territory as a source of food. This caused ranchers to see wolves as pests and call for their elimination. In 1906, the U.S. Forest Service was in the business of killing wolves for ranchers. They used a number of methods. Denning entailed finding a wolf den and killing all but one pup. When the adults responded to the pup's cries, they in turn were killed, quickly eliminating an entire family. The Forest Service dispersed poisoned carcasses for wolves to scavenge. This method kills indiscriminately, though, including killing the ranchers' dogs. Hunting from the air was also popular. Planes or helicopters ran the wolves until they were exhausted, and then hunters would shoot them from the air or step out and shoot them. This government-sponsored killing continues today. In 2013, USDA Wildlife Services killed more than two million animals, including coyotes, beavers, bears, and birds. In 2015, the number was 3.2 million and included wolves, cougars, bobcats, foxes, and prairie dogs.[23]

A story that brings these complicated relationships together is the 1972 book *Julie of the Wolves* and the 1994 sequel *Julie*, by Jean Craighead George. Gray wolves (*Canis lupus*) are two to three feet high at the shoulder, weigh between 57 and 130 pounds, and can run up to 30 miles an hour and cover 100 to 260 square miles in a day.[24] This makes them formidable for any human to encounter, not to mention a young girl who is lost on the Alaskan tundra. And yet, in these books, the girl and the wolves become companions. The girl's name is Miyax, and she is an Eskimo[25] (Inuit) from Mekoryuk whose mother is dead and whose father is presumed dead. Her English name is Julie. Her father had promised her in marriage to the son of a family friend. When she turns thirteen, she is sent to Barrow, Alaska, and married. She is not happy, afraid of her husband and her father-in-law when he drinks. One day she decides to leave. But she gets lost on her journey and finds herself in need of food. She builds a sod house near a wolf den and settles in to befriend the wolves. She is not worried about being harmed. While white people (*gussak*) talk of wolves eating humans, her people knew wolves to be brothers.

"Miyax stared hard at the regal black wolf, hoping to catch his eye. She must somehow tell him that she was starving and ask him for food. This could be done she knew, for her father, an Eskimo hunter, had done so."[26] But he had never explained how it could be done. She watches the wolves to see how they communicate with each other to signal friendship, and she gives them names. The regal black male leader she names Amaroq, which is an Eskimo word for wolf. She names the lead female Silver, a low-ranking adult is Jello, the gray is Nails, the smallest pup is Sister, and the three tawny pups are Zing, Zat, and Zit. The black male pup she calls Kapu after her father. She realizes she understands Amaroq when he bares his teeth and tells her to lie down. "He had talked to her not with his voice, but with his ears, eyes, and lips, and he had even commended her with a wag of his tail."[27] She notices that the pups play like human children—wrestling, chasing, and playing tug-of-war. She notices that they all bite Amaroq gently under the chin, and he gently takes their noses in his mouth. When showing submission, they pull their ears back and make themselves small. She is able to signal a pup to lie down and use the call to come home to call the pups to her. She learns to narrow her eyes and move forward when challenged. When Amaroq comes close, she gets down on her belly and pats him under the chin. He wags his tail in friendship, and Miyax becomes one of the pack.[28]

Over time, she realizes that the pups put their noses in the corner of an adult's mouth to get them to regurgitate food. She gets Jello to come near with a grunt-whine. She puts her hand over his nose to say she is in charge and then puts her hand in the corner of his mouth. He pulls away. But Kapu seems to understand and comes over and nuzzles Jello, who then regurgitates food. Miyax puts her mouth over Kapu's nose and then puts the food in her pot.[29] Later the wolves take down a caribou near her camp. After the wolves eat, she takes her share. Now she has food beyond the lichens and ferns that she had been eating.

The wolves also offer her protection. They chase a grizzly away from her. At first, she wonders why the grizzly was awake so early. Then she realizes it is the white man's hunting season. The wolves will be in danger now, as hunters are paid to kill them. Miyax remembers that this is why "[w]olves did not like civilization. Where they had once dwelled all over North America they now lived in remote parts of Canada, in only two of the lower forty-eight states, and in the wilderness of Alaska."[30] Miyax's father, Kapugen, thought the bounty on the wolves was also the *gussaks'* way of making sure the Eskimos could not survive. "'When the wolves are gone there will be too many caribou grazing the grass and the lemmings will starve. Without the lemmings the foxes and birds and weasels will die. Their passing will end smaller lives upon which even man depends, whether he knows it or not, and the top of the world will pass into silence.'"[31] So, as she comes closer to civilization, Miyax tries to tell the wolves to stay behind. But then the plane comes. Shots ring out. Amaroq sends Kapu away, and the plane follows Amaroq and shoots him. He dies. The plane returns to shoot Kapu, who was running back to Amaroq. The plane returns once more, but they do not land and collect their bounty. Miyax sees the men laughing; later she hears Silver and the other wolves howling in sorrow. Kapu is not dead, though, and Miyax nurses him back to health. With Amaroq's death, Miyax realizes that all of civilization is red with the blood of the wolf. She also sees the pack begin to disintegrate without their leader and not eat well. Kapu returns to the pack and begins leading the hunts.[32] Miyax knows it's time to leave the wolves when she meets some people who tell her that her father is alive. When she returns to the village and finds him, though, she realizes that he was flying the plane that carried the sportsman who shot Amaroq. Distressed, she leaves his house to live like an Eskimo.

Published in 1972, *Julie of the Wolves* was in many ways ahead of its time. The importance of wolves for the ecosystem was made clear, and the complex social structure of a wolf pack was presented in a way that showed the many parallels between humans and wolves. The novel also showed the disparity between indigenous cultures and the white settlers who hunted for sport or money. Written when just a few people were arguing for the reintro-duction of wolves to their historical territories, and when most Western peo-ples still called for the extermination of wolves to protect livestock and game animals, this book presented a challenge to the status quo. More than two decades later, George wrote a sequel that further complicated the issues. In *Julie*, Miyax has returned to her father's house, where she learns that he is in charge of a musk oxen herd that provides an industry and income for the entire village. He hunts wolves to protect the herd and to make money for the village. The musk oxen themselves were native to the region but had been hunted to extinction when the Eskimos were given guns. The U.S. government was working to reintroduce them to the wild and was supporting captive herds for the *qivit* industry. Julie helps care for the musk oxen. She also worries that, since the herd resides in her wolf pack's territory, Kapu and the pack might come near and get killed.

Her father has married a woman from Minnesota, and he tells Julie that, in Minnesota, if a wolf kills livestock, the government sends people to kill the wolf. "They shoot the ones that compete with humans. They think that is fair. That is how it is between humans and wolves in Minnesota." Julie responds, "We are different. We know the wolf is from the earth and must live so we can all live."[33] When her father says that Eskimos now live by Minnesota rules, Julie reminds him that he taught her to live by Eskimo rules of respect. After the pack kills a musk ox, her father reluctantly agrees to let her try to convince the pack to hunt elsewhere. She finds Kapu's pack and once again makes herself part of the family. Befriending the one pup, she carries the pup in the direction she wants the pack to move. But just when they are on the verge of entering a place rich with game, the wolves stop and won't follow. They won't cross the line of their territory. Julie realizes that Silver, Kapu's mother, has a mate on the other side of the line. She acts as a go-between, and the two groups combine into one pack and begin to hunt. This action keeps the wolves away for a while, but since the musk oxen were in their territory, the wolves considered them fair game. Hearing that wolves had been seen in the area, her father goes to protect his herd. When Julie arrives, though, she finds he'd set the herd free. "'There they are again,' he said. 'The wolf and the little oxen of the north.'"[34]

Many native peoples regard the wolf as kin and a sovereign tribe of their own. Many human tribes have clans named for the wolf. The Hopi, Navajo, Cherokee, Seminole, Penobscot, Algonquian, and Chippewa all see the wolf as a spiritual guide and ally. The Makah and Quileute peoples see wolves as their ancestors. A Quileute elder notes, "We learned from the wolf how to survive and how to be more human. How to honor our elders, to protect and provide for our families—and we learned from wolves the loyalty you need to really belong to a tribe."[35]

Rather than seeing wolves as kin or nations deserving of respect, the European colonists had seen the wolf as an enemy to be eliminated. This continues today with many livestock ranchers who worry the wolves will kill their livestock, and with hunters who see wolves as competition for game species such as elk and deer. Wolves are master hunters, but they are successful in only a small fraction of their hunts. Their hearing and smell are far superior to those of humans. Their vision is also quite acute, though they are nearsighted and limited in color range. They are highly social mammals. Packs or families can have up to fifty members, but most range between four and seven. They travel twenty miles or more a day in search of food.[36] While they usually work together to bring down prey, some wolves are also adept solo hunters. They eat what they can of each kill, but inevitably their kills are shared by coyotes, bears, and birds. By keeping the elks constantly on the move, the wolves' presence allows trees and grasses some reprieve, which brings back antelopes and beavers. There are more berries for bears. Since the wolves keep coyotes in check, rodents and rabbits rebound and increase the presence of raptors, weasels, and foxes. The elk numbers themselves increase as well. This kind of effect is described as a trophic cascade.[37] The presence of the wolves interacts in complex ways with climate conditions, the limited space allowed to the free-living animals, human hunting, and fire policies (to name a few considerations). While debate continues about which factors impact other factors, scientists agree that wolves make a difference: "Fire, climate change, drought, hunting, elk and willow growth, wolves, bison, beaver—all of these elements work together to shape story-as-ecology. And science needs time to understand and tell these not-so-simple stories."[38]

THE CALL OF THE WILD AND WHITE FANG

In this chapter, I am focusing the discussion on gray wolves. It should be noted, though, that the red wolf is even more endangered, and conservation efforts focus on cross-breeding them with coyotes, with whom they share a vocabulary as well as genetics.[39] Wolves and dogs also still share much in common and can interbreed. Novels such as Jack London's *Call of the Wild* and *White Fang* build on people's love for dogs in order to take them into the world of the wolf. Like Melville, who used contemporaneous knowledge about whales when writing *Moby-Dick*, London drew on the knowledge of the time to give an account of the behavior of dogs, wolves, and dog/wolf hybrids. While some saw his use of dogs as narrators as a bad version of anthropomorphism, London argued that he only used mental and instinctual responses that could be justified by scientific knowledge of the day. He wrote that be believed "his accounts of dogs' mental and emotional lives were precise" and their behavior could be explained by "instinct, sensation, and by simple reasoning."[40] In both books, the reader gains knowledge and sympathy for wolves, while at the same time they are being challenged to reconsider the nature of the dogs with whom they live and the ethics of their relationships with them.

Both books are very much inspired by particular readings of evolutionary theory, and there are obvious themes of a kind of "survival of the fittest." The language of the novels replicates the "primitive" and "savage" as being opposed to the "civilized," though the canine heroes of each book end up blurring those lines. In *Call of the Wild*, the reader meets Buck, a dog, kidnapped from his home in California and sent to Alaska to become a sled dog. In *White Fang*, the reader follows a wolf/dog hybrid who is born in the wild in Alaska, becomes a sled dog, and ends up as a pet dog in California. While Buck's journey requires him to get in touch with his wolf instincts in order to fight and survive, White Fang must learn to accept the rules of humans and curb his wolf instincts in order to have a home.

In *Call of the Wild*, London gives an account of the reality of many dogs who were kidnapped, beaten, starved, and shipped to Alaska. Many died in fights with other dogs, others from the cold and hard work. By watching the other dogs, Buck learns to dig a bed in the snow to stay warm, he learns to eat first, and he learns to steal food. His first theft of food "marked Buck as fit to survive in the hostile Northland environment. It marked his adaptability, his capacity to adjust himself to changing conditions, the lack of which would have meant swift and terrible death. It marked, further, the decay or going to pieces of his moral nature, a vain thing and a handicap in the ruthless struggle for existence." He steals and fights to live. He learns to break ice so he can drink and to chew the ice out from between his toes. He learns by experience, but London also paints a picture of the wolf awakening in the dog. "The domesticated generations fell from him. In vague ways he remembered back to the youth of the breed, to the time the wild dogs ranged in packs through the primeval forest and killed their meat as they ran it down." He, in some sense, already knew how to hunt and fight. "It was no task for him to learn to fight with cut and slash and the quick wolf snap. In this manner had fought forgotten ancestors. They quickened the old life within him, and . . . when on the still cold nights, he pointed his nose at a star and howled long and wolflike, it was his ancestors, dead and dust, pointing nose at star and howling down through the centuries and through him."[41] Once he becomes the lead dog and has a place by the fire, Buck thinks of (but does not miss) his earlier life. The old memories are weak compared to "the instincts (which were but the memories of his ancestors become habits) which . . . quickened and became alive again."[42]

In 2020, a movie version of *The Call of the Wild* was released, starring Harrison Ford.[43] The movie remains largely faithful to the book but with some interesting points of emphasis. With the exception of the people who kidnap and take Buck to Alaska, and the greedy greenhorn prospector—Hal—who tries to get Buck to cross thinning ice, the people in Buck's life treat him as an intelligent and feeling being. The humans with whom he lives in California understand him as mischievous and a bit out of control, but when he destroys a table of food at a party, he is talked to about his behavior and asked to think about what he's done. When he is on the team for the mail sled, he is shown to be observant and thoughtful as he quickly learns from the humans and the other dogs what he is supposed to do. There is an interesting choice to have this sled operated by a couple. The man, Perrault, is apparently from Africa, and the woman, Francoise, is at least part Native Alaskan. Perrault talks to Buck, while Francoise scoffs at the idea that Buck can understand and doesn't believe he'll make a good sled dog. When Buck saves her life, though, she warms up to him and also begins talking to him. When Buck refuses to pull unless he's the lead dog, Francoise even says that Buck knows something Perrault does not. When Buck ends up on Hal's team, however, his intelligence is not valued. John Thornton saves Buck from Hal's cruelty because he already has a bond with Buck. In the movie, Buck crosses paths with Thornton on several occasions and does him a favor each time. This situation creates an obligation for Thornton. Throughout the film, Buck sees images of his wolf ancestors, which push him to gain knowledge and courage, and he eventually joins up with a wolf.

Even as London (and the recent film) portrays the awakening of some kind of inner wolf, Buck is saved from the lash and the club by human love when Thornton saves him from Hal. Buck feels love for Thornton and worries about losing him, but Buck still feels wild. "Faithfulness and devotion, things born of fire and roof, were his; yet he retained his wildness and wiliness. He was a thing of the wild, come in from the wild to sit by Thornton's fire, rather than a dog of the soft Southland stamped with the marks of generations of civilization."[44] In the book, Buck eventually follows a wolf into the forest and makes friends—his "wood brother"—but he returns to Thornton. He starts hunting his own food and sleeping away from the camp. One day he returns to find Thornton and the others in the camp dead. They had been killed by a local tribe, and Buck begins attacking those who are dancing in celebration of their victory. While he mourns his loss, he also takes pride in the fact that he killed men. He realizes it was only men's weapons that made them strong.[45] In the recent movie, this ending is altered. Thornton is killed by Hal, from whom Thornton had rescued Buck. Instead of attacking Hal, Buck pushes him into a burning cabin where Hal dies. This ending is more realistic regarding where the threat to life lay for white prospectors in Alaska—that is, they were more likely to be killed by other white prospectors than by native peoples. Having Buck push the man into a burning building, though, prevents the audience from seeing the final and violent relinquishing of Buck's remaining dogness. Either way, though, with nothing left to tie him to humans, Buck joins a wolf pack. Even as he comes to lead a family pack of his own, he visits the site of Thornton's death every summer.

By contrast, *White Fang* opens with a scene of wolves hunting two men and their dogs. The wolves start by killing and eating the dogs when the men camp for the night. When the men catch sight of the female who's been stalking them, she is cinnamon in color and seems doglike, as well as truly wolf. One man chases the wolves, but when he runs out of ammunition, he is killed and eaten.[46] London makes it clear that this happens during a time of famine, suggesting it was an unusual event. In the last one hundred years, only two people have been killed by wild wolves in North America. In contrast, since 2002 thirty-five people have been killed by bears, since 1990 eleven have been killed by cougars, and twenty to thirty people are killed annually by dogs. Another hundred people are killed by humans hunting.[47]

As the reader gets to know the she-wolf and her mate One-Eye, London describes general pack dynamics and hunting practices. When she has her first litter of pups, she keeps the male at a distance until he proves to be a gentle provider. Most of the litter has the reddish hue of their mother, but one looks just like his wolf father. The pups are fierce and curious as they begin to learn about the world. But famine takes its toll, and only the gray pup survives. Following One-Eye on his search for food, London also introduces the reader to a lynx who unsuccessfully takes on a porcupine. Not long after this, One-Eye is killed by a lynx, making things desperate for White Fang and his mother.[48]

He has to learn about the world fast in order to survive. "But the cub was learning. His misty little mind had already made an unconscious classification. There were live things and things not alive. Also, he must watch out for the live things. The things not alive remained always in one place; but the live things moved about, and there was no telling what they might do."[49] London describes encounters with birds, squirrels, weasels, hawks, twigs, rivers, and pebbles. When White Fang stumbles into a ptarmigan nest and eats the chick, he is attacked by the returning mother. He quickly goes from being scared to fighting: "All the fighting blood of his breed was up in him and surging through him. This was living, though he did not know it. He was realizing his own meaning in the world; he was doing that for which he was made—killing meat and battling to kill it."[50] Later, as hunger returns, he begins studying animals in earnest so he will know how to hunt them. After his mother brings him a lynx kitten as a meal, the mother lynx visits them. This is his first real fight, and he saves his mother. He also learns that it is eat or be eaten. "The lynx-mother would have eaten him had she not herself been killed and eaten. . . . He was a killer."[51]

When White Fang first encounters humans, he feels that they have mastery and power. He cannot move. One of the Native Americans picks him up, and White Fang bites him. The man hits him with a club. White Fang's cries call his mother, who comes to protect him. When one of the Native Americans calls her by her name, Kiche, she crouches down and wags her tail. She is a wolf/dog hybrid who had left the tribe during a time of famine. White Fang experiences the sensation of being petted and having his stomach rubbed. He snarls and enjoys it—confused.[52] He comes to see the humans as gods whom he must obey or face clubs and whips. "He belonged to them as all dogs belonged to them. His actions were theirs to command. His body was theirs to maul, to stamp upon, to tolerate."[53]

Then White Fang's mother is given away to another tribe in payment of a debt. He tries to follow her and is beaten. He fights and bites, and he is beaten more.[54] While he comes to a kind of truce with the humans, the dogs in the camp are always attacking him, and White Fang "became wickeder and more ferocious than it was his natural right to be. Savageness was a part of his make-up, but the savageness thus developed exceeded his make-up. He acquired a reputation for wickedness amongst the man-animals themselves."[55] Being a wolf, he was assumed to be trouble. He eventually kills a dog and becomes an outcast from the pack. When the tribe prepares to move, White Fang leaves the camp and hides so they will leave without him. Soon, though, he feels lonely and cold. "His bondage had softened him. Irresponsibility had weakened him."[56] Wanting protection and companionship, he goes in search of the camp and gives himself to the humans. "At last he lay at the master's feet, into whose possession he now surrendered himself, voluntarily, body and soul. Of his own choice he came in to sit by man's fire and to be ruled by him."[57]

When famine once again comes, the dogs eat each other, the humans eat the dogs, and White Fang is left to fend for himself. He returns to the camp when the famine is over. This is a fateful decision, as he is then taken by Gray Beaver to Klondike, where he sees his first white man. "As compared with the Indians he had known, they were to him another race of beings, a race of superior gods. They impressed him as possessing superior power, and it is on power that a god-head rests."[58] A man named Beauty Smith tries to buy White Fang, but Gray Beaver won't sell him. Smith regularly brings alcohol to Gray Beaver, though, and Gray Beaver "got the thirst." Gray Beaver eventually sells White Fang to Smith for alcohol. White Fang proves difficult to catch, and he escapes and returns to Gray Beaver several times. Smith beats him and seems to enjoy it. He teases White Fang until he hates everyone and everything. Then Smith uses White Fang to make money in dog fights—a reality still with us today. White Fang's experience and his ferocity make him unbeatable. When he has fought and beaten all the dogs, wolves and lynx are trapped to fight him, and he wins. Out of competitors, a bulldog arrives in town. This dog is different, and White Fang looks to be losing. Smith begins to kick and curse him. At this point, Weedon Scott intervenes to break up the fight and take White Fang with him.[59]

Scott is a different kind of man, and he decides to see what kindness can do for White Fang. He sits with him, talks to him, and gives him meat. Eventually he is able to pet White Fang. "Weedon Scott had set himself the task of redeeming White Fang—or rather, of redeeming mankind from the wrong it had done White Fang. It was a matter of principle and conscience."[60] White Fang becomes devoted to Scott and becomes the lead dog on his sled team. When Scott takes a trip, White Fang stops eating and becomes sick. When Scott returns, though, White Fang rallies, wags his tail, and snuggles (something he had never done before). This presents a problem, as Scott is returning to California and needs to leave White Fang behind. When it is time to leave, he locks White Fang in the cabin and heads for the boat, only to find White Fang waiting for him on the deck of the boat, having jumped through the cabin window. White Fang is now on his way to California, where he has to learn *not* to fight with dogs, *not* to eat chickens, and *not* to attack other humans when they hug his master. He begins to learn these lessons, but he is not permitted to sleep in the house. The master's wife, though, often secretly lets him in at night. When a criminal comes to the house to seek revenge on Scott's father, who is a judge, White Fang kills the man and earns the undying love and trust of the family. However, White Fang is badly injured in the altercation. The nursing he receives during his long recuperation further bonds him to the family. Here, as in *Call of the Wild*, what is emphasized is the possibility of mutual loyalty and trust between the human and the canine. In contrast to *Call of the Wild*, where the dog leaves his loyalty to humans and transfers it to the wolves, *White Fang* ends with the wolf living among the humans. Today, many wolves are living in closer contact with humans than they have in the last two hundred years.

WOLF REINTRODUCTION

Today the story of the wolf is closer to home for many living in the Rocky Mountains and the western United States. The idea of reintroducing wolves in Yellowstone National Park has always been controversial, but in 1995, it became a reality when Canadian wolves were released. By 2003, there were 174 wolves living in fourteen families. Some had also left the park. There was another release in Idaho, and wolves began moving south from Canada, resulting in a Northern Rockies wolf population of about seventeen hundred.[61] Wolf tourism became very popular in the area. The number of wolves in the park declined to about one hundred by 2010. Disease, wolf conflicts, and prey availability contributed to the natural decline. This made it harder to spot wolves in the park, though, as did the return of legal wolf hunting outside the park. Poachers had always posed a threat, and some wolves had been killed for preying on livestock (though only two hundred of the five million cattle in Montana, Idaho, and Wyoming were lost this way in any given year). Legal hunting, with no buffer around the park, made it impossible to protect any of the park's wolves. Some believed that poachers and hunters actually targeted collared wolves to send a message. In the first three weeks of Montana's 2009 hunt, four of the ten wolves in one park family had been killed. By the end of that season, 258 wolves had been killed in Montana and Idaho (Wyoming's hunt was still tied up in court at that time). After much political wrangling, Montana and Idaho were permitted to continue their hunts in 2011, and Wyoming's management plan declared most of the state a predator zone in which wolves could be killed for any reason. While Montana limited their hunt to 220 wolves, Idaho declared no limit and made plans to bring back a trapping season. Pressure to remove gray wolves from the endangered species list continued to grow in other places that now had wolves migrating across their state boundaries. Oregon, Washington, and Colorado began to join the debates about wolves. [62]

The hunting of wolves in Alaska continued throughout, even though 70 percent of Alaskans oppose killing wolves. "Under Governor Sarah Palin wolves were shot from helicopters and wolf dens were gassed to kill pups, and in 2007 her office 'offered 180 volunteer pilots and aerial hunters a $150 cash prize for turning in the legs of freshly killed wolves.'" In 2016, the U.S. Fish and Wildlife Service banned aerial hunting in the wildlife refuge, but other hunting and trapping continues since wolves were declared furbearers and big game animals. They are also hunted to increase caribou numbers, though fewer wolves has not meant more caribou. The number of wolves in Denali Park is at an all-time low, with just fifty-one wolves in thirteen packs. "In 2014 state wildlife officials gunned down the entire radio-collared Lost Creek pack—eleven wolves killed in a single day, which wiped out twenty years of research." So many wolves (ninety) have been killed around the Yukon-Charley Rivers National Park that the National Park Service ended a twenty-three-year study there. [63]

The loss of collared wolves means lost data to scientists, loss of tourists to the park, loss of money to the surrounding communities, and lost taxpayer money. The loss of taxpayer money is made more ironic when more taxpayer money is spent to kill wolves on behalf of ranchers who were compensated for their lost livestock. By 2010, more than twelve hundred wolves had been killed by the same government that had introduced them. While "one federal agency was reintroducing predators on public land, a second was leasing adjacent land to ranchers, and a third was dispatching trappers or men in helicopters to kill those same predators when they inevitably crossed paths with livestock." [64]

For the wolves, though, each death threatened the survival of a whole family and meant loss of genetic and cultural diversity within the still small wolf population as a whole. Many argue that we need to move beyond simply counting wolves and begin paying more attention to their complexity and base coexistence practices on helping families maintain their social integrity. [65] The number of wolves in North America poses no real threat to livestock, elk, or humans, but there are still those who want wolves eliminated. There are others, though, who are equally passionate about having a world with wolves. When a hunter legally killed the female leader (known as O-Six) of one of the most-watched families in Yellowstone, backlash followed. When, a few months later, U.S. Fish and Wildlife proposed delisting wolves throughout the lower forty-eight states, comments poured in, and the proposal was rejected. Wyoming's management plan was declared inadequate, and the fall hunt there was canceled. Wolves in the Upper Midwest were also returned to the endangered list after hunters and trappers in Wisconsin and Minnesota had killed more than fifteen hundred wolves in just three years. [66]

Each wolf killed means a lost individual personality, emotional distress in that wolf's family, lost knowledge, and lost help in support of the family. When a leader is killed, it usually means the end of the family group altogether. The remaining leader may languish or leave in search of another mate, since they won't mate with their relatives. The other wolves must find a new family (risking attack) or try to make it on their own. Lone wolves, and young wolves who have not yet perfected their hunting skills, are often those who are desperate enough to prey on livestock. Killing wolves disrupts family groups and actually increases the probability that wolves will kill livestock. There are ways to coexist, though.

Washington's Wolf Advisory Group (WAG) is one model working to encourage nonlethal protection methods among ranchers in Washington, Oregon, and California. With ninety wolves living in nineteen families, Washington is motivated to find ways wolves, ranchers, hunters, hikers, and conservationists can coexist. Made up of ranchers, hunters, and wolf advocates, WAG works to find compromise and common ground. Ranchers who promise to practice conflict avoidance can get daily alerts about wolves in their area from wildlife officials. They can then send range riders to those areas and move livestock if wolves become active in particular grazing locations. They also need to practice deterrence by removing carcasses. Other nonlethal methods include guard dogs, flashing lights, sirens, stun guns, and flapping cloth. If livestock are killed, these farmers are compensated for the loss. Wood River Wolf Project promotes similar measures in Idaho working with sheep farmers. [67] WAG reached an agreement that, in order to move to a lethal response against wolves, there need to "be four qualifying wolf depredations in one calendar year or six in two consecutive years. And in order for the depredation by a wolf or wolf pack to count as a strike against it the rancher must have removed all attractants, such as bone piles or carcasses, and have used at least one method of nonlethal deterrence at the time of the wolf attack." [68] While this was a compromise, it offered more protection than other wolves in North America enjoy. The policy was put into action in 2016 when Washington's Profanity Pack was killed.

Public outcry about the killing of the Profanity Pack was strong, and many members of WAG were saddened and frustrated by having to take an action that they did not support. Members of the pack had predated on livestock the requisite number of times, despite deterrence efforts. The compromises made when arriving at the protocol for taking lethal action against wolves had been necessary to keep the wide array of constituents at the table and willing to work to improve the lives of wolves by actively investing in methods of deterrence rather than falling back on old habits of seeking the elimination of wolves. At the time, the president of Defenders of Wildlife was saddened by the devastating loss but focused on the future: "This might be hard for some wolf advocates to digest, but the reality is that without the cooperation of ranchers, wolves don't have a chance in this landscape." A statement from WAG reaffirmed their commitment to the "long-term recovery and public acceptance of wolves" and asked people to "engage in respectful and civil dialogue as we work through these challenging events. We believe that ultimately we can create conditions where everyone's values are respected."[69] This is a contemporary example of the kind of pragmatist-informed and publicly engaged philosophy practiced by Jane Addams.

As stated in chapter 1, Addams is best known for her peace activism and work at Hull House. She was guided by a deep commitment to an inclusive democracy. She also thought that it is both better and more effective to work with people in a problematic situation to change that situation rather than for someone from outside or above to try to impose a solution. Working with others, one is more likely to have a fuller understanding of the problems at hand and to propose solutions that will have the support of those involved. Working in this way, she found that "progress has been slower perpendicularly, but incomparably greater because lateral."[70] To ameliorate a problematic situation means to make it better, not to fix it completely or once and for all. This approach requires humility with regard to one's own positions, recognizing that we are each fallible and only have a partial perspective on any given issue. It also requires respecting those involved in both the problem and the proposed responses. This means respecting, listening to, and working and compromising with those with whom one disagrees. This takes courage. It is easier for people to act on their convictions when they are sure they are correct and they are in a position to impose their will on a situation. It is harder and scarier to be open to having one's ideas changed and to be willing to compromise in order to achieve concrete improvements for those in need. This was the situation faced by those participating in WAG. Addams's commitment to this kind of approach rested on her understanding of individuals and communities always in complex relationships and situations that required collective inquiry and sympathetic understanding. Ethics and politics both needed to move beyond a focus on individual rights and responsibilities to embrace a social perspective.

Addams and pragmatists generally are committed to the idea of an open, pluralistic, and changing universe in which humans try to navigate their continuously developing embodied and conscious existence amid the lives of other continuously developing embodied and conscious existences. Doing this constructively and respectfully requires acknowledging one's own limited perceptions, knowledge, and understanding and living consciously as a fallible being. It requires that one seek out the perspectives, knowledges, and understandings of others who are differently situated in order to live intelligently and experimentally. Rather than fixing knowledge in place once and for all, espousing beliefs that are warranted by one's experience and putting them to work in the world to improve or ameliorate conditions becomes the task at hand. WAG has done much to ameliorate the situation for wolves, and it serves as a model for other states. At the same time, it needs to continue to reevaluate its policies and approaches and embrace perspectives currently not being considered. An important step going forward would be for WAG to include the voices and perspectives of Native Americans.

LIVING WELL WITH WOLVES AND CATS

Oregon now has more than one hundred wolves. One of those wolves, OR7, was the first wolf to migrate to California, helping to reintroduce wolves there as well. OR7 returned to Oregon, where he is no longer protected since wolves lost their place on the state's Endangered Species List in 2015. Convicted of killing livestock, the original alpha male in Oregon, OR4, and his family were run down by a helicopter and then shot in 2016.[71] The dominance of the livestock industry still holds sway in these decisions and overrides general public opinion, though it is worth noting that much of that public still wants to be able to eat inexpensive hamburgers.[72]

In contrast, the Nez Perce tribe, who have long lived on the land that is now Oregon, have taken in wolves from the Sawtooth and Owyhee packs, and they run the Wolf Education and Research Center.[73] Other indigenous peoples point out that they have no voice in WAG, even though they have had long relationships with wolves and other North American wildlife. Having been sickened, killed, and relocated in much the same way that the wolf has been, Native Americans want their voices heard. David Bearshield is a member of Guardians of Our Ancestors' Legacy and works to protect grizzly bears. He noted, "Tribal societies have always observed wolf packs and learned their societal concepts. For example, it's not just a female wolf who raises pups; it's also a family responsibility. Wolves also taught tribal peoples about hunting and tracking. Our tribal scouts are called 'wolves.' These scouts would signal when buffalo or relatives or enemies were close."[74] This reciprocal relationship continues as the Nez Perce and other tribes offer wolves protection and ongoing respect.

When WAG met in the aftermath of the killing of the Profanity Pack, the meeting opened with a prayer from Jimmy St. Goddard of the Montana Blackfoot, in which he asked the farmers and ranchers to understand that the wolf is holy to the Blackfoot. He continued, "We want to teach the children that we can all come together." This was followed by a song.[75] While this was an important step for WAG, people at the same meeting pointed out that there were no tribal representatives on WAG. As one woman noted, this perspective is important because "wolves and our people have been erased from public lands. . . . Wolves are our kin, our creators. My brother is from the Wolf Clan, and in our stories the wolf is part of our identity." A Cowlitz leader pointed out that the rancher in question had repeatedly put livestock in harm's way, rather than working to minimize the threat of loss: "It is not the fault of our sacred animals. They did not ask to have their home range invaded by careless livestock owners." Protect the Wolves, a Native American wildlife conservation program, sent a letter to the state arguing that such lethal removal violated their treaty and religious rights.[76] Protect the Wolves is not only focused on wolves; it also seeks to be a voice for what "our wolves, bison, grizzlies, cougars, and wild horses need to help ensure their safety and Creator-given right to live wild and free."[77] The group promotes education, as well as advocacy for wolves and other wildlife. "Education of the younger generations is important as they will be the keepers of our sacred species for coming generations. We will always encourage civil and intelligent debate while discouraging attacks on anyone who has a different opinion or lifestyle. We are not interested in running an advocacy group that attacks hunters or trappers on a personal level."[78]

This approach, as well as the demand to be at the table, is very much in keeping with pragmatist commitments and the approach of Jane Addams. It is also in keeping with ecowomanist commitments. Recall from chapter 1 that Alice Walker created the term *womanist* to distinguish what she had in mind from the term *feminist*. Womanism has a richer hue than feminism as it is more inclusive of women of color and their experiences. In her poem "Democratic Womanism," Walker states the need for, and the possibilities of, democratic womanism, socialist womanism, and democratic socialist womanism. She relates this to the needs of the frail earth as well as the needs of women of color. Given the strong connections in Walker's work between social justice issues and concerns about the environment and other animal beings, the idea of ecowomanism was born. Given the parallel oppressions faced by women of color and the rest of nature, ecowomanism complicates much ecofeminist analysis even while sharing many of the same commitments. In the same poem, Walker writes, "The male leaders / of Earth / appear to have abandoned / their very senses / though most appear / to live now / entirely / in their heads. / They murder humans and other / animals / forests and rivers and mountains / every day / they are in office." Walker thinks womanism can build a dream that changes this "brutally enforced complicity / in the assassination / of Mother earth."[79] Walker herself says, "My activism—cultural, political, spiritual—is rooted in my love of nature and my delight in human beings."[80] Despite the devastation and injustice she sees, like Addams, she remains committed to the work of making things better through cooperative and democratic action. Since the roots of these pragmatist commitments can be found in Native American philosophies (as was discussed in chapter 5), this is very much in keeping with Walker's womanist stance.

Walker's poem "Racism Dates Us" has the subtitle "Speciesism Does Too." She writes that both racism and speciesism make us feel good by making us feel superior. She shares the pragmatist impulse toward pluralism and fallibilism. She writes that she learned "the futility of expecting anyone, including oneself, to be perfect. People who go about seeking to change the world, to diminish suffering, to demonstrate any kind of enlightenment, are often as flawed as anybody else." This shared fallibilism, though, "opens us to courage and compassion."[81] On her view, we need this courage and compassion to face what humans have done to the rest of nature. This approach requires not only changes in practices but also a change in mind-set (a change in ontology). She argues that to change, we must decolonize our spirits and "return reverence to the Earth, thereby saving it, in this fearful-of-Nature, spiritually colonized age."[82] This will entail reining in consumeristic and individualistic ways of living. She writes, "Everything in Nature is warning us / to hurry up / and share."[83] Social and political change, for Walker, is only possible if a personal and spiritual change also occurs.

Walker worships "the Earth as God—representing everything—and Nature as its spirit," aligning herself with pagan spiritualities. She reaches back to her ancestors (African, Celtic, and Native American) to recover "their Earth-centered female reverencing religions" and to argue that in such religions Nature accepts and is pleased with however she made you.[84] She supports the animistic view of minded nature already discussed with regard to Plumwood and Kimmerer, and she worries about the dangerous messages that come from patriarchal religions that replicate the model of human exceptionalism. She offers her poem, "We Have a Beautiful Mother," to all women of color (and like-minded others) who come to see that "we are the daughters of Mother Earth." In the poem, she invokes the image of being born from the earth's ocean womb and being safe in "her green lap / immense / Her brown embrace / eternal / Her blue body / everything / we know."[85]

She believes we need to embrace this "Earth-centered female reverencing" approach or risk a slow and painful destruction of all life. Using the Sioux word *Wasichu* (meaning "he who takes the fat"), Walker asks, "Who has not been / invaded / by the Wasichu?" in her poem "Who?" Not the people, trees, water, rocks, air, or even the moon.[86] Similarly, in "No One Can Watch the Wasichu," she notes that the Wasichu not only harm other humans but also "[h]e is scalping / the earth / till she runs / into the ocean / The dust of her / flight / searing / our sight."[87] The mind-set and ethic of the *Wasichu* is one of extractive use and exploitation and is not compatible with respectful coexistence. Walker writes, "Let us consider the depletion of the ozone; let us consider homelessness and the nuclear peril; let us consider the destruction of the rainforests—in the name of the almighty hamburger. Let us consider the poisoned apples and the poisoned water and the poisoned air, and the poisoned earth."[88] Let us consider the cougar and the wolf as well.

Chapter Eight

Living with Animals Revisited

Now that we have examined some particular accounts of how humans have chosen to live with some specific animal others, it might be helpful to reconsider such choices. It should now be clear that how human choices impact the lives of other animal beings is quite complicated. The ideas we have about who and what counts morally have great power to shape our understanding of what it means to live well and respectfully. The role of the philosopher on a pragmatist ecofeminist account is to help people sort through the ongoing difficulties rather than to provide some principle to settle them. Raising awareness of the complicated nature of the issues, and finding ways to negotiate provisional responses in the midst of competing claims, is the task at hand.

For example, someone eating a vegan diet in an effort to minimize animal suffering and death may contribute to the death of apes by consuming products with palm oil (a common ingredient in many vegetarian and vegan foods). Someone advocating to end the slaughter of horses may cause more horses to suffer if closing slaughter facilities results in horses being held longer and shipped farther before being slaughtered. Someone who is vegetarian and doesn't want to consume the flesh of other animals may be saved by a pig valve or medicine tested on cats. As many of the philosophical perspectives discussed in this book point out, being human is wrapped up in living (and dying) with other animal beings. Given human continuity with the rest of nature, and the relationships of interdependence that frame our existence (and possible flourishing), we need to wrestle with questions of how to live with other animal beings in order to have sustaining and sustainable lives. The acceptance of our ontological relatedness opens up new possibilities, but it also forces us to face difficult responsibilities. Rather than just trying to avoid the ethical issues by finding ways of living that do not include interaction with, or use of, other animal beings, it is important to think through better and worse ways to navigate these complex relationships.

For example, many of the animal beings discussed in this book are, or have been, used in scientific research—apes, monkeys, cattle, horses, dogs, cats, mice, and rats. Apes and monkeys, for instance, have been used in Alzheimer's research, HIV research, aging research, vaccine research, drug research, surgical procedures, and more. Despite pressure to reduce the use of animals in such research, the number is actually going up. There were seventy-six thousand nonhuman primates used in research or held in breeding facilities in 2017. This is an increase of 22 percent from 2015. At the same time, the National Institutes of Health stopped funding invasive research using chimpanzees, and many of those chimpanzees are now housed in sanctuaries. While animal advocates feel good about this change, it may be a contributor to the increased use of monkeys even as debates about the results of such research continue. "The public wants more cures, but fewer animals," says Cindy Buckmaster, board chair of the Washington, DC–based Americans for Medical Progress, which supports animal studies. "They can't have it both ways."[1] In the United States, support for the use of animals in research is divided. Fifty-two percent of adults say they oppose the use of animals in scientific research, and 62 percent of women say they oppose using animals in such research. In March 2018, legislation was passed that limited the use of dogs in research conducted by the U.S. Department of Veterans Affairs.[2]

The push by many animal advocates to end all research involving other animal beings has reduced the overall use of animals and pushed the research community to develop ethical guidelines for such use. An Institutional Animal Care and Use Committee (IACUC) is required at any institution receiving federal funds for such research. This committee must include a veterinarian, a non-science person, and a community member in addition to scientists, animal care personnel, and human safety officers. As with the Wolf Advisory Group (discussed in chapter 7), the idea is to have a plurality of perspectives giving voice to a range of concerns associated with any particular research project. I currently serve on my university's IACUC. I personally find it to be a very difficult task. Following Addams's example, though, I also think it is important work. While I do worry that the use of animals in much research is a habit that is supported by the industry supplying the animals and the funding agencies that support such research under the assumption that it is the best way to get trustworthy results, I don't think it is realistic to end all such research now or in the near future. I don't think many of those who oppose such research really want this result, either. Most people in the United States are reliant on a whole host of drugs to deal with blood pressure, heart disease, cancer, and pain. Most undergo one or more surgeries that were initially developed on other animals and informed by research conducted with other animals—from organ transplants (sometimes using organs and tissues from other-than-human animals) to the more common LASIK surgery to improve eyesight.

Vaccines are another important tool in maintaining the health of humans and other animals. Dogs, cats, and horses routinely receive a host of vaccines, as do many of their human partners. Animal research was involved in the development of vaccines for polio, meningitis, typhus, whooping cough, smallpox, tetanus, measles, cholera, and more. Current research focused on developing vaccines for Ebola and the Zika virus has involved mice and primate studies.[3] While there have been refinements and a reduction in the number of animals used, most scientists believe live models are necessary to study the complexities of immunity. Further, while mice and rats can provide some information, such research often fails to transfer well to humans. Large animals—such as rabbits, pigs, sheep, cattle, and horses—are preferred for such testing (before moving to late-stage testing in primates), and pigs are seen as a particularly reliable model given the similarity between their physiology and immune system and that of humans.[4] Such research is seen as necessary because human behavior has been increasing the introduction of pathogenic microbes to human populations. For instance, in "Large Animal Models for Vaccine Development and Testing," the authors write,

> With continuing increased growth and geographic expansion of human populations, intrusion of agriculture into previously untouched areas of the native environment, and disturbances in ecosystems and a redistribution of natural hosts and vectors due to climate change, humans are increasingly coming into contact with wild animals and their microbial repertoire (Patz et al. 2004; Pulliam et al. 2012; Webb et al. 2010). This change in contact between humans and other species has led to a dramatic increase in the number of emerging infectious diseases (EIDs) (Jones et al. 2008). In addition, more intensive global travel and trade have increased the risk that pathogens can be spread widely and have increased opportunities to infect multiple hosts.[5]

Wildlife markets are one of the main sources of current contact. With multiple species kept and slaughtered in cramped and filthy conditions, disease spread is almost inevitable. As David Benatar writes, "Simply put, the coronavirus pandemic is a result of our gross maltreatment of animals."[6] Ironically, while COVID-19 emerged in humans as a result of disrespectful care and use of other animal beings, the research to create a vaccine for COVID-19 will involve the use and death of a host of other animal beings. Only a few months into the COVID-19 pandemic, mice, monkeys, cats, dogs, ferrets, chickens, and horses were already being used in such research.[7] Benatar argues that rather than only reacting to a pandemic, we ought to take steps to prevent them. This would entail altering human behavior (perhaps less travel), agriculture (less disturbance of ecosystems), and better treatment of animals (both as potential pets and as potential sources of food). He writes, "Real prevention requires taking steps to minimize the chances of the virus or other infectious agents emerging in the first place. One of a number of crucial measures would be a more intelligent—and more compassionate—appraisal of our treatment of nonhuman animals, and concomitant action."[8]

It is also worth mentioning, as Benatar does, that at the same time that we use and kill animals for the sake of such biomedical research, we throw away one of the most transformative breakthroughs in modern medicine—antibiotics. The use of antibiotics to promote growth in livestock is a major contributor to the problem of antibiotic resistance. In one case (the emergence of COVID-19), our disrespect for other animal beings creates new health threats for human beings, and in the other (the emergence of antibiotic resistance), our disrespect for other animal beings removes or diminishes the effectiveness of a host of lifesaving drugs on which both human and other animal beings depend. Overuse of antibiotics in livestock animals (who suffer and die) wastes the suffering and loss of lives involved in the development of antibiotics, further compounding the disrespect and requiring even more animals in research to find replacement drugs.[9] While wiser use of various animals (including humans) in such research is important, and further refinement and reduction of use is preferable, giving up such research also has a host of ethical problems, as death from injuries and preventable diseases comes with suffering and loss of its own kind.

This doesn't mean that people are wrong to see much about the lives and deaths of animals used in research (especially research for commercial products) as involving many ethical problems. But is banning all such research the right response? Pressure to do this in the United States has actually resulted in decreasing the welfare of the animals used in research and criminalizing many activities of animal advocacy groups. Fearing the actions of animal advocates who might destroy labs and remove animals, most animal research facilities are hidden and employ many security measures. This situation often means less space for the animals and no (or very limited) access to outdoor spaces. At my university, this is the case for the owls used for breeding and in educational research. They once had an enclosure that included outdoor access. Fearing that animal advocates would release the owls, they were moved to an indoor aviary.

The point here, then, is that using other animal beings in scientific research is a complex question that is not served by simple all-or-nothing approaches to the ethical or political concerns in which it is involved. We need thoughtful, informed, ongoing inquiry into such questions and a willingness to make changes in an effort to ameliorate the problems. This process will have to be ongoing, as there are no fully unproblematic ways to live with other beings—human or other-than-human—and there will always be new emerging situations and concerns. This is where the pragmatist commitment to pluralistic, inclusive, and democratic inquiry is important, as is the commitment to holding ideas tentatively and being willing to revise beliefs and work to change habits as the need arises.

A pragmatist method of inquiry is also helpful when considering issues about what to eat (or not eat). While many try to find a diet that addresses all ethical and political concerns, a pragmatist approach is more contextual and revisable in light of emerging information and concerns. While not eating animals may reduce the suffering and deaths of some animals, it may result in increasing the suffering and deaths of other animals. Wildlife in particular may be harmed by clearing more land for crop production and in order to protect crops from being eaten or trampled. While much cropland currently is used to grow crops to feed livestock, a simple switch to growing food to feed humans and their animal companions would not result in all the food that would be needed. Is it a marked improvement to kill elephants and deer to prevent them from destroying crops rather than killing wolves to prevent them from killing and eating cattle or sheep? Is it better to poison and kill a whole host of insects and microbes (and other "pests") to protect crops than to eat animals who grazed on land that is not covered in chemicals? At the same time, the current methods of raising and slaughtering animals for food in the United States, or raising them for by-products such as milk and honey, contributes to a whole host of environmental and health problems. Unreflective consumption of animals and animal products is not ethical, nor is it sustainable. These are just a few examples to remind us all that growing and distributing food of any kind involves ethical and political problems that are not solved by any particular injunction or prescription.

For those seeking to escape the specter or moral compromise, and take refuge in some kind of moral absolute, it might make more sense to focus on using land and resources currently dedicated to luxury products such as coffee, tea, chocolate, and sugar for growing food for humans. But it seems even fewer people are willing to make that move than are willing to stop eating other animals. Forest clearing to grow coffee kills monkeys; sugarcane production kills rats and pollutes waterways, thereby harming aquatic life; cocoa farming harms a variety of primates.[10] These products contribute to loss of habitat, pollution, and the direct deaths of animals. And none of this has yet really taken up the human suffering involved in both crop and animal production—farm workers exposed to pesticides and unfair labor practices, forced labor, child labor, and slaughterhouse workers injured and fired for exposing safety concerns about either their working conditions or the meat being sold.[11]

There are also complications in advocating for single-issue animal protections. The ban on the slaughter of horses (for food) and the push to only adopt dogs (rather than purchase puppies from breeders) are just two examples. Rather than use the slaughtering of horses for meat in the United States as an opportunity to draw attention to the problems with current slaughterhouse practices for all animals (including humans), animal advocates instead made the horse a special animal deserving of special protections. While there are admirable motivations involved with this move, it served to reinforce the dualistic value hierarchies critiqued by ecofeminists and ecowomanists, and it did little to change how humans relate to other animals slaughtered for food. In addition, it may have done little to actually prevent the suffering and slaughter of horses (as discussed in chapter 3).

Similarly, opposition to puppy mills that produce and house excessive numbers of animals in unethical and unhealthy conditions is often framed as opposition to all breeding of dogs. This approach fails to account for the differences between puppy mills and reputable and responsible breeders. While there are good reasons to oppose many of the practices used in breeding "purebred" dogs with a focus on a particular appearance, it is again not an all-or-nothing concern. Some dogs are bred for specialized tasks such as herding or protecting sheep or sniffing out drugs.[12] The presence of livestock guardian dogs, who exist through the combination of breeding and training, helps prevent the deaths of many coyotes and wolves (as discussed in chapter 7). In order to ameliorate the lives of both the domesticated and the nondomesticated animal beings with whom we are in relation, it is probably necessary to let go of many absolutistic positions.

Plumwood's pragmatist ecofeminist call for an ethic of respectful use is well positioned to make sense of the complicated and intertwined lives of human and other animal beings. Supported by the work of ecowomanists, such as Alice Walker, and native scholars, such as Robin Wall Kimmerer, an approach to social, political, and ethical concerns takes fuller shape. They all weave together elements of a pragmatist ecofeminist approach to living with animals that understands humans as part of nature, and honors and respects the rest of nature and other animal beings while also acknowledging human dependence on them. They all acknowledge the ongoing importance of negotiating and improving human relationships with the rest of nature and the need to continually adapt in order to respond to mistakes. They all take a pluralist perspective and seek inclusive social and political processes for improving how humans coexist with other animal beings. They all acknowledge the agency of the rest of nature and see humans as partners rather than dominators. They all acknowledge a spectrum of sameness and difference among various creatures, including humans. They all acknowledge the possibility of communication among species and the possibility of cultural exchange and influence across species. A dialogical ethic that stands ready to revise positions and experiment with ways of living together emerges from this ontological relatedness and animistic approach to knowing the world.

Trying to find ways to help make the agency of nature more visible and so encourage the dialogical, partnership ethic suggested by Plumwood and others, Kimmerer searches for a word to represent "the simple but miraculous state of just being" that could replace the common use of the word *it*. In Potawatomi, *Aakibmaadiziiwin* means "a being of the earth." From that word, she takes *ki* to signify a being of the living earth. Not *he* or *she*, but *ki*. So that when the robin warbles on a summer morning, we can say, "*Ki* is singing up the sun. *Ki* runs through the branches on squirrel feet, *ki* howls at the moon, *ki*'s branches sway in the pine-scented breeze, all alive in our language as in our world." This can be paired with the plural *kin*, which already has many related meanings in English. "The mending we need will require reweaving the relationship between humans and our more-than-human kin. Maybe now, in this time when the myth of human exceptionalism has proven illusory, we will listen to intelligences other than our own, to kin."[13] If we don't do more to listen to, learn from, and respect other animal beings—our kin—we will continue to miss the complex interactions among all life. We will continue to either ignore the needs, interests, and desires of other animal beings or focus on single issues without grappling with the complex intersections among issues such as farming, ranching, hunting, biomedical research, environmental policies, and personal relationships with pets. Humans need to remember that their lives and deaths are intertwined with the rest of nature; they need to remember that to be human is to be related to the rest of life, not separate from or superior to it.

Notes

PREFACE AND INTRODUCTION

1. Barbara Natterson-Horwitz and Kathryn Bowers, *Zoobiquity: The Astonishing Connection between Human and Animal Health* (New York: Vintage Books, 2013), 312.

2. Karin Brulliard, "The Next Pandemic Is Already Coming, Unless Humans Change How We Interact with Wildlife, Scientists Say," *Washington Post*, April 3, 2020, https://www.washingtonpost.com/science/2020/04/03/coronavirus-wildlife-environment/.

3. Brulliard, "The Next Pandemic Is Already Coming."

4. Natterson-Horwitz and Bowers, *Zoobiquity*, 311.

5. Natterson-Horwitz and Bowers, *Zoobiquity*, 19.

6. Brulliard, "The Next Pandemic Is Already Coming."

7. Louise Boyle, "Jane Goodall Calls for Global Ban on Wildlife Trade and End to 'Destructive and Greedy Period of Human History,'" *Independent*, April 11, 2020, https://www.independent.co.uk/environment/jane-goodall-interview-animal-markets-wildlife-trafficking-a9458611.html.

8. Michael J. Caduto and Joseph Bruchac, *Keepers of the Animals: Native American Stories and Wildlife Activities for Children*, with a foreword by Vine Deloria Jr. (Golden, CO: Fulcrum, 1997).

9. I use the term *fishes* instead of the more commonly accepted term *fish* to highlight the plurality among those animal beings classified as fish.

1. LIVING WITH ANIMALS

1. Humans today also have reproductive technologies that can be used to limit or augment reproduction.

2. There were several sequels to this film in the early 2000s.

3. Hugh Lofting, "Dr. Dolittle's Circus," in *Dr. Dolittle: A Treasury* (Philadelphia: Lippincott, 1967), 40.

4. Lofting, *Dr. Dolittle: A Treasury*, 74, 115, 127.

5. Alice Walker, "Frida, the Perfect Familiar," in *Anything We Love Can Be Saved* (New York: Random House 1997), 127–33, 129.

6. Karen E. Lange, "Eating for Tomorrow: Why Eating More Plant-Based Meals Matters," *All Animals* (June/July/August 2019), 24.

7. J. Poore and T. Nemecek, "Reducing Food's Environmental Impacts through Producers and Consumers," *Science* 360, no. 6392 (2018): 987–89, http://science.sciencemag.org/content/360/6392/987.

8. Poore and Nemecek, "Reducing Food's Environmental Impacts," 990–91.

9. It is important to note that some theorists use these same perspectives to argue that the current human treatment of other-than-human animals is fine as it is.

10. For fuller accounts, see Erin McKenna, *Pets, People, and Pragmatism* (New York: Fordham University Press, 2013); Erin McKenna, *Livestock: Food, Fiber, and Friends* (Athens: University of Georgia Press, 2018). For more on pragmatism, see Erin McKenna and Scott L. Pratt, *American Philosophy: From Wounded Knee to the Present* (New York: Bloomsbury, 2015).

11. Charles S. Peirce, *The Collected Papers of Charles Sanders Peirce*, ed. Charles Hartshorne, Paul Weiss, and Arthur W. Burks (New York: Thoemmes Continuum, 1997), 5:613.

12. Peirce, *Collected Papers*, 7:379.

13. William James, "A World of Pure Experience," in *The Writing of William James*, ed. John J. McDermott (Chicago: University of Chicago Press, 1977), 195.

14. William James, "The Will to Believe," in *The Writing of William James*, ed. John J. McDermott (Chicago: University of Chicago Press, 1977), 725.

15. John Dewey, *Human Nature and Conduct*, in *The Middle Works of John Dewey*, ed. Jo Ann Boydston (Carbondale, Illinois: Southern Illinois University Press), 14:11.

16. Jane Addams, *Democracy and Social Ethics*, ed. Charlene Haddock Seigfried (Urbana: University of Illinois Press, 2002), 69.

17. I think there are ways that pragmatism provides important correctives to some versions of ecofeminism/ecowomanism and some ways that ecofeminism/ecowomanism provides important correctives to some versions of pragmatism, but that discussion is not the focus here.

18. Alice Walker, *In Search of Our Mothers' Gardens: Womanist Prose* (Fort Washington, PA: Harvest Books, 1983), xi.

2. CHIMPANZEES AND OTHER PRIMATES

1. H. A. Heyes, *Curious George* (Boston: Houghton Mifflin, 1941).

2. Dale Peterson, *Eating Apes* (Berkeley: University of California Press, 2003), 123.

3. Roger Fouts, *Next of Kin: My Conversations with Chimpanzees* (New York: Avon Books, 1997), 43.

4. Thomas M. Butynski, "Africa's Great Apes," in *Great Apes and Humans: The Ethics of Coexistence*, ed. Benjamin B. Beck et al. (Washington, DC: Smithsonian Institution Press, 2001), 27.

5. Heyes, *Curious George*, 48.

6. H. A. Heyes, *Curious George Takes a Job* (Boston: Houghton Mifflin, 1947).

7. Fouts, *Next of Kin*, 43.

8. H. A. Heyes, *Curious George Gets a Medal* (Boston: Houghton Mifflin, 1957).

9. Fouts, *Next of Kin*, 25–26.

10. *Chimposium Script* (Ellensburg, WA: Chimpanzee and Human Communication Institute, 2000).

11. I want to be clear that this is far from the only example of such work. Koko the gorilla, who died in 2018 at the age of forty-seven, also used ASL to communicate. Inspired by the work with Washoe, Penny Patterson began a similar study with Koko. Sue Savage-Rumbaugh is well known for her work with Kanzi and his computer lexigrams. While Kanzi is a bonobo, Rumbaugh had started such research with chimpanzees using sign language. She and her then husband Duane Rumbaugh later created a vocabulary of lexigrams in order to address concerns about apes just mimicking signs they were seeing or humans seeing signs when the apes were just moving their hands. With the lexigrams, a computer recorded what "sign" was touched.

Not to be left out of the mix, similar work has been done with orangutans. Chantek, who died at thirty-nine in 2017, is also well known. Lyn Miles began working with Chantek in 1978 when he was nine months old. Like Washoe, he was cross-fostered and taught ASL in the course of his everyday activities. In addition to language work and work on problem solving, Chantek was known for lying or deceiving the humans around him to get what he wanted. Work at the Smithsonian National Zoo's think tank features the cognitive capacity of orangutans and gorillas and explores emotions such as guilt and shame.

While ape language research has dominated the field for quite some time, it is important to note that the same year Washoe died, so did another famous nonhuman language user—Alex the gray parrot. Irene Pepperberg is well known for her work with Alex (and other parrots) and language use, counting, and categorization. Dolphins have also been used in sign language research, and that research has shown that dolphins understand the importance of word order for the meaning of a sentence. They've also shown that dolphins can understand abstract ideas like "do something new."

12. Fouts, *Next of Kin*, 265.

13. Val Plumwood, *Environmental Culture: The Ecological Crisis of Reason* (New York: Routledge, 2002), 102–5.

14. John Rawls, *A Theory of Justice* (Cambridge, MA: Belknap Press, 1971).

15. For important discussions of these points, see Carole Pateman's *The Sexual Contract* (Stanford, CA: Stanford University Press, 1988) and Charles Mills's *The Racial Contract* (Ithaca, NY: Cornell University Press, 1997).

16. Roger Fouts, "Darwinian Reflections on Our Fellow Apes," in *Great Apes and Humans: The Ethics of Coexistence*, ed. Benjamin E. Beck et al. (Washington, DC: Smithsonian Institution Press, 2001), 206.

17. Deborah Bird Rose, "Val Plumwood's Philosophical Animism: Attentive Interactions in the Sentient World," *Environmental Humanities* 3, no. 1 (2013), 104.

18. Gisela Kaplan and Lesley J. Rogers, *The Orangutans: Their Evolution, Behavior, and Future* (Cambridge, MA: Perseus, 2000), 56–62.

19. "Project Chantek," Chantek Foundation, https://chantek.org/project-chantek.

20. David Beasley, "U.S. Orangutan Chantek, 'the Ape Who Went to College,' Dies at 39," Reuters Environment, August 8, 2017, https://www.reuters.com/article/us-georgia-orangutan/u-s-orangutan-chantek-the-ape-who-went-to-college-dies-at-39-idUSKBN1AO29J.

21. There are a number of sanctuaries, including the Fauna Foundation in Canada where the last living members of Washoe's family—Tatu and Loulis—now live. Others include the Center for Great Apes, Chimp Haven, Primarily Primates, Project Chimps, and the Primate Rescue Center.

22. Chimpanzee Sanctuary Northwest, https://chimpsnw.org.

23. Phillip Low, "The Cambridge Declaration on Consciousness," ed. Jaak Panksepp, Diana Reiss, David Edelman, Bruno Van Swinderen, Philip Low, and Christof Koch, presented at the Francis Crick Memorial Conference on Consciousness in Human and Non-Human Animals, Churchill College, University of Cambridge, July 7, 2012, http://fcmconference.org/img/CambridgeDeclarationOnConsciousness.pdf.

24. Humane Society of the United States, "Animals Used in Biomedical Research FAQ," https://www.humanesociety.org/animals/monkeys/qa/questions_answers.html.

25. United States Department of Agriculture, *Animal Welfare Act and Animal Welfare Regulations*, 2017.

26. A. Michele Schuler and Christian R. Abee, "Enrichment for Nonhuman Primates," 3, Department of Health and Human Services, 2005, https://olaw.nih.gov/sites/default/files/Squirrel_Monkeys.pdf.

27. Mary Anne Warren, "The Moral Status of Great Apes," in *Great Apes and Humans: The Ethics of Coexistence*, ed. Benjamin E. Beck et al. (Washington, DC: Smithsonian Institution Press, 2001), 326–27.

3. HORSES AND CATTLE

1. Equo, "The Horse Industry by the Numbers," January 16, 2017, https://www.ridewithequo.com/blog/the-horse-industry-by-the-numbers.

2. "Race to Save Thoroughbreds from Slaughter," *Animal Times* 24, no. 3 (Fall 2009), 12.

3. For more on these particular concerns, see my book *Pets, People, and Pragmatism* (New York: Fordham University Press, 2013).

4. Equo, "The Horse Industry by the Numbers."

5. All breeds of horses have various physical issues, but since the quarter horse is the most popular breed in the United States, and the one most commonly used to work cattle, it is an important focus here.

6. Kentucky Equine Research Staff, "Common Genetic Diseases in Quarter Horses," *Equinews*, March 8, 2013, https://ker.com/equinews/common-genetic-diseases-quarter-horses/.

7. Lyla June Johnston, "Yes World, There Were Horses in Native Culture before the Settlers Came," *Indian Country Today*, July 3, 2019, https://newsmaven.io/indiancountrytoday/news/yes-world-there-were-horses-in-native-culture-before-the-settlers-came-JGqPrqLmZk-3ka-IBqNWiQ.

8. Native American Legends, "The Orphan Boy and the Elk Dog: A Blackfoot Legend," https://www.firstpeople.us/FP-Html-Legends/TheOrphanBoyAndTheElkDog-Blackfoot.html.

9. Ann Nolan Clark, *Bringer of the Mystery Dog—Sunk Wan Wak'an Agli Kin He*, Sioux text by Emil Afraid of Hawk, illustrated by Oscar Howe (United States Indian Service, 1943), Hathi Trust Digital Library, https://babel.hathitrust.org/cgi/pt?id=uc1.b5120464&view=1up&seq=14.

10. David Quammen, "People of the Horse," *National Geographic* 225, no. 3 (March 2014), https://www.national geographic.com/magazine/2014/03/native-american-horse/.

11. American Civil War Homepage, "Life and Death of the Civil War Horse: From Barn to Battlefield to Bullets to Burial," in *Civil War Horse History and Facts: Union and Confederate Horses*, http://www.thomaslegion.net/americancivilwar/totalcivilwarhorseskilled.html.

12. United States Foundation for the Commemoration of the World Wars, "Horse Heroes: By the Numbers," https://www.worldwar1centennial.org/index.php/brookeusa-statistics.html.

13. Anna Sewell, *Black Beauty* (Racine, WI: Whitman, 1965), 230.

14. Sewell, *Black Beauty*, 241.

15. Charlotte Perkins Gilman, "When I Was a Witch," in *The Charlotte Perkins Gilman Reader*, ed. Ann J. Lane (New York: Pantheon Books, 1980), 22.

16. Charlotte Perkins Gilman, *His Religion and Hers* (Westport, CT: Hyperion Press, 1923), 150–51.

17. Charlotte Perkins Gilman, *Moving the Mountain* (New York: Charlton, 1911), 74.

18. Charlotte Perkins Gilman, *Herland* (New York: Pantheon Books, 1979 [1915]), 47–48.

19. Sewell, *Black Beauty*, 203.

20. Sewell, *Black Beauty*, 192.

21. Sewell, *Black Beauty*, 22.

22. Aurelia Schuetz, Kate Farmer, and Konstnaze Kruege, "Social Learning across Species: Horses (*Equus caballus*) Learn from Humans by Observation," *Animal Cognition* 20, no. 3 (May 2017), 567.

23. Sewell, *Black Beauty*, 19.

24. Sewell, *Black Beauty*, 157.

25. It is important to note the wide variation in these practices among different kinds and levels of shows. Even with these differences taken into account, though, horses have many more rules in place to protect their welfare than do other livestock animals.

26. Charlotte Perkins Gilman, *Women and Economics: A Study of the Economic Relation between Men and Women as a Factor in Social Evolution* (New York: Harper & Row, 1966), 43–44.

27. Carol Adams, "Why I Became a Vegetarian," *Carol J. Adams* (blog), September 6, 2015, https://caroljadams.com/carol-adams-blog/why-i-became-a-vegetarian.

28. Alice Walker, "Am I Blue," Genius, https://genius.com/Alice-walker-am-i-blue-annotated.

29. Alice Walker, "Human Sunrise," in *The Cushion in the Road: Meditation and Wandering as the Whole World Awakens to Being in Harm's Way* (New York: New Press, 2013), 50.

30. Melanie Harris, *Ecowomanism: African American Women and Earth-Honoring Faiths* (Maryknoll, NY: Orbis Books, 2017).

31. Alice Walker, "Treasure," in *Anything We Love Can Be Saved* (New York: Random House, 1997); Alice Walker, "African Images: Glimpses from a Tiger's Back," in *Her Blue Body Everything We Know: Earthling Poems, 1965–1990 Complete* (San Diego, CA: Harcourt Brace Jovanovich, 1991), 145.

32. Alice Walker, "Letter to People for the Ethical Treatment of Animals," in *Anything We Love Can Be Saved* (New York: Random House, 1997), 168–69.

33. A. Breeze Harper, "Revisiting Racialized Consciousness and Black Female Vegan Experiences: An Interview," Sistah Vegan Project, December 6, 2009, http://www.sistahvegan. com/2009/12/06/revisiting-racialized-consciousness-and-black-female-vegan-experiences-an-interview/.

34. Delicia Dunham, "On Being Black and Vegan," in *Sistah Vegan: Black Female Vegans Speak on Food, Identity, Health, and Society*, ed. A. Breeze Harper (New York: Lantern Books, 2010), 44.

35. A. Breeze Harper, "Social Justice Beliefs and Addiction to Uncompassionate Consumption: Food for Thought," in *Sistah Vegan: Black Female Vegans Speak on Food, Identity, Health, and Society*, ed. A. Breeze Harper (New York: Lantern Books, 2010), 23, 29.

36. Harper writes after Plumwood's death, but there is considerable overlap in their views as well. Plumwood understands the logic of domination to be the logic of colonization.

37. Val Plumwood, *Environmental Culture: The Ecological Crisis of Reason* (New York: Routledge, 2002), 163.

38. Plumwood, *Environmental Culture*, 159.

39. Val Plumwood, "Animals and Ecology: Toward a Better Integration," in *The Eye of the Crocodile*, ed. Lorraine Shannon (Canberra: Australian National University Press, 2012), 78.

40. Plumwood, "Animals and Ecology," 81.

41. United States Department of Agriculture, Economic Research Service, "Livestock & Meat Domestic Data," https://www.ers.usda.gov/data-products/livestock-meat-domestic-data.aspx.

42. Juliet Clutton-Brock, "Domesticates in Ancient India and Southeast Asia," in *Animals as Domesticates: A World View through History* (East Lansing: Michigan State University Press, 2012), 86–87.

43. Larry C. Price and Debbie M. Price, "India: Toxic Tanneries," *Pulitzer Center Newsletter*, March 9, 2017, https://pulitzercenter.org/reporting/india-toxic-tanneries. It is also important to note the toxic conditions of the tanning industry for the workers and the environment.

44. While wild cattle no longer really exist, in the United States today there are both free-living and domesticated populations of horses, ponies, donkeys, and burros. These populations often interact with the lives and deaths of domesticated cattle. In many cases, the populations of these groups threaten to surpass the carrying capacity of the limited land humans allow for them, and that carrying capacity is expected to include the grazing of cattle as well. Determining what the optimal populations of these various herds are is complicated and controversial. So, too, are the methods for limiting populations. In the 1930s, it was common to kill them and use their meat for pet food. When this practice became unpopular, and then illegal with the passing of the Wild Free-Roaming Horses and Burro Act in 1971, the Bureau of Land Management moved to rounding up and adopting out ponies, horses, donkeys, and burros. There are now competitions for trainers to prepare these animals for successful adoptions. However, there are still ethical problems with making these animals live in confinement and with some of the attempts to rehome them. Working with these animals requires knowledge and skills many regular horse people do not have. This may be especially true for those who adopt donkeys or burros. Further, this program has been used to work around prohibitions on killing and selling these animals for meat: people would adopt these animals and then sell them to dealers who had them slaughtered. One motivation behind the outlawing of horse slaughter in the United States in 2014 was to try to stop this practice. Horses are still shipped to Mexico and Canada for slaughter, however, and it's hard to keep track of every adopted animal. So many people urge the use of contraception to keep these populations at "manageable" levels.

Just like horses, though, despite this special status, many cattle are overloaded, worked too hard, and killed for food and fiber. The situation of cattle and horses around the globe is very much like the story told in *Black Beauty*. They are both still commonly used as "beasts of burden" to haul goods, plow fields, and move people. In this context, it is also important to note that mules, donkeys, and burros are also used as pack animals and for transportation. For many of these animals, there is less understanding of their needs and interests, and they are treated as if they were horses. But they aren't horses. They have different social orders and higher levels of pain tolerance, and they benefit from different training techniques.

45. Varun Nambiar, "India Court Rules in Favor of Legal Person Status for All Animals," *Jurist*, June 3, 2019, https://www.jurist.org/news/2019/06/india-court-rules-in-favor-of-legal-person-status-for-all-animals/.

46. Black Feet Nation, "Iinnii Buffalo Spirit Center," https://blackfeetnation.com/iinnii-buffalo-spirit-center/.

47. Jens Finke, "Maasai—Livestock—Cattle," Blue Gecko, http://www.bluegecko.org/kenya/tribes/maasai/livestock.htm.

48. Sebastian Felix Braun, *Buffalo Inc.: American Indians and Economic Development* (Norman: University of Oklahoma Press, 2008), 46.

49. This quote is taken from a phone conversation in February 2020.

50. The same can be said for the difference between working lines and show lines in most dog breeds.

51. Nicolette Hahn Niman, *Defending Beef: The Case for Sustainable Meat Production* (Hartford, VT: Chelsea Green, 2014), 39, 75, 96.

52. Erin McKenna, *Livestock: Food, Fiber, and Friends* (Athens: University of Georgia Press, 2018), 64–65.

4. PIGS AND POULTRY

1. F. Bailey Norwood and Jayson L. Lusk, *Compassion by the Pound: The Economics of Farm Animal Welfare* (Oxford: Oxford University Press, 2011), 116–17.

2. Norwood and Lusk, *Compassion by the Pound*, 120.

3. Pork Checkoff, "Life Cycle of a Market Pig," https://www.pork.org/facts/pig-farming/life-cycle-of-a-market-pig/.

4. Mark Essig, *Lesser Beasts: A Snout-to-Tail History of the Humble Pig* (New York: Basic Books, 2015), 238.

5. United States Department of Agriculture, Economic Research Service, "Livestock & Meat Domestic Data," https://www.ers.usda.gov/data-products/livestock-meat-domestic-data.aspx.

6. Simon Fairlie, *Meat: A Benign Extravagance* (Hartford, VT: Chelsea Green, 2010).

7. Essig, *Lesser Beasts*, 238.

8. Barry Estabrook, *Pig Tales: An Omnivore's Quest for Sustainable Meat* (New York: Norton, 2015), 222.

9. The cost of humanely raised and ecologically sustainable meat would not be higher than meat from industrial operations if the industrial operations had to pay for the pollution their operations cause.

10. Byron Stein, "Introduction to Commercial Duck Farming," Department of Primary Industries, NSW Government, 2012, http://www.dpi.nsw.gov.au/__data/assets/pdf_file/0009/442854/introduction-to-commercial-duck-farming.pdf.

11. Farm Transparency Project, "Age of Animals Slaughtered," October 12, 2017, https://www.aussieabattoirs.com/facts/age-slaughtered.

12. In her book *Interspecies Ethics* (New York: Columbia University Press, 2014), Cynthia Willett argues that individuals are really nested communities of many organisms. We are each actually "a living web of interspecies communities" (71), each of which helps shape our immune systems, our brains, and our feelings. Microorganisms make us who we are (84).

13. The predominant animal rights views of Tom Regan and animal welfare views of Peter Singer do not challenge the logic, only the placement and treatment of some within the logic.

14. Dick King-Smith, *Babe: The Gallant Pig* (New York: Crown, 1983), 17.

15. Val Plumwood, "'Babe': The Tale of the Speaking Meat," in *The Eye of the Crocodile*, ed. Lorraine Shannon (Canberra: Australian National University Press, 2012), 56.

16. Plumwood, "'Babe,'" 57–58.

17. Plumwood, "'Babe,'" 65.

18. Mike Pearl, "'Babe' Is Now 20-Years-Old, and So Is Star James Cromwell's Animal Rights Crusade," *Vice*, August 6, 2015, https://www.vice.com/en_us/article/4wb3jw/babe-is-20-years-old-so-is-star-james-cromwells-animal-rights-crusade-382.

19. Interestingly, Plumwood uses the same kind of critique to argue against some forms of veganism. She argues that veganism reinforces the animal/plant binary and maintains the value hierarchy that privileges animal life over plant life. This backgrounds the dependence on plant life that holds for all animals and attempts to erase the complex interdependencies found in ecosystems.

20. Hal Herzog, *Some We Love, Some We Hate, Some We Eat* (New York: HarperCollins, 2010), 167.

21. Herzog, *Some We Love*, 167–69.

22. Norwood and Lusk, *Compassion by the Pound*, 114, 116–17, 123.

23. United Egg Producers, "U.S. Egg Production and Hen Population," https://united-egg.com/facts-stats/.

24. Andrew Lawler, *Why Did the Chicken Cross the World? The Epic Saga of the Bird That Powers Civilization* (New York: Atria Books, 2016), 239–42.

25. Something to keep in mind when reading a "no forced molting" label on a carton of eggs.

26. Essig, *Lesser Beasts*, 170.

27. King-Smith, *Babe*, 14–15.

28. Alice Walker, foreword to *The Dreaded Comparison: Human and Animal Slavery*, by Marjorie Spiegel, 2nd ed. (New York: Mirror Books, 1989), 13.

29. Walker, foreword to *The Dreaded Comparison*, 14.

30. Christine M. Korsgaard, *Fellow Creatures: Our Obligations to Other Animals* (Oxford: Oxford University Press, 2018). Korsgaard's position shares something with a pragmatist and feminist approach as she understands value to be perspectival. These various values should be respected, and other creatures should not be treated as mere means. She grants sentience, intelligence, and self-awareness to most other creatures but reserves rationality for humans. This position does not support a notion of human superiority for her, though, and she argues that we should stop using other animals in many of the ways we currently do (e.g., for food and research). But she understands the world to be set up in a way that such use is often unavoidable; she suggests that the dictum that ought to apply does not apply here, and we should do the best we can with regard to other animals and do our best to treat them in ways that are consistent with their own good. Rather than focusing on animals, most of the book focuses on presenting and defending a highly modified Kantian perspective against utilitarian views. This focus limits her ability to truly acknowledge the limits of the Kantian approach on this issue.

31. Plumwood, "'Babe,'" 68.

32. Plumwood, "'Babe,'" 72.

33. Plumwood, "'Babe,'" 74.

34. Plumwood, "'Babe,'" 73.

35. Plumwood, "'Babe,'" 61.

5. WHALES AND FISHES

1. Brain Fagan, *Fishing: How the Sea Fed Civilization* (New Haven, CT: Yale University Press, 2017), 173, 303.

2. Jim Robbins, "Orcas of the Pacific Northwest Are Starving and Disappearing," *New York Times*, July 9, 2018, https://www.nytimes.com/2018/07/09/science/orcas-whales-endangered.html.

3. Diana Reiss, *The Dolphin in the Mirror* (New York: Houghton Mifflin Harcourt, 2011), 199.

4. National Oceanic and Atmospheric Association (NOAA) Fisheries, "Formal Rulemaking on Proposed MMPA Waiver and Hunt Regulations Governing Gray Whale Hunts by the Makah Tribe," https://fisheries.noaa.gov/action/formal-rulemaking-proposed-mmpa-waiver-and-hunt-regulations-governing-gray-whale-hunts-makah.

5. Roger Payne, *Among Whales* (New York: Scribner, 1995), 253.

6. Payne, *Among Whales*, 116–17.

7. Payne, *Among Whales*, 274–88.

8. Payne, *Among Whales*, 298.

9. Payne, *Among Whales*, 253–60.

10. Herman Melville, *Moby-Dick: A Norton Critical Edition*, ed. Hershel Parker and Harrison Hayford (New York: Norton, 2002), 97–98.

11. Melville, *Moby-Dick*, 98.

12. Melville, *Moby-Dick*, 172.

13. Melville, *Moby-Dick*, 139–40, 152–55.

14. Melville, *Moby-Dick*, 173, 175–76.

15. Melville, *Moby-Dick*, 180. Melville notes that whales will often change direction while under water. He calls this behavior deceitful. In contemporary research, one measure used to judge the intelligence of other-than-human animals is whether they engage in deceitful behavior. This is taken as an indication of self-awareness, the awareness of other minds, and intentional planning.

16. Melville, *Moby-Dick*, 231–33.

17. Melville, *Moby-Dick*, 212.

18. Melville, *Moby-Dick*, 198, 277.

19. Melville, *Moby-Dick*, 282.

20. Melville, *Moby-Dick*, 352.

21. Melville, *Moby-Dick*, 354.

22. Melville, *Moby-Dick*, 300–308.

23. Melville, *Moby-Dick*, 203.

24. Melville, *Moby-Dick*, 241.

25. Melville, *Moby-Dick*, 326.

26. Melville, *Moby-Dick*, 240–41.

27. Melville, *Moby-Dick*, 242.

28. Melville, *Moby-Dick*, 242, 266, 317.

29. Reiss, *The Dolphin in the Mirror*, 84.

30. Bernd Würsig and Heidi C. Pearson, "Dolphin Society: Structure and Function," in *Dolphin Communication and Cognition: Past, Present, and Future*, ed. Denise L. Herzing and Christine M. Johnson (Cambridge, MA: MIT Press, 2015), 91–93.

31. Reiss, *The Dolphin in the Mirror*, 122, 127.

32. Hal Whitehead and Luke Randall, *The Cultural Lives of Whales and Dolphins* (Chicago: University of Chicago Press, 2015), 103–7, 111.

33. Whitehead and Randall, *The Cultural Lives of Whales and Dolphins*, 128–30.

34. Whitehead and Randall, *The Cultural Lives of Whales and Dolphins*, 133.

35. Whitehead and Randall, *The Cultural Lives of Whales and Dolphins*, 139–42.

36. Whitehead and Randall, *The Cultural Lives of Whales and Dolphins*, 11, 19, 32.

37. Whitehead and Randall, *The Cultural Lives of Whales and Dolphins*, 65.

38. Whitehead and Randall, *The Cultural Lives of Whales and Dolphins*, 19, 80.

39. Whitehead and Randall, *The Cultural Lives of Whales and Dolphins*, 19, 87–88.

40. Whitehead and Randall, *The Cultural Lives of Whales and Dolphins*, 19, 72, 92, 94.

41. Whitehead and Randall, *The Cultural Lives of Whales and Dolphins*, 270.

42. Alain Locke and B. J. Stern, *When Peoples Meet: A Study in Race and Culture Contacts* (New York: Hinds, 1946), 11.

43. Alain Locke, "Pluralism and Intellectual Democracy," in *The Philosophy of Alain Locke: Harlem Renaissance and Beyond* (Philadelphia: Temple University Press, 1989), 64.

44. Ted Benton, *Natural Relations: Ecology, Animal Rights, and Social Justice* (London: Verso, 1993), 53–54.

45. Reiss, *The Dolphin in the Mirror*, 138, 179–81.

46. Würsig and Pearson, "Dolphin Society: Structure and Function," 77–79.

47. Reiss, *The Dolphin in the Mirror*, 173, 182–88; Würsig and Pearson, "Dolphin Society: Structure and Function," 90.

48. Lori Marino, "The Brain: Evolution, Structure, and Function," in *Dolphin Communication and Cognition: Past, Present, and Future*, ed. Denise L. Herzing and Christine M. Johnson (Cambridge, MA: MIT Press, 2015), 4, 8, 11.

49. Marino, "The Brain," 5–6, 9.

50. Marino, "The Brain," 10, 13.

51. Adam A. Pack, "Experimental Studies of Dolphin Cognition," in *Dolphin Communication and Cognition: Past, Present, and Future*, ed. Denise L. Herzing and Christine M. Johnson (Cambridge, MA: MIT Press, 2015), 176–88.

52. Payne, *Among Whales*, 276.

53. Payne, *Among Whales*, 305–13.

54. Reiss, *The Dolphin in the Mirror*, 111; Nick Pyenson, *Spying on Whales: The Past, Present, and Future of Earth's Most Awesome Creatures* (New York: Viking Press, 2018), 33.

55. Pyenson, *Spying on Whales*, 30, 32.

56. Payne, *Among Whales*, 241.

57. Bernd Heinrich, *Life Everlasting: The Animal Way of Death* (Boston: Mariner Books, 2013), 158–63.

58. Heinrich, *Life Everlasting*, 163.

59. Pyenson, *Spying on Whales*, 118–29.

60. "The Gift of the Whale," as told in *Keepers of the Animals: Native American Stories and Wildlife Activities for Children*, by Michael J. Caduto and Joseph Bruchac, with a foreword by Vine Deloria Jr. (Golden, CO: Fulcrum, 1997), 205.

61. Michael J. Caduto and Joseph Bruchac, *Keepers of the Animals: Native American Stories and Wildlife Activities for Children*, with a foreword by Vine Deloria Jr. (Golden, CO: Fulcrum, 1997), 210.

62. Pyenson, *Spying on Whales*, 2.

63. World Wildlife Fund, "Decreasing Fishstocks," https://wwf.panda.org/knowledge_hub/endangered_species/cetaceans/threats/fishstocks/.

64. Gillian Flaccus, "Oregon Begins Killing Sea Lions after Relocation Fails," *AP News*, January 11, 2019, https://apnews.com/7e0991fa9f7f404e904bb271999b6e59.

65. Fagan, *Fishing*, 173.

66. Fagan, *Fishing*, 178.

67. Jim Lichatowich, *Salmon without Rivers: A History of the Pacific Salmon Crisis* (Washington, DC: Island Press, 1999), 204.

68. Lichatowich, *Salmon without Rivers*, 29.

69. Lichatowich, *Salmon without Rivers*, 91.

70. "Salmon Boy," as told in *Keepers of the Animals: Native American Stories and Wildlife Activities for Children*, by Michael J. Caduto and Joseph Bruchac, with a foreword by Vine Deloria Jr. (Golden, CO: Fulcrum, 1997), 95–97.

71. Lichatowich, *Salmon without Rivers*, 34.

72. Caduto and Bruchac, *Keepers of the Animals*, 98.

73. Fagan, *Fishing*, 164–65, 167.

74. "Chicken of the Sea Parent Company Commits to Combating Slavery in Thai Fishing Industry," *Green American Magazine*, no. 109 (Fall 2017), 5.

75. Fagan, *Fishing*, 169.

76. World Wildlife Fund, "Facts," https://www.worldwildlife.org/species/tuna.

77. Fagan, *Fishing*, 163.

78. Vine Deloria Jr., foreword to *Keepers of the Animals: Native American Stories and Wildlife Activities for Children*, by Michael J. Caduto and Joseph Bruchac (Golden, CO: Fulcrum, 1997), xi.

79. Deloria, foreword to *Keepers of the Animals*, xii.

80. Robin Wall Kimmerer, "Weaving Traditional Ecological Knowledge into Biological Education: A Call to Action," *BioScience* 52, no. 5 (May 2002), 432.

81. Kimmerer, "Weaving Traditional Ecological Knowledge," 434.

82. Kimmerer, "Weaving Traditional Ecological Knowledge," 435.

83. Scott L. Pratt, *Native Pragmatism: Rethinking the Roots of American Philosophy* (Bloomington: Indiana University Press, 2002), xi.

84. Pratt, *Native Pragmatism*, xiii–xiv.

85. Pratt, *Native Pragmatism*, xvi.

86. Kimmerer, "Weaving Traditional Ecological Knowledge," 432–38, 436.

87. Robin Wall Kimmerer, *Braiding Sweetgrass: Indigenous Wisdom and Scientific Knowledge* (Minneapolis, MN: Milkweed Editions, 2015), 382–83.

88. Robin Wall Kimmerer, "Speaking of Nature," *Orion*, June 12, 2017, https://orionmagazine.org/article/speaking-of-nature/.

89. Robin Wall Kimmerer, "A Grammar of Animacy," *Anthropology of Consciousness* 28, no. 2 (Fall 2017), 133.

90. Kimmerer, "Speaking of Nature."

6. PESTS

1. Bernd Heinrich, *Life Everlasting: The Animal Way of Death* (Boston: Mariner Books, 2013), 26–30.

2. Heinrich, *Life Everlasting*, 35.

3. Heinrich, *Life Everlasting*, 112.

4. Heinrich, *Life Everlasting*, 130.

5. "How Poison Came into the World," as told in *Keepers of the Animals: Native American Stories and Wildlife Activities for Children*, by Michael J. Caduto and Joseph Bruchac, with a foreword by Vine Deloria Jr. (Golden, CO: Fulcrum, 1997), 121.

6. "How Grandmother Spider Named the Clans" and "How the Spider Symbol Came to the People," as told in *Keepers of the Animals: Native American Stories and Wildlife Activities for Children*, by Michael J. Caduto and Joseph Bruchac, with a foreword by Vine Deloria Jr. (Golden, CO: Fulcrum, 1997), 29–32.

7. Michael J. Caduto and Joseph Bruchac, *Keepers of the Animals: Native American Stories and Wildlife Activities for Children*, with a foreword by Vine Deloria Jr. (Golden, CO: Fulcrum, 1997), 32–33.

8. Rachel Carson, *Silent Spring* (Boston: Houghton Mifflin, 1962), 127.

9. Carson, *Silent Spring*, 297.

10. Lori Gruen, *Entangled Empathy: An Alternative Ethics for Our Relationships with Animals* (New York: Lantern Books, 2015), 3.

11. Gruen, *Entangled Empathy*, 67.

12. Gruen, *Entangled Empathy*, 70–71.

13. Alina Bradford, "Mouse Facts: Habits, Habitat & Types of Mice," *Live Science*, June 26, 2014, https://www.livescience.com/28028-mice.html.

14. Alina Bradford, "Facts about Rats," *Live Science*, September 30, 2015, https://www.livescience.com/52342-rats.html.

15. Vera Gorbunova, Michael J. Bozzella, and Andrei Seuanov, "Rodents for Comparative Aging Studies: From Mice to Beavers," *Age* 30, no. 2–3 (2008), 111.

16. In this book, I leave aside the question of developing such relationships with rivers, mountains, trees, or ecosystems. I hope to develop that possibility in a future book.

17. E. B. White, *Charlotte's Web* (New York: Harper & Row, 1952), 39–40, 48.

18. White, *Charlotte's Web*, 41.

19. White, *Charlotte's Web*, 46.

20. White, *Charlotte's Web*, 49, 51, 61, 77.

21. White, *Charlotte's Web*, 80.

22. White, *Charlotte's Web*, 90, 94.

23. White, *Charlotte's Web*, 114.

24. White, *Charlotte's Web*, 140.

25. White, *Charlotte's Web*, 146.

26. White, *Charlotte's Web*, 163.

27. White, *Charlotte's Web*, 167.

28. White, *Charlotte's Web*, 171.

29. Gruen, *Entangled Empathy*, 64, 39.

30. Gruen, *Entangled Empathy*, 130.

31. Lori Gruen, *Ethics and Animals: An Introduction* (Cambridge: Cambridge University Press, 2011), 103.

32. Prairie dogs find themselves embroiled in another kind of conflict at First Peoples Buffalo Jump State Park (FPBJ) in Montana, where their burrowing activity now poses a threat to maintaining Native American historical sites that the park preserves for tourism and some Native Americans use for ceremonial sites. The FPBJ Draft Prairie Dog Management Plan from 2016 suggests using live trapping and translocation, physical and natural barriers, raptor perches, toxicants including zinc phosphide and anti-coagulants, lethal trapping, and aluminum phosphide (27). This report makes no mention of consulting with native peoples about this management plan. First Peoples Buffalo Jump State Park, "Draft Prairie Dog Management Plan

and Environmental Assessment," October 2016, http://stateparks.mt.gov/news/publicNotices/environmental-assessments/pn_0063.html.

33. Donna Lybecker, Berton Lee Lamb, and Phadrea D. Ponds, "Public Attitudes and Knowledge of Black-Tailed Prairie Dogs: A Common and Controversial Species," *BioScience* 52, no. 7 (July 2002), 607, 609.

34. American Society of Mammalogists, "Resolution on Prairie Dogs," http://www.mammalogy.org/committees/resolutions/resolution-of-prairie-dogs.

35. Sebastian Felix Braun, *Buffalo Inc.: American Indians and Economic Development* (Norman: University of Oklahoma Press, 2008), 114.

36. Linda Black Elk, "Native Science: Understanding and Respecting Other Ways of Thinking," *Rangelands* 38, no. 1 (2016), 3.

37. Quoted in Braun, *Buffalo Inc.*, 58.

38. With protection, populations of wolves in Europe are starting to recover, and they face conflicts with those who raise livestock animals similar to those found in the United States.

39. Karen E. Lange, "Better Off Alive," *All Animals* (September/October 2018), 18. The article appears online on the Humane Society of the United States website: https://www.humanesociety.org/news/better-alive.

40. Lange, "Better Off Alive," 20.

41. Lange, "Better Off Alive," 21.

42. It is important to note that coyotes are not the only animals killed in contests. Foxes, wolves, and cougars are also regularly targeted. In addition, there are contests focused on "bears, bobcats, crows, deer, feral pigs, frogs, groundhogs, pheasants, porcupines, prairie dogs, opossums, rabbits, rattlesnakes, skunks, squirrels and turkeys" (Lange, "Better Off Alive," 22).

43. Jes Burns, "Oregon Governor Approves Ban on Predator Control 'Cyanide Bombs,'" Oregon Public Broadcasting, May 9, 2019, https://www.opb.org/news/article/oregon-cyanide-bombs-predators-livestock-farming/.

44. Lange, "Better Off Alive," 21.

45. Caduto and Bruchac, *Keepers of the Animals*, 3.

46. Marsha C. Boi, ed., *Stars Above, Earth Below: American Indians and Nature* (Niwot, CO: Roberts Rinehart, 1998), 55–57.

7. CATS AND CANINES

1. Robert H. Busch, *The Wolf Almanac, New and Revised: A Celebration of Wolves and Their World* (Guilford, CT: Lyons Press, 2007), 115.

2. Busch, *The Wolf Almanac*, 43.

3. Brenda Peterson, *Wolf Nation: The Life, Death, and Return of Wild American Wolves* (Boston: Da Capo, 2017), 106.

4. Busch, *The Wolf Almanac*, 1.

5. Jeanna Bryner, "House Cats' Wild Ancestor Found," *Live Science*, June 28, 2007, https://www.livescience.com/7299-house-cats-wild-ancestor.html.

6. Jerry Kobalenko, *Forest Cats of North America: Cougars, Bobcat, Lynx* (Buffalo, NY: Firefly Books, 1997), 107.

7. Kobalenko, *Forest Cats*, 4.

8. Rudyard Kipling, *The Jungle Book* (New York: Macmillan, 1894; Project Gutenberg, 2006, last updated 2016), 42, https://www.gutenberg.org/files/236/236-h/236-h.htm.

9. Joy Adamson, *Born Free: A Lioness of Two Worlds* (New York: Pantheon Books, 1960), 148.

10. Kobalenko, *Forest Cats*, 4.

11. Kobalenko, *Forest Cats*, 38–44.

12. Kobalenko, *Forest Cats*, 10, 15.

13. Kobalenko, *Forest Cats*, 52.

14. Kobalenko, *Forest Cats*, 8–12.

15. Kobalenko, *Forest Cats*, 84.

16. California Department of Fish and Wildlife, "Verified Mountain Lion-Human Attacks," https://wildlife.ca.gov/Conservation/Mammals/Mountain-Lion/Attacks.

17. Kobalenko, *Forest Cats*, 80–83.

18. Kobalenko, *Forest Cats*, 12, 83.

19. Kobalenko, *Forest Cats*, 23–26.

20. Kobalenko, *Forest Cats*, 30–34, 37.

21. Peterson, *Wolf Nation*, 244. This mirrors the intentional introduction of diseases, such as smallpox, in order to kill Native Americans.

22. Peterson, *Wolf Nation*, 16, 79.

23. Peterson, *Wolf Nation*, 6–9.

24. Daniel Dyer, "A Reader's Companion," in *The Call of the Wild*, by Jack London (Norman: University of Oklahoma Press, 1995), 220.

25. The term *Eskimo* has fallen out of favor in recent years, but it is used here because that is the word that appears in the original book.

26. Jean Craighead George, *Julie of the Wolves*, illustrated by John Schoenherr (New York: HarperCollins, 1972), 6.

27. George, *Julie of the Wolves*, 15.

28. George, *Julie of the Wolves*, 18–25.

29. George, *Julie of the Wolves*, 31–34.

30. George, *Julie of the Wolves*, 133.

31. George, *Julie of the Wolves*, 134.

32. George, *Julie of the Wolves*, 140–50.

33. Jean Craighead George, *Julie*, illustrated by Wendell Minor (New York: HarperCollins, 1994), 113.

34. George, *Julie*, 221.

35. Peterson, *Wolf Nation*, 14.

36. Busch, *The Wolf Almanac*, 32–34, 47, 73.

37. Nate Blakeslee, *American Wolf: A True Story of Survival and Obsession in the West* (New York: Crown, 2017), 183–86; Peterson, *Wolf Nation*, 70.

38. Peterson, *Wolf Nation*, 77.

39. Peterson, *Wolf Nation*, 164.

40. Daniel Dyer, introduction to *The Call of the Wild*, by Jack London (Norman: University of Oklahoma Press, 1995), xxx.

41. Jack London, *The Call of the Wild*, with an illustrated reader's companion by Daniel Dyer (Norman: University of Oklahoma Press, 1995), 18–19.

42. London, *The Call of the Wild*, 34–35.

43. The 1935 film based on the book really had very little to do with dogs and wolves at all.

44. London, *The Call of the Wild*, 52.

45. London, *The Call of the Wild*, 65–72.

46. Jack London, *White Fang* (New York: Arcadia House, 1950), 3–35.

47. Peterson, *Wolf Nation*, 105.

48. London, *White Fang*, 73–84.

49. London, *White Fang*, 91–92.

50. London, *White Fang*, 94.

51. London, *White Fang*, 109.

52. London, *White Fang*, 113–19.

53. London, *White Fang*, 131.

54. London, *White Fang*, 137–40.

55. London, *White Fang*, 143. The use of the word *savage* here is in keeping with the times and the savage/civilized divide that was present in anthropology and other disciplines. Humans who were deemed to be savage were seen as beastlike.

56. London, *White Fang*, 152.

57. London, *White Fang*, 156–57.

58. London, *White Fang*, 195.

59. London, *White Fang*, 216–40.

60. London, *White Fang*, 259.

61. Blakeslee, *American Wolf*, 14, 23.

62. Blakeslee, *American Wolf*, 66–67, 110–12, 132, 190–93, 196.

63. Peterson, *Wolf Nation*, 46–47.

64. Blakeslee, *American Wolf*, 131.

65. Peterson, *Wolf Nation*, 146.

66. Blakeslee, *American Wolf*, 102–5, 249–51.

67. Peterson, *Wolf Nation*, 125–26, 201.

68. Peterson, *Wolf Nation*, 149–50.

69. Peterson, *Wolf Nation*, 209.

70. Jane Addams, *Democracy and Social Ethics*, ed. Charlene Haddock Seigfried (Urbana: University of Illinois Press, 2002), 69.

71. Peterson, *Wolf Nation*, 189, 192.

72. To help keep things in perspective, it is worth noting that in "North America, healthy wild wolves have not been documented to kill anyone since European colonization" (348) and that "livestock depredations are rare, that competition for wild ungulates is minimal, and there have been virtually no restrictions of human recreational or commercial activities to enhance wolf survival and restoration" (346). Edward E. Bangs et al., "Managing Wolf-Human Conflict in the Northwestern United States," in *People and Wildlife: Conflict or Coexistence?*, ed. Rosie Woodroffe, Simon Thirgood, and Alan Rabinowitz (New York: Cambridge University Press, 2005).

73. Peterson, *Wolf Nation*, 198.

74. Peterson, *Wolf Nation*, 250.

75. Peterson, *Wolf Nation*, 210.

76. Peterson, *Wolf Nation*, 212.

77. Twowolves, "Cowlitz Tribal Newspaper Article Was Printed," Protect the Wolves, May 25, 2017, https://protectthewolves.com/cowlitz-tribal-news-paper-article-was-printed/.

78. Twowolves, "Cowlitz Tribal Newspaper Article Was Printed."

79. Alice Walker, "Democratic Womanism," in *The World Will Follow Joy* (New York: New Press, 2015), 177–78.

80. Alice Walker, introduction to *Anything We Love Can Be Saved* (New York: Random House, 1997), xxii.

81. Alice Walker, introduction to *Anything We Love Can Be Saved*, xxv.

82. Alice Walker, "The Only Reason You Want to Go to Heaven Is That You Have Been Driven Out of Your Mind (Off Your Land and Out of Your Lover's Arms)," in *Anything We Love Can Be Saved* (New York: Random House, 1997), 4.

83. Alice Walker, "After Many Years and Much Silliness," in *The World Will Follow Joy* (New York: New Press, 2015), 185.

84. Walker, "The Only Reason You Want to Go to Heaven," 9, 17, 25–26.

85. Alice Walker, "What Can I Give My Daughters, Who Are Brave?" in *Anything We Love Can Be Saved* (New York: Random House, 1997), 106–7.

86. Alice Walker, "Who?" in *Her Blue Body Everything We Know: Earthling Poems, 1965–1990 Complete* (San Diego, CA: Harcourt Brace Jovanovich, 1991), 378.

87. Alice Walker, "No One Can Watch the Wasichu," in *Her Blue Body Everything We Know: Earthling Poems, 1965–1990 Complete* (San Diego, CA: Harcourt Brace Jovanovich, 1991), 385.

88. Alice Walker, "The Right to Life: What Can the White Man Say to the Black Woman?" in *Her Blue Body Everything We Know: Earthling Poems, 1965–1990 Complete* (San Diego, CA: Harcourt Brace Jovanovich, 1991), 446.

8. LIVING WITH ANIMALS REVISITED

1. David Grimm, "Record Number of Monkeys Being Used in U.S. Research," *Science* (November 2018), https://www.sciencemag.org/news/2018/11/record-number-monkeys-being-used-us-research.

2. Mark Strauss, "Americans Are Divided over the Use of Animals in Scientific Research," Pew Research Center, August 16, 2018, https://www.pewresearch.org/fact-tank/2018/08/16/americans-are-divided-over-the-use-of-animals-in-scientific-research/.

3. Kent Scientific Corporation, "Animal Research Plays a Key Role in Developing Important Vaccines," June 25, 2018, https://www.kentscientific.com/blog/animal-research-plays-a-key-role-in-developing-important-vaccines/.

4. Volker Gerdts et al., "Large Animal Models for Vaccine Development and Testing," *ILAR Journal* (Institute for Laboratory Animal Research) 56, no. 1 (May 2015), https://academic.oup.com/ilarjournal/article/56/1/53/661264.

5. Gerdts et al., "Large Animal Models."

6. David Benatar, "Our Cruel Treatment of Animals Led to the Coronavirus: The Conditions That Lead to the Emergence of New Infectious Diseases Are the Same Ones That Inflict Horrific Harms on Animals," The Stone, *New York Times*, April 13, 2020, https://www.nytimes.com/2020/04/13/opinion/animal-cruelty-coronavirus.html.

7. Tim McDonnell, "How Monkeys, Ferrets, and Horses Are Helping Scientists Fight Covid-19," *Quartz*, April 13, 2020, https://qz.com/1837094/how-lab-animals-are-helping-scientists-fight-covid-19/.

8. Benatar, "Our Cruel Treatment of Animals Led to the Coronavirus."

9. It is also worth noting that the problematic conditions of livestock slaughter in the United States are now becoming more apparent, as meat processing plants have been centers of the COVID-19 outbreak. Rather than change our eating habits, though, these plants have been ordered to remain in operation despite the risk to human health in the plant and the surrounding communities.

10. David Biello, "My Morning Cup of Coffee Kills Monkeys," *Scientific American*, June 6, 2012, https://blogs.scientificamerican.com/observations/my-morning-cup-of-coffee-kills-monkeys/; "Sugar Cane Farming's Toll on the Environment," *World Wildlife Magazine* (Summer 2015), https://www.worldwildlife.org/magazine/issues/summer-2015/articles/sugarcane-farming-s-toll-on-the-environment; Brandon Keim, "The Surprisingly Complicated Math of How Many Wild Animals Are Killed in Agriculture," *Anthropocene*, July 18, 2018, https://www.anthropocenemagazine.org/2018/07/how-many-animals-killed-in-agriculture/; B. Fischer and A. Lamey, "Field Deaths in Plant Agriculture," *Journal of Agricultural and Environmental Ethics* 31, no. 4 (2018): 409–28; "Illegal Cocoa Farms Threaten Primates," *Science Connected*, April 2, 2015, https://magazine.scienceconnected.org/2015/04/illegal-cocoa-farms-threaten-primates/.

11. I do take up some of these issues in my book *Livestock: Food, Fiber, and Friends*, but there are many good books exposing the darker side of the human costs of our food production systems.

12. Dogs who can sense a person's dropping insulin levels or the onset of a seizure also come about as a result of both breeding and training.

13. Robin Wall Kimmerer, "Speaking of Nature," *Orion*, June 12, 2017, https://orionmagazine.org/article/speaking-of-nature/.

Bibliography

Adams, Carol. "Why I Became a Vegetarian." *Carol J. Adams* (blog), September 6, 2015. https://caroljadams.com/carol-adams-blog/why-i-became-a-vegetarian.

Adamson, Joy. *Born Free: A Lioness of Two Worlds*. New York: Pantheon Books, 1960.

Addams, Jane. *Democracy and Social Ethics*. Edited by Charlene Haddock Seigfried. Urbana: University of Illinois Press, 2002.

American Civil War Homepage. "Life and Death of the Civil War Horse: From Barn to Battlefield to Bullets to Burial." In *Civil War Horse History and Facts: Union and Confederate Horses*. http://www.thomaslegion.net/americancivilwar/totalcivilwarhorseskilled.html.

American Society of Mammalogists. "Resolution on Prairie Dogs." http://www.mammalogy.org/committees/resolutions/resolution-of-prairie-dogs.

Bale, Rachael. "This Government Program's Job Is to Kill Wildlife." *National Geographic*, February 12, 2016. https://www.nationalgeographic.com/news/2016/02/160212-Wildlife-Services-predator-control-livestock-trapping-hunting/.

Bangs, Edward E., et al. "Managing Wolf-Human Conflict in the Northwestern United States." In *People and Wildlife: Conflict or Coexistence?*, edited by Rosie Woodroffe, Simon Thirgood, and Alan Rabinowitz, 340–56. New York: Cambridge University Press.

Barth, Friedrich G. *A Spider's World: Senses and Behavior*. Translated by M. A. Biedermann-Thorson. New York: Springer, 2002.

Beasley, David. "U.S. Orangutan Chantek, 'the Ape Who Went to College,' Dies at 39." Reuters Environment, August 8, 2017. https://www.reuters.com/article/us-georgia-orangutan-idUSKBN1AO29J.

Benatar, David. "Our Cruel Treatment of Animals Led to the Coronavirus: The Conditions That Lead to the Emergence of New Infectious Diseases Are the Same Ones That Inflict Horrific Harms on Animals." The Stone, *New York Times*, April 13, 2020. https://www.nytimes.com/2020/04/13/opinion/animal-cruelty-coronavirus.html.

Benton, Ted. *Natural Relations: Ecology, Animal Rights, and Social Justice*. London: Verso, 1993.

Biello, David. "My Morning Cup of Coffee Kills Monkeys." *Scientific American*, June 6, 2012. https://blogs.scientificamerican.com/observations/my-morning-cup-of-coffee-kills-monkeys/.

Big Cat Rescue. "Bobcats Are Often Targets of Sport Hunters." December 5, 2010. https://bigcatrescue.org/bobcats-are-often-targets-of-sport-hunters/.

Big Cats Wild Cats. "Wild Cats of North America." https://bigcatswildcats.com/countries/wild-cats-north-america/.

Black Elk, Linda. "Native Science: Understanding and Respecting Other Ways of Thinking." *Rangelands* 38, no. 1 (2016): 3–4.

Black Feet Nation. "Iinnii Buffalo Spirit Center." https://blackfeetnation.com/iinnii-buffalo-spirit-center/.

Blakeslee, Nate. *American Wolf: A True Story of Survival and Obsession in the West.* New York: Crown, 2017.

Boi, Marsha C., ed. *Stars Above, Earth Below: American Indians and Nature.* Niwot, CO: Roberts Rinehart, 1998.

Boyle, Louise. "Jane Goodall Calls for Global Ban on Wildlife Trade and End to 'Destructive and Greedy Period of Human History.'" *Independent*, April 11, 2020. https://www.independent.co.uk/environment/jane-goodall-interview-animal-markets-wildlife-trafficking-a9458611.html.

Bradford, Alina. "Facts about Rats." *Live Science*, September 30, 2015. https://www.livescience.com/52342-rats.html.

———. "Mouse Facts: Habits, Habitat & Types of Mice." *Live Science*, June 26, 2014. https://www.livescience.com/28028-mice.html.

Bradley, Richard A. *Common Spiders of North America.* Berkeley and Los Angeles: University of California Press, 2013.

Braun, Sebastian Felix. *Buffalo Inc.: American Indians and Economic Development.* Norman: University of Oklahoma Press, 2008.

Brown, Sheila. "The Six Wildcats of North America." Owlcation, last updated December 13, 2018. https://owlcation.com/stem/The-Four-Wildcats-of-North-America.

Brulliard, Karin. "The Next Pandemic Is Already Coming, Unless Humans Change How We Interact with Wildlife, Scientists Say." *Washington Post*, April 3, 2020. https://www.washingtonpost.com/science/2020/04/03/coronavirus-wildlife-environment/.

Bryner, Jeanna. "House Cats' Wild Ancestor Found." *Live Science*, June 28, 2007. https://www.livescience.com/7299-house-cats-wild-ancestor.html.

Buotte, Polly C., Maurice G. Hornocker, and Toni K. Ruth. *Yellowstone Cougars: Ecology before and during Wolf Restoration.* Louisville: University Press of Colorado, 2019.

Burns, Jes. "Oregon Governor Approves Ban on Predator Control 'Cyanide Bombs.'" Oregon Public Broadcasting, May 9, 2019. https://www.opb.org/news/article/oregon-cyanide-bombs-predators-livestock-farming/.

Busch, Robert H. *The Wolf Almanac, New and Revised: A Celebration of Wolves and Their World.* Guilford, CT: Lyons Press, 2007.

Butynski, Thomas M. "Africa's Great Apes." In *Great Apes and Humans: The Ethics of Coexistence*, edited by Benjamin B. Beck et al., 3–56. Washington, DC: Smithsonian Institution Press, 2001.

Byers, Thomas. "U.S. Poisonous Spiders: Black Widow, Brown Recluse, & Hobo." Dengarden, last updated January 18, 2018. https://dengarden.com/pest-control/Spider-Information.

Caduto, Michael J., and Joseph Bruchac. *Keepers of the Animals: Native American Stories and Wildlife Activities for Children.* Foreword by Vine Deloria Jr. Golden, CO: Fulcrum, 1997.

California Department of Fish and Wildlife. "Verified Mountain Lion–Human Attacks." https://wildlife.ca.gov/Conservation/Mammals/Mountain-Lion/Attacks.

Carson, Rachel. *Silent Spring.* Boston: Houghton Mifflin, 1962.

Centers for Disease Control and Prevention. "Venomous Spiders." https://www.cdc.gov/niosh/topics/spiders/default.html.

Chantek Foundation. "Project Chantek." https://chantek.org/project-chantek.

"Chicken of the Sea Parent Company Commits to Combating Slavery in Thai Fishing Industry." *Green American*, no. 109 (Fall 2017).

Chimpanzee Sanctuary Northwest. https://chimpsnw.org.

Chimposium Script. Ellensburg, WA: Chimpanzee and Human Communication Institute, 2000.

Clark, Ann Nolan. *Bringer of the Mystery Dog—Sunk Wan Wak'an Agli Kin He*. Sioux text by Emil Afraid of Hawk. Illustrated by Oscar Howe. United States Indian Service, 1943. Hathi Trust Digital Library. https://babel.hathitrust.org/cgi/pt?id=uc1.b5120464&view=1up&seq=14.

Clutton-Brock, Juliet. "Domesticates in Ancient India and Southeast Asia." In *Animals as Domesticates: A World View through History*, 81–98. East Lansing: Michigan State University Press, 2012.

Cougar Fund. "Historical Timeline." https://www.cougarfund.org/education/historical-timeline/.

Culin, Joseph, Herbert W. Levi, and Lorna R. Levi. "Spider: Arachnid." In *Encyclopaedia Britannica Online*, last updated June 1, 2020. https://www.britannica.com/animal/spider-arachnid.

Deloria, Vine, Jr. Foreword to *Keepers of the Animals: Native American Stories and Wildlife Activities for Children*, by Michael J. Caduto and Joseph Bruchac. Golden, CO: Fulcrum, 1997.

Dewey, John. *Human Nature and Conduct*. In *The Middle Works of John Dewey*. Vol. 14, edited by Jo Ann Boydston. Carbondale: Southern Illinois University Press, 1988.

Dunham, Delicia. "On Being Black and Vegan." In *Sistah Vegan: Black Female Vegans Speak on Food, Identity, Health, and Society*, edited by A. Breeze Harper, 42–46. New York: Lantern Books, 2010.

Dyer, Daniel. Introduction to *The Call of the Wild*, by Jack London. Norman: University of Oklahoma Press, 1995.

———. "A Reader's Companion." In *The Call of the Wild*, by Jack London. Norman: University of Oklahoma Press, 1995.

Equo. "The Horse Industry by the Numbers." January 16, 2017. https://www.ridewithequo.com/blog/the-horse-industry-by-the-numbers.

Essig, Mark. *Lesser Beasts: A Snout-to-Tail History of the Humble Pig*. New York: Basic Books, 2015.

Estabrook, Barry. *Pig Tales: An Omnivore's Quest for Sustainable Meat*. New York: Norton, 2015.

Fagan, Brian. *Fishing: How the Sea Fed Civilization*. New Haven, CT: Yale University Press, 2017.

Fairlie, Simon. *Meat: A Benign Extravagance*. Hartford, VT: Chelsea Green, 2010.

Farm Transparency Project. "Age of Animals Slaughtered." October 12, 2017. https://www.aussieabattoirs.com/facts/age-slaughtered.

Finke, Jens. "Maasai—Livestock—Cattle." Blue Gecko. http://www.bluegecko.org/kenya/tribes/maasai/livestock.htm.

First Peoples Buffalo Jump State Park. "Draft Prairie Dog Management Plan and Environmental Assessment." October 2016. http://stateparks.mt.gov/news/publicNotices/environmental-assessments/pn_0063.html.

Fischer, B., and A. Lamey. "Field Deaths in Plant Agriculture." *Journal of Agricultural and Environmental Ethics* 31, no. 4 (2018): 409–28.

Flaccus, Gillian. "Oregon Begins Killing Sea Lions after Relocation Fails." *AP News*, January 11, 2019. https://apnews.com/7e0991fa9f7f404e904bb271999b6e59.

Flores, Dan. *Coyote America: A Natural and Supernatural History*. New York: Basic Books, 2016.

Fouts, Roger. "Darwinian Reflections on Our Fellow Apes." In *Great Apes and Humans: The Ethics of Coexistence*, edited by Benjamin E. Beck et al., 191–211. Washington, DC: Smithsonian Institution Press, 2001.

———. *Next of Kin: My Conversations with Chimpanzees*. New York: Avon Books, 1997.

George, Jean Craighead. *Julie*. Illustrated by Wendell Minor. New York: HarperCollins, 1994.

———. *Julie of the Wolves*. Illustrated by John Schoenherr. New York: HarperCollins, 1972.

Gerdts, Volker, et al. "Large Animal Models for Vaccine Development and Testing." *ILAR Journal* (Institute for Laboratory Animal Research) 56, no. 1 (May 2015): 53–62. https://academic.oup.com/ilarjournal/article/56/1/53/661264.

"The Gift of the Whale." As told in *Keepers of the Animals: Native American Stories and Wildlife Activities for Children*, by Michael J. Caduto and Joseph Bruchac, with a foreword by Vine Deloria Jr., 205. Golden, CO: Fulcrum, 1997.

Gilman, Charlotte Perkins. *Herland*. New York: Pantheon Books, 1979. Originally published in 1915.

———. *His Religion and Hers*. Westport, CT: Hyperion, 1923.

———. *The Man-Made World, or Our Androcentric Culture*. Amherst, NY: Humanity Books, 2001.

———. *Moving the Mountain*. New York: Charlton, 1911.

———. "When I Was a Witch." In *The Charlotte Perkins Gilman Reader*, edited by Ann J. Lane, 21–31. New York: Pantheon Books, 1980.

———. *With Her in Ourland: Sequel to Herland*. Edited by Mary Jo Deegan and Michael R. Hill. Westport, CT: Greenwood, 1997.

———. *Women and Economics: A Study of the Economic Relation between Men and Women as a Factor in Social Evolution*. New York: Harper & Row, 1966.

Gonzaga, Marcelo O., and Carmen Viera, eds. *Behaviour and Ecology of Spiders: Contributions from the Neotropical Region*. New York: Springer, 2018.

Gorbunova, Vera, Michael J. Bozzella, and Andrei Seuanov. "Rodents for Comparative Aging Studies: From Mice to Beavers." *Age* 30, no. 2–3 (2008): 111–19.

Grimm, David. "Record Number of Monkeys Being Used in U.S. Research." *Science* (November 2018). https://www.sciencemag.org/news/2018/11/record-number-monkeys-being-used-us-research.

Gruen, Lori. *Entangled Empathy: An Alternative Ethics for Our Relationships with Animals*. New York: Lantern Books, 2015.

———. *Ethics and Animals: An Introduction*. Cambridge: Cambridge University Press, 2011.

Harper, A. Breeze. "Revisiting Racialized Consciousness and Black Female Vegan Experiences: An Interview." Sistah Vegan Project, December 6, 2009. http://www.sistahvegan.com/2009/12/06/revisiting-racialized-consciousness-and-black-female-vegan-experiences-an-interview/.

———, ed. *Sistah Vegan: Black Female Vegans Speak on Food, Identity, Health, and Society*. New York: Lantern Books, 2010.

———. "Social Justice Beliefs and Addiction to Uncompassionate Consumption: Food for Thought." In *Sistah Vegan: Black Female Vegans Speak on Food, Identity, Health, and Society*, edited by A. Breeze Harper, 20–41. New York: Lantern Books, 2010.

Harris, Melanie. *Ecowomanism: African American Women and Earth-Honoring Faiths*. Maryknoll, NY: Orbis Books, 2017.

Heinrich, Bernd. *Life Everlasting: The Animal Way of Death*. Boston: Mariner Books, 2013.

Herberstein, Marie Elisabeth, ed. *Spider Behaviour: Flexibility and Versatility*. Cambridge: Cambridge University Press, 2011.

Herzing, Denise L., and Christine M. Johnson, eds. *Dolphin Communication and Cognition: Past, Present, and Future*. Cambridge, MA: MIT Press, 2015.

Herzog, Hal. *Some We Love, Some We Hate, Some We Eat*. New York: HarperCollins, 2010.

Heyes, H. A. *Curious George*. Boston: Houghton Mifflin, 1941.

———. *Curious George Gets a Medal*. Boston: Houghton Mifflin, 1957.

———. *Curious George Takes a Job*. Boston: Houghton Mifflin, 1947.

"How Grandmother Spider Named the Clans." As told in *Keepers of the Animals: Native American Stories and Wildlife Activities for Children*, by Michael J. Caduto and Joseph Bruchac, with a foreword by Vine Deloria Jr., 29–30. Golden, CO: Fulcrum, 1997.

"How Poison Came into the World." As told in *Keepers of the Animals: Native American Stories and Wildlife Activities for Children*, by Michael J. Caduto and Joseph Bruchac, with a foreword by Vine Deloria Jr., 121. Golden, CO: Fulcrum, 1997.

"How the Spider Symbol Came to the People." As told in *Keepers of the Animals: Native American Stories and Wildlife Activities for Children*, by Michael J. Caduto and Joseph Bruchac, with a foreword by Vine Deloria Jr., 31. Golden, CO: Fulcrum, 1997.

Humane Society of the United States. "Animals Used in Biomedical Research FAQ." Accessed August 23, 2018. https://www.humanesociety.org/animals/monkeys/qa/questions_answers. html.

"Illegal Cocoa Farms Threaten Primates." *Science Connected*, April 2, 2015. https://magazine.scienceconnected.org/2015/04/illegal-cocoa-farms-threaten-primates/.

Insect Identification. "North American Spiders." https://www.insectidentification.org/spiders.asp.

James, William. "The Will to Believe." In *The Writing of William James*, edited by John J. McDermott. Chicago: University of Chicago Press, 1977.

———. "A World of Pure Experience." In *The Writing of William James*, edited by John J. McDermott. Chicago: University of Chicago Press, 1977.

Johnston, Lyla June. "Yes World, There Were Horses in Native Culture before the Settlers Came." *Indian Country Today*, July 3, 2019. https://newsmaven.io/indiancountrytoday/news/yes-world-there-were-horses-in-native-culture-before-the-settlers-came-JGqPrqLm Zk-3ka-IBqNWiQ.

Kaplan, Gisela, and Lesley J. Rogers. *The Orangutans: Their Evolution, Behavior, and Future*. Cambridge, MA: Perseus, 2000.

Kaston, B. J. "Some Little Known Aspects of Spider Behavior." *American Midland Naturalist* 73, no. 2 (1965): 336–56.

Keim, Brandon. "The Surprisingly Complicated Math of How Many Wild Animals Are Killed in Agriculture." *Anthropocene*, July 18, 2018. https://www.anthropocenemagazine.org/2018/07/how-many-animals-killed-in-agriculture/.

Kent Scientific Corporation. "Animal Research Plays a Key Role in Developing Important Vaccines." June 25, 2018. https://www.kentscientific.com/blog/animal-research-plays-a-key-role-in-developing-important-vaccines/.

Kentucky Equine Research Staff. "Common Genetic Diseases in Quarter Horses." *Equinews*, March 8, 2013. https://ker.com/equinews/common-genetic-diseases-quarter-horses/.

Ketcham, Christopher. "A Biocentrist History of the West." *Harper's Magazine*, February 15, 2016. https://harpers.org/blog/2016/02/a-biocentrist-history-of-the-west/.

———. "The Rogue Agency." *Harper's Magazine*, March 2016. https://harpers.org/archive/2016/03/the-rogue-agency/.

Kimmerer, Robin Wall. *Braiding Sweetgrass: Indigenous Wisdom and Scientific Knowledge.* Minneapolis, MN: Milkweed Editions, 2015.

———. "A Grammar of Animacy." *Anthropology of Consciousness* 28, no. 2 (Fall 2017): 128–34.

———. "Speaking of Nature." *Orion*, June 12, 2017. https://orionmagazine.org/article/speaking-of-nature/.

———. "Weaving Traditional Ecological Knowledge into Biological Education: A Call to Action." *BioScience* 52, no. 5 (May 2002): 432–38.

King-Smith, Dick. *Babe: The Gallant Pig.* New York: Crown, 1983.

Kipling, Rudyard. *The Jungle Book.* New York: Macmillan, 1894. Project Gutenberg, 2006, last updated 2016. https://www.gutenberg.org/files/236/236-h/236-h.htm.

Kobalenko, Jerry. *Forest Cats of North America: Cougars, Bobcat, Lynx.* Buffalo, NY: Firefly Books, 1997.

Korsgaard, Christine M. *Fellow Creatures: Our Obligations to Other Animals.* Oxford: Oxford University Press, 2018.

Lange, Karen E. "Better Off Alive." *All Animals* (September/October 2018): 18–22.

———. "Eating for Tomorrow: Why Eating More Plant-Based Meals Matters." *All Animals* (June/July/August 2019): 22–25.

Lawler, Andrew. *Why Did the Chicken Cross the World? The Epic Saga of the Bird That Powers Civilization.* New York: Atria Books, 2016.

Lichatowich, Jim. *Salmon without Rivers: A History of the Pacific Salmon Crisis.* Washington, DC: Island Press, 1999.

Locke, Alain. "Pluralism and Intellectual Democracy." In *The Philosophy of Alain Locke: Harlem Renaissance and Beyond.* Philadelphia: Temple University Press, 1989.

Locke, Alain, and B. J. Stern. *When Peoples Meet: A Study in Race and Culture Contacts.* New York: Hinds, 1946.

Lofting, Hugh. "Dr. Dolittle's Circus." In *Dr. Dolittle: A Treasury.* Philadelphia: Lippincott, 1967.

London, Jack. *The Call of the Wild.* With an illustrated reader's companion by Daniel Dyer. Norman: University of Oklahoma Press, 1995.

———. *White Fang.* New York: Arcadia House, 1950.

Low, Phillip. "The Cambridge Declaration on Consciousness." Edited by Jaak Panksepp, Diana Reiss, David Edelman, Bruno Van Swinderen, Philip Low, and Christof Koch. Presented at the Francis Crick Memorial Conference on Consciousness in Human and Non-Human Animals, Churchill College, University of Cambridge, July 7, 2012. http://fcmconference.org/img/CambridgeDeclarationOnConsciousness.pdf.

Lusk, Jayson L., and F. Bailey Norwood. *Compassion by the Pound: The Economics of Farm Animal Welfare.* New York: Oxford University Press, 2011.

Lybecker, Donna, Berton Lee Lamb, and Phadrea D. Ponds. "Public Attitudes and Knowledge of Black-Tailed Prairie Dogs: A Common and Controversial Species." *BioScience* 52, no. 7 (July 2002): 607–13.

Maasai Wilderness Conservation Trust. "The Maasai." http://maasaiwilderness.org/maasai/.

Marino, Lori. "The Brain: Evolution, Structure, and Function." In *Dolphin Communication and Cognition: Past, Present, and Future*, edited by Denise L. Herzing and Christine M. Johnson, 3–18. Cambridge, MA: MIT Press, 2015.

McDonnell, Tim. "How Monkeys, Ferrets, and Horses Are Helping Scientists Fight Covid-19." *Quartz*, April 13, 2020. https://qz.com/1837094/how-lab-animals-are-helping-scientists-fight-covid-19/.

McKenna, Erin. *Livestock: Food, Fiber, and Friends.* Athens: University of Georgia Press, 2018.

———. *Pets, People, and Pragmatism.* New York: Fordham University Press, 2013.

McKenna, Erin, and Scott L. Pratt. *American Philosophy: From Wounded Knee to the Present.* New York: Bloomsbury, 2015.

Mekonnen, Serkalem. "Brown Recluse Spider Bites." Poison Control, October 2014. https://www.poison.org/articles/2014-oct/brown-recluse-spider-bites.

Melville, Herman. *Moby-Dick: A Norton Critical Edition.* Edited by Hershel Parker and Harrison Hayford. New York: Norton, 2002.

Mills, Charles. *The Racial Contract.* Ithaca, NY: Cornell University Press, 1997.

Milne, Lorus Johnson, and Margery Milne. *The Audubon Society Field Guide to North American Insects and Spiders.* New York: Knopf, 1996.

Mullen, William. "Lincoln Park Zoo out to Save Chimps from Private Pet Trade." *Chicago Tribune,* August 25, 2010. https://www.chicagotribune.com/news/ct-xpm-2010-08-25-ct-met-chimpcare-20100825-story.html.

Nambiar, Varun. "India Court Rules in Favor of Legal Person Status for All Animals." *Jurist,* June 3, 2019. https://www.jurist.org/news/2019/06/india-court-rules-in-favor-of-legal-person-status-for-all-animals/.

National Oceanic and Atmospheric Association (NOAA) Fisheries. "Formal Rulemaking on Proposed MMPA Waiver and Hunt Regulations Governing Gray Whale Hunts by the Makah Tribe." https://fisheries.noaa.gov/action/formal-rulemaking-proposed-mmpa-waiver-and-hunt-regulations-governing-gray-whale-hunts-makah.

———. "Makah Tribal Whale Hunt." https://www.fisheries.noaa.gov/west-coast/makah-tribal-whale-hunt.

———. "Some Good News for Pacific Bluefin Tuna." August 10, 2018. https://www.fisheries.noaa.gov/news/some-good-news-pacific-bluefin-tuna.

Native American Legends. "The Orphan Boy and the Elk Dog: A Blackfoot Legend." https://www.firstpeople.us/FP-Html-Legends/TheOrphanBoyAndTheElkDog-Blackfoot.html.

Natterson-Horwitz, Barbara, and Kathryn Bowers. *Zoobiquity: The Astonishing Connection between Human and Animal Health.* New York: Vintage Books, 2013.

Niman, Nicolette Hahn. *Defending Beef: The Case for Sustainable Meat Production.* Hartford, VT: Chelsea Green, 2014.

Norwood, F. Bailey, and Jayson L. Lusk. *Compassion by the Pound: The Economics of Farm Animal Welfare.* Oxford: Oxford University Press, 2011.

Pack, Adam A. "Experimental Studies of Dolphin Cognition." In *Dolphin Communication and Cognition: Past, Present, and Future,* edited by Denise L. Herzing and Christine M. Johnson, 175–200. Cambridge, MA: MIT Press, 2015.

Pateman, Carol. *The Sexual Contract.* Stanford, CA: Stanford University Press, 1988.

Payne, Roger. *Among Whales.* New York: Scribner, 1995.

PBS. "Wolf Wars: America's Campaign to Eradicate the Wolf." September 14, 2008. http://www.pbs.org/wnet/nature/the-wolf-that-changed-america-wolf-wars-americas-campaign-to-eradicate-the-wolf/4312/.

Pearl, Mike. "'Babe' Is Now 20-Years-Old, and So Is Star James Cromwell's Animal Rights Crusade." *Vice,* August 6, 2015. https://www.vice.com/en_us/article/4wb3jw/babe-is-20-years-old-so-is-star-james-cromwells-animal-rights-crusade-382.

Peirce, Charles S. *The Collected Papers of Charles Sanders Peirce.* Edited by Charles Hartshorne, Paul Weiss, and Arthur W. Burks. 8 vols. New York: Thoemmes Continuum, 1997.

Peterson, Brenda. *Wolf Nation: The Life, Death, and Return of Wild American Wolves.* Boston: Da Capo, 2017.

Peterson, Dale. *Eating Apes*. Berkeley: University of California Press, 2003.

Plumwood, Val. "Animals and Ecology: Toward a Better Integration." In *The Eye of the Crocodile*, edited by Lorraine Shannon, 77–90. Canberra: Australian National University Press, 2012.

———. "'Babe': The Tale of the Speaking Meat." In *The Eye of the Crocodile*, edited by Lorraine Shannon, 55–75. Canberra: Australian National University Press, 2012.

———. *Environmental Culture: The Ecological Crisis of Reason*. New York: Routledge, 2002.

Poore, J., and T. Nemecek. "Reducing Food's Environmental Impacts through Producers and Consumers." *Science* 360, no. 6392 (2018): 987–92. http://science.sciencemag.org/content/360/6392/987.

Pork Checkoff. "Life Cycle of a Market Pig." https://www.pork.org/facts/pig-farming/life-cycle-of-a-market-pig/.

Pratt, Scott L. *Native Pragmatism: Rethinking the Roots of American Philosophy*. Bloomington: Indiana University Press, 2002.

Price, Larry C., and Debbie M. Price. "India: Toxic Tanneries." *Pulitzer Center Newsletter*, March 9, 2017. https://pulitzercenter.org/reporting/india-toxic-tanneries.

Project Coyote. "The Gray Wolf (*Canis lupus*)." http://www.projectcoyote.org/carnivores/wolf/.

———. "Learn about North America's 'Song Dog.'" http://www.projectcoyote.org/carnivores/coyote/.

Pyenson, Nick. *Spying on Whales: The Past, Present, and Future of Earth's Most Awesome Creatures*. New York: Viking Press, 2018.

Quammen, David. "People of the Horse." *National Geographic* 225, no. 3 (March 2014). https://www.nationalgeographic.com/magazine/2014/03/native-american-horse/.

"Race to Save Thoroughbreds from Slaughter." *Animal Times* 24, no. 3 (Fall 2009): 12.

Rawls, John. *A Theory of Justice*. Cambridge, MA: Belknap Press, 1971.

Reid, Robin S. "Amboseli: 'Cattle Create Trees, Elephants Create Grassland' in the Shadow of Kilimanjaro." In *Savannas of Our Birth: People, Wildlife, and Change in East Africa*, 184–201. Berkeley: University of California Press, 2012.

Reiss, Diana. *The Dolphin in the Mirror*. New York: Houghton Mifflin Harcourt, 2011.

Robbins, Jim. "Orcas of the Pacific Northwest Are Starving and Disappearing." *New York Times*, July 9, 2018. https://www.nytimes.com/2018/07/09/science/orcas-whales-endangered.html.

Rose, Deborah Bird. "Val Plumwood's Philosophical Animism: Attentive Interactions in the Sentient World." *Environmental Humanities* 3, no. 1 (2013): 93–109.

"Salmon Boy." As told in *Keepers of the Animals: Native American Stories and Wildlife Activities for Children*, by Michael J. Caduto and Joseph Bruchac, with a foreword by Vine Deloria Jr., 95–97. Golden, CO: Fulcrum, 1997.

Schuetz, Aurelia, Kate Farmer, and Konstnaze Kruege. "Social Learning across Species: Horses (*Equus caballus*) Learn from Humans by Observation." *Animal Cognition* 20, no. 3 (May 2017): 567–73.

Schuler, A. Michele, and Christian R. Abee. "Enrichment for Nonhuman Primates." Department of Health and Human Services, 2005. https://olaw.nih.gov/sites/default/files/Squirrel_Monkeys.pdf.

Sen Nag, Oishimaya. "The Wild Cats of North America." WorldAtlas, June 26, 2018. https://www.worldatlas.com/articles/how-many-species-of-wild-cats-are-found-in-north-america.html.

Sewell, Anna. *Black Beauty*. Racine, WI: Whitman, 1965.

Smithsonian National Museum of Natural History. "What Does It Mean to Be Human?" Last updated December 2, 2019. http://humanorigins.si.edu/evidence/genetics.

Soloway, Rose Ann Gould. "Black Widow Spider Bites Can Be Dangerous." Poison Control, June 2012. https://www.poison.org/articles/2012-jun/black-widow-spiders.

Spider ID. "Spiders in United States." https://spiderid.com/locations/united-states/.

———. "Spider Taxonomy." https://spiderid.com/taxonomy/.

Stein, Byron. "Introduction to Commercial Duck Farming." Department of Primary Industries, NSW Government, 2012. http://www.dpi.nsw.gov.au/__data/assets/pdf_file/0009/442854/introduction-to-commercial-duck-farming.pdf.

Strauss, Mark. "Americans Are Divided over the Use of Animals in Scientific Research." Pew Research Center, August 16, 2018. https://pewresearch.org/fact-tank/2018/08/16/americans-are-divided-over-the-use-of-animals-in-scientific-research.

"Sugar Cane Farming's Toll on the Environment." *World Wildlife Magazine* (Summer 2015). https://www.worldwildlife.org/magazine/issues/summer-2015/articles/sugarcane-farming-s-toll-on-the-environment.

Twowolves. "Cowlitz Tribal Newspaper Article Was Printed." Protect the Wolves, May 25, 2017. https://protectthewolves.com/cowlitz-tribal-news-paper-article-was-printed/.

United Egg Producers. "U.S. Egg Production and Hen Population." https://unitedegg.com/facts-stats/.

United States Department of Agriculture. *Animal Welfare Act and Animal Welfare Regulations.* 2017.

United States Department of Agriculture, Economic Research Service. "Livestock & Meat Domestic Data." https://www.ers.usda.gov/data-products/livestock-meat-domestic-data.aspx.

United States Foundation for the Commemoration of the World Wars. "Horse Heroes: By the Numbers." https://www.worldwar1centennial.org/index.php/brookeusa-statistics.html.

Venomous, Poisonous, Dangerous, and Other Wonders. "North America's Most Venomous Spiders." https://sites.google.com/site/venomousdangerous/spiders/n-america-s-most-venomous-spiders.

Walker, Alice. "African Images: Glimpses from a Tiger's Back." In *Her Blue Body Everything We Know: Earthling Poems, 1965–1990 Complete*, 7–52. San Diego, CA: Harcourt Brace Jovanovich, 1991.

———. "After Many Years and Much Silliness." In *The World Will Follow Joy*, 184–85. New York: New Press, 2015.

———. "Am I Blue." Genius. https://genius.com/Alice-walker-am-i-blue-annotated.

———. "Democratic Womanism." In *The World Will Follow Joy*, 171–79. New York: New Press, 2015.

———. Foreword to *The Dreaded Comparison: Human and Animal Slavery*, by Marjorie Spiegel. 2nd ed. New York: Mirror Books, 1989.

———. "Frida, the Perfect Familiar." In *Anything We Love Can Be Saved*, 127–33. New York: Random House, 1997.

———. "Human Sunrise." In *The Cushion in the Road: Meditation and Wandering as the Whole World Awakens to Being in Harm's Way*, 47–55. New York: New Press, 2013.

———. *In Search of Our Mothers' Gardens: Womanist Prose*. Fort Washington, PA: Harvest Books, 1983.

———. Introduction to *Anything We Love Can Be Saved*, xxi–xxv. New York: Random House, 1997.

———. "Letter to People for the Ethical Treatment of Animals." In *Anything We Love Can Be Saved*, 168–69. New York: Random House, 1997.

———. "No One Can Watch the Wasichu." In *Her Blue Body Everything We Know: Earthling Poems, 1965–1990 Complete*, 384–86. San Diego, CA: Harcourt Brace Jovanovich, 1991.

———. "The Only Reason You Want to Go to Heaven Is That You Have Been Driven Out of Your Mind (Off Your Land and Out of Your Lover's Arms)." In *Anything We Love Can Be Saved*, 3–26. New York: Random House, 1997.

———. "The Right to Life: What Can the White Man Say to the Black Woman?" In *Her Blue Body Everything We Know: Earthling Poems, 1965–1990 Complete*, 442–48. San Diego, CA: Harcourt Brace Jovanovich, 1991.

———. "Treasure." In *Anything We Love Can Be Saved*, 144–46. New York: Random House, 1997.

———. "What Can I Give My Daughters, Who Are Brave?" In *Anything We Love Can Be Saved*, 89–107. New York: Random House, 1997.

———. "Who?" In *Her Blue Body Everything We Know: Earthling Poems, 1965–1990 Complete*, 378. San Diego, CA: Harcourt Brace Jovanovich, 1991.

Warren, Mary Anne. "The Moral Status of Great Apes." In *Great Apes and Humans: The Ethics of Coexistence*, edited by Benjamin E. Beck et al., 313–28. Washington, DC: Smithsonian Institution Press, 2001.

Wernick, Adam. "A Successful Whale Hunt in Northern Canada Revives an Ancient Inuit Tradition." *The World*, August 11, 2014. https://www.pri.org/stories/2014-08-11/successful-whale-hunt-northern-canada-revives-ancient-inuit-tradition.

White, E. B. *Charlotte's Web*. New York: Harper & Row, 1952.

Whitehead, Hal, and Luke Randall. *The Cultural Lives of Whales and Dolphins*. Chicago: University of Chicago Press, 2015.

Wild Earth Guardians. "War on Wildlife: A Report on the U.S. Department of Agriculture's 'Wildlife Services' Program." Revised January 2017. http://pdf.wildearthguardians.org/site/DocServer/WoW_report17_Hi_but_lo.pdf.

Willett, Cynthia. *Interspecies Ethics*. New York: Columbia University Press, 2014.

Williams, Jim. *Path of the Puma: The Remarkable Resilience of the Mountain Lion*. Ventura, CA: Patagonia Books, 2018.

Wollstonecraft, Mary. *A Vindication of the Rights of Woman*. New York: Modern Library, 2001. Originally published in 1792.

World Wildlife Fund. "Decreasing Fishstocks." https://wwf.panda.org/knowledge_hub/endangered_species/cetaceans/threats/fishstocks/.

———. "Facts." https://www.worldwildlife.org/species/tuna.

Worrall, Simon. "How the Most Hated Animal in America Outwitted Us All." *National Geographic*, August 7, 2016. https://www.nationalgeographic.com/news/2016/08/coyote-america-dan-flores-history-science/.

WotCat. "Wild Cats of North America." https://www.wotcat.com/wildlife/Mammal/North%20America.html.

Würsig, Bernd, and Heidi C. Pearson. "Dolphin Society: Structure and Function." In *Dolphin Communication and Cognition: Past, Present, and Future*, edited by Denise L. Herzing and Christine M. Johnson, 77–106. Cambridge, MA: MIT Press, 2015.

Index